The Kaisers

Theo Aronson

CORGI BOOKS
A DIVISION OF TRANSWORLD PUBLISHERS LTD
A NATIONAL GENERAL COMPANY

THE KAISERS
A CORGI BOOK 0 552 09393 9

Originally published in Great Britain
by Cassell & Co. Ltd.

PRINTING HISTORY

Cassell edition published 1971
Cassell edition second impression 1971
Corgi edition published 1973

This book is set in Baskerville 10/11 pt.

Corgi Books are published by Transworld Publishers Ltd.,
Cavendish House, 57–59 Uxbridge Road, Ealing,
London, W.5.

Made and printed in Great Britain by
Richard Clay (The Chaucer Press), Ltd., Bungay, Suffolk.

**NOTE: The Australian price appearing on the
back cover is the recommended retail price.**

For R. I. B. Webster

CONTENTS

ILLUSTRATIONS

Wilhelm I, the simple, courteous, autocratic King of Prussia, later first German Emperor of the Second Reich.

The inauguration of the Second German Reich in the Galerie des Glaces at Versailles. Wilhelm I stands in the centre of the dais with Crown Prince Frederick at his right hand. Bismarck, in white uniform, stands at the foot of the steps.

The liberal, mercurial Queen Augusta of Prussia, who afterwards became the Empress Augusta.

Kaiser Wilhelm I in old age.

The Empress Augusta in old age.

Otto von Bismarck, the astute and ruthless Iron Chancellor, who led the Hohenzollern dynasty to greatness.

A conference at German Headquarters during the Franco-Prussian War. Wilhelm I is seated left, Bismarck seated right. Crown Prince Frederick is standing left foreground.

The liberal, sensitive Crown Prince Frederick of Prussia, afterwards Kaiser Frederick III.

The brilliant, emotional Crown Princess Victoria, painted in Venetian costume, at the age of thirty-eight.

The marriage of Victoria (Vicky), the Princess Royal, to Prince Frederick Wilhelm (Fritz) of Prussia, in the Chapel Royal, St. James's Palace.

The Crown Princess with Prince Wilhelm, aged seventeen, photographed during the less stormy period of their relationship. His crippled left arm is kept hidden from the camera.

The showy, neurotic, vainglorious Kaiser Wilhelm II.

Princess Auguste Viktoria (Dona) at the time of her marriage to Prince Wilhelm.

Kaiser Wilhelm II delivering the Speech from the Throne at the opening of the Reichstag, 1888.

The widowed Empress Frederick.

AUTHOR'S NOTE

The year 1888, during which three Kaisers reigned in Germany, saw the climax of a conflict that had torn the ruling Hohenzollern family apart for over a quarter of a century. This book tells the story of that family feud. It is a study of the six leading protagonists, or rather, of these protagonists in relation to each other. The six characters are Kaiser Wilhelm I and the Empress Augusta, Kaiser Frederick III and the Empress Victoria, Kaiser Wilhelm II and, most important of all, Prince Otto von Bismarck. Together, for some thirty years of Germany's history, the six of them were locked in a fierce ideological struggle, creating an extraordinary maelstrom at the very centre of national life.

Although this family vendetta raged throughout Bismarck's years of power (indeed, his Herculean presence was largely responsible for the conflict) this book is not a study of his career. Only where the Iron Chancellor's policies directly affect relations between the various members of the House of Hohenzollern are they dealt with in any detail; otherwise they are simply mentioned *en passant*. Still less is this a history of the Second Reich. The focus, throughout the study, is on the Hohenzollern dynasty; this is a book which deals with personalities first, politics second. It is an account of a domestic conflict which was, in many ways, a microcosm of a national conflict.

It will be noticed that whereas I have spelt the name 'Wilhelm' in the German fashion, I have used the English version of 'Frederick', on the assumption that this will be more acceptable to English-speaking readers than the German 'Friedrich'.

I am grateful for the help I have received from Dr Anton Ritthaler of the Hausarchiv, Burg Hohenzollern, Munich, and

11

Dr Branig of the Geheimes Staatsarchiv, Berlin. I must thank also the Bibliothèque Nationale, Paris, the Library of Congress, Washington and the British Museum, London. I am indebted for information, material, advice and help to Mrs Ilse Rooseboom, Miss Ann Seeliger, Miss Julie Mullard, Professor Dennis A. Davey, Dr Klaus Schmidt, Mr Anton Reinhardt and Mr Brocas Harris. I am grateful to Miss Myra Conradie for putting her superb genealogical tables at my disposal. To those many people who have helped me during my visits to Germany and to the von Eicken family of Munich for their hospitality, I am deeply indebted. As always, without the assistance, encouragement and expert advice of Mr Brian Roberts, this book would never have been written. I should like to thank the publishers of the following books for permission to quote copyright material: *Letters of the Empress Frederick*, edited by Sir Frederick Ponsonby (Macmillan, 1928); ABP International, *My Early Life*, Wilhelm II (Methuen, 1926); and *The Letters of Queen Victoria*, edited by G. E. Buckle (John Murray, 1907–32).

PROLOGUE

VERSAILLES
1871

On a snowy day in January 1871 old King Wilhelm of Prussia was proclaimed first Emperor of the re-established German Reich. This momentous proclamation did not take place, as might have been expected, in the Prussian capital of Berlin, but within the mirrored splendour of the Galerie des Glaces at Versailles. The German army, fighting the French, had its headquarters at Versailles; with the Franco-Prussian War in its seventh month, the triumphant Germans were still laying siege to a shelled and starving Paris. Indeed, it was the succession of victories on the part of the combined armies of the various German states that had finally made possible the inauguration of the new German Empire. The last barriers to the unification of the assorted kingdoms, principalities, grand duchies and free cities of Germany, under Prussia, had been swept away on the floodtide of military success. It was thus no more than fitting that the Second Reich should be proclaimed in the palace in which the victorious German army was now established.

That morning's snowfall had prevented the proposed procession from the Préfecture, where King Wilhelm was living, to the palace of Versailles, and so it was not until the King had alighted from his closed carriage at the State Entrance that the ceremonial could begin. While, outside, the cannon thundered in salute, the seventy-four-year-old King, wearing the uniform of the First Regiment of Guards and trailing an impressively bemedalled retinue, passed down an avenue of soldiers and mounted the great staircase to the Galerie des Glaces. As he entered the vast white and gold hall, the clocks struck noon. Slowly, through the uniformed throng reflected into infinity in the mirrored walls, he made his way to the dais at the far end of the room. There he stood, tall, erect, fresh-complexioned and white-whiskered, surveying the brilliant scene with those still keen blue eyes. Below him, on either side of the dais, stood helmeted cuirassiers with drawn swords and gleaming breast-plates. On his right stood his only son, the thirty-nine-year-old Crown Prince Frederick. Taller, and even more luxuriantly bearded than his father, the Crown Prince was wearing the uniform of a Prussian Field-Marshal. On the King's left stood his only son-in-law, the Grand Duke of Baden. Behind them, in a great semi-circle, shuffled the various kings, princes, grand dukes and dukes who reigned over the conglomeration of states that were about to be unified into a new German Empire. Over their heads swayed a bright assortment of regimental colours and above all sprawled a gigantic painted allegory of the Grand Monarque, Louis XIV, himself, bearing the not in-appropriate inscription, '*Le Roi gouverne par lui-même*'.

Slightly apart from this galaxy of royalties and conspicuous in his white cuirassier's uniform, stood the one man who, more than any other, had made possible this day's ceremony: Otto von Bismarck. As much as for King Wilhelm, this was the crowning moment of Bismarck's career. Without him, the King of Prussia would never have been proclaimed German Emperor. 'It was on my own shoulders,' claimed Bismarck in typically self-satisfied fashion, 'that I carried him to the imperial throne.'

That this day's ceremony was, above all, a military one, was very largely Bismarck's doing. The new Reich had been created by force of arms—or, in the Chancellor's own words, 'not by speeches and majority votes, but by blood and iron'—and by force of arms it would be maintained. A military Em-pire was being inaugurated in the Galerie des Glaces that day, and a military Empire it was to remain. The deputation from the Reichstag—the North German parliament—which had been allowed, a month before, to come to Versailles to beg the King to accept the imperial crown, played no part in the pro-ceedings. This was an affair of kings, princes, nobles and gen-erals.

With his Chancellor's attitude King Wilhelm was in com-plete agreement. Indeed, in his determination to keep the oc-casion free of any taint of democracy, the King had been even more resolute than Bismarck. It had been with considerable difficulty that the more practical Chancellor had persuaded the autocratic old King to receive the parliamentary deputation at all. The King had all along made it quite clear that it was by request of the princely rulers of the various German states, and not to satisfy the more genuine aspirations of the German liberals, that he was accepting the crown. The new Empire might be a constitutional monarchy in theory but it was certainly not going to be one in practice. *Gottesgnadentum*—the Divine Right of Kings—was much more to the taste of both Wilhelm and his Chancellor. 'German patriotism, to be active and effective,' claimed Bismarck, 'needs as a rule to be dependent upon a dynasty ... the German's love of the fatherland needs a prince on whom he can concentrate his attachment.'

In Wilhelm of Prussia—simple, conservative, tenacious and courtly—Bismarck, and the Germans, had just such a prince.

The ceremony opened with the chanting of a chorale by the military choir and then, from a temporary altar, the Court preacher Rogge conducted the service. His 'short, impassioned' sermon was followed by the heartfelt singing on the part of the entire assembly of the old Lutheran hymn *Nun danket alle Gott*. The old monarch stepped forward and in 'a loud yet broken voice', read out the declaration proclaiming the re-establishment of the German Empire and the vesting of the imperial dignity in himself and his descendants 'for all time to come, in accordance with the unanimous will of the German peoples'.

After Bismarck had read out the new Emperor's address to the nation, the Grand Duke of Baden stepped forward and, raising his helmet into the air, shouted, 'Long live his Imperial Majesty, Kaiser Wilhelm!' His cry was followed by a tempest of cheering and a frantic waving of swords and helmets. The standards were dipped and the military band burst into *Heil dir im Siegerkranz*. Dropping to his knees, the Crown Prince kissed his father's hand. His impulsive act of homage was repeated by all the lesser royalties until even the austere-looking old King was reduced to tears.

This surge of Teutonic emotion on the part of the company gathered in the Galerie des Glaces was not without justification. It was indeed a glorious moment for the German people. It marked the fulfilment of a long-cherished dream. As recently as ten years before—the year of the coronation of Wilhelm as King of Prussia—Germany had been a collection of thirty-eight independent states. Two of them, Austria and, to a lesser extent, Prussia, had been Great Powers; some of them—Bav-

aria, Württemberg, Hanover and Saxony—had been fairly important kingdoms; the majority of them had been insignificant
principalities and grand duchies, sometimes so small that they
had been all but impossible to find on a map. These states had
been the flotsam of the wreck of the First Reich—that haphazardly organized Holy Roman Empire founded by Charlemagne in 800 and destroyed by Napoleon just over a thousand
years later. Loosely combined in the Deutscher Bund, they had
tended to look to Austria, as the greatest among them, for
leadership. Yet within the space of a decade Prussia had
wrested the leadership of Germany from Austria and, by waging
this successful war against France, had brought the remaining states of Germany under her control. With the proclamation of Wilhelm I as German Emperor, Prussia, from having
been the least of the Great Powers of Europe, emerged as the
dominant nation on the Continent, with its King—now Kaiser
—as the leading sovereign. It was, indeed, a time for high emotion.

'Tears ran down my cheeks,' wrote the historian Heinrich
von Sybel on the morrow of the ceremony at Versailles. 'By
what have we deserved the grace of God, that we are allowed to
live to see such great and mighty deeds? What for twenty years
was the substance of all our wishes and efforts, is now fulfilled
in such an immeasurably magnificent way.'

And the new Kaiser himself? What did he feel on this, the
most auspicious day, not only of his own career, but in the
history of the House of Hohenzollern of which he was the
head? The date, 18 January, was significant, for it marked the
anniversary of the crowning, at Königsberg in 1701, of the first
Hohenzollern as King of Prussia. In those far-off days Prussia
had been no more than a third-rate kingdom set amidst the
sandy, wind-blown wastes of north-eastern Germany. Compared with the other states that went to make up the First
Reich, Prussia had been considered poor, savage and insignificant. Not until the reign of Wilhelm's great grand-uncle, Frederick the Great, in the mid-eighteenth century, had Prussia
enjoyed some measure of importance. And even though Frederick had fashioned it into one of the first-class powers of
Europe, it had remained the least among them; 'regarded', as
Disraeli once put it, 'if not respected'.

What then, were the thoughts of this latest Hohenzollern,
now proclaimed Emperor in the mightiest nation on the Con-

tinent; master of a territory that stretched from the Baltic Sea to the Alps, from the borders of Russia to the very gates of Paris? What emotions were passing through the mind of this autocratic old man as the loyal cheers echoed and re-echoed through the once-proud palace of the French kings and the drawn swords and spiked helmets flashed silver in the blaze of the chandeliers?

The ceremony marked, he admitted in a letter to his wife, now the Empress Augusta, 'the most unhappy day of my life'.

PART ONE

THE HOHENZOLLERNS OF PRUSSIA

CHAPTER ONE

THE DYNASTY

1

Wilhelm of Prussia was a simple man. There was a quality of artlessness about him which neither age nor experience had been able to tarnish. At the time of his proclamation as Emperor in 1871, he remained as unaffected, as guileless, as conscientious, as disciplined, as unswerving and as sensible as he had ever been. And, by the same token—for he had both the strengths and the weaknesses of simplicity—he remained as limited, as stubborn, as unimaginative and as reactionary. The surge of events, the thrust of new ideas through which he had lived, had had precious little effect on that uncomplicated mind; the tenets which were to carry him to the very threshold of the twentieth century (for he would live to be over ninety) were those which had been rooted during his eighteenth-century boyhood. Prejudices which should have been swept away by a succession of revolutionary tidal waves remained firmly fixed in his mind. The three ruling passions of his life—for Prussia, for the army and for the principle of Absolutism—were as strong in his old age as they had been in his youth. He was an anachronism; honest, well-intentioned and just, but an anachronism none the less.

Several factors were responsible for his obscurantism. An inborn conservatism, the militarism of his early environment and the vicissitudes of his boyhood had all played a part in the shaping of his outlook. His father, King Frederick Wilhelm III of Prussia, had been a narrow-minded autocrat; his mother, Queen Louise, had been the brave and beautiful figure who had at one stage symbolized Prussia's defiance of the all-conquering Napoleon. Prince Wilhelm had been born in 1797— the very year in which his father had succeeded to the throne of Prussia—and before he was many years old his mother could write that, 'Unless I am mistaken, our son Wilhelm will be like his father—simple, straightforward and sensible.'

Every passing year confirmed her opinion. Whereas his elder brother, the Crown Prince, showed signs of a more extravagant turn of mind, Wilhelm's interests seemed confined to military matters. In this he received every encouragement. Since the days of Frederick the Great, the tone of the Prussian Court had been unquestionably martial. It was therefore considered quite natural that at the age of ten he should enter the army with the rank of second-lieutenant. But the beginnings of his military career were singularly inglorious. By then the Prussian army had been routed by Napoleon at the battle of Jena and the Prussian royal family forced to leave Berlin.

The story of the following years was one of flight, poverty and humiliation. This period of exile had a profound effect on the young Prince Wilhelm. It bred in him a love of stability, a taste for austerity and an unshakeable belief in the need for an invincible army. By the time the victorious Allied forces went clattering into Paris after the defeat of Napoleon, the seventeen-year-old Prince Wilhelm of Prussia—who was among their number—was an unquestioning supporter of that pre-Revolutionary system which the short-sighted conquerors were preparing to reimpose on a transformed Europe.

The ensuing years merely confirmed the Prince's conservatism. His list of 'principles', personally compiled for his confirmation at Charlottenburg, was a high-minded, almost priggish, collection of maxims dealing with such things as the obligation of princes, mental and spiritual culture and the avoidance of intemperance and sensuality—'which degrade human nature to the lowest depths'. He swore that he would scrupulously discharge the duties of his position and, 'whilst sternly exhorting my subjects to carry out their obligations', would act kindly towards them.

Even love, where it threatened to disturb the established pattern, had to be renounced. At the age of twenty-four he fell in love with a cousin, Princess Elisa Radziwill. Her mother was Princess Louise of Prussia, the King's cousin; her father was Prince Anton Radziwill, a descendant of the family that had once ruled Poland. One would have considered such ancestry illustrious by any standards but it seems not to have been quite illustrious enough for the Prussian royal family. Wilhelm, as the second son of the King of Prussia, was expected to marry a princess of royal blood only; the Radziwills, however well born, were not a reigning House. Try as it might—for Prince Wilhelm was passionately in love and Princess Elisa was, in every other way, eminently suitable—the King's ministry could not see its way clear to allowing this *mésalliance*. The marriage, it was decided regretfully, 'would not be in keeping with the Prince's rank according to all provisions and legal titles'. The sympathetic King tried to persuade, first the Tsar and then one of his more suitably married brothers to adopt Elisa as their daughter but the plan never materialized. Inevitably, after the affair had dragged on for years, Wilhelm renounced Elisa. Faced with a choice between love and the possibility of breaking the royal code, he chose the path of duty.

The heartbroken Elisa, in the best traditions of that romantic age, faded away and died, while Prince Wilhelm, no less in character, kept her picture on his desk until his own death, over half a century later. 'I always think of her,' he confided to a friend when he was over eighty; 'she was, and is still, the guiding star of my life!'

When Wilhelm eventually married, at the age of thirty-two in 1829, he chose the eighteen-year-old and generally acceptable Princess Augusta of Saxe-Weimar as his bride. She was to prove herself to be made of sterner stuff than the elusive Elisa.

Once Wilhelm had renounced Elisa Radziwill, his passions were restricted to the strengthening of the Prussian army and the upholding of the principle of monarchist absolutism. He adored soldiering. He adored it, not only for its own sake but because he regarded the army as the main prop of the monarchy. In his mind, Crown and army were inexorably linked. 'It is for the army to defend [the Crown],' he once announced to a military deputation, 'and Prussia's kings have never known the army waver in its loyalty.' Prussian soldiers must protect their King, not only against foreign invasion but, almost more important, against the rising tide of democracy at home. 'The tendency of the revolutionary and Liberal Party in Europe is to pull down all the pillars, by degrees, on which the Sovereign's power and prestige depend...' he warned. 'It is natural that the armies should still be the first and foremost of these pillars, and the more they are inspired by a true military spirit, the more difficult it is to get at them.'

Between liberalism and anarchy, Prince Wilhelm saw very

little difference. Give the constitutionalists an inch, he reckoned, and they would take a yard. 'The fashionable doctrine is to extort everything from the King through the masses, and, in the last resort, through rebellion,' he declared, 'but it is the first duty of every loyal subject, particularly of the officials and, beneath them again, of the soldiers, to put down any such teaching.'

Gradually the conservatives came to look upon Prince Wilhelm as their champion. Tall, handsome, with the ramrod back and heel-clicking punctiliousness of a Prussian soldier, he seemed the very epitome of the old order. In the Prussia of Prince Wilhelm's day, this old order was upheld by the class known as the Junkers. These Junkers were landowning noblemen, sometimes rich, quite often impoverished, but almost always proud, narrow-minded and conservative, with a ruthless determination to resist reform and to hang on to their special privileges. As they were royalist to a man, it was from their ranks that the Prussian monarchs recruited all their army officers and administrators; 'because the sons of the nobility defend the country, and their race is so good', Frederick the Great had once said, it was important that the preferential treatment of the Junkers be continued. Prince Wilhelm was in complete agreement with this state of affairs. The death of his father and the accession of his childless elder brother as King Frederick Wilhelm IV merely enhanced his position *vis-à-vis* the Junkers.

A more complex, but less unyielding man than his younger brother, King Frederick Wilhelm IV was alive to the need for some sort of change in the regime. It was not that he was any more liberal than Wilhelm but, as something of a visionary, he dreamed of resurrecting the old German Reich. In this, the King's vague schemes coincided with those of the German liberals. They too, longed for a unified German state as opposed to the present loose federation of states. But whereas their nationalism was democratically inspired, his was almost feudal. What the German liberals wanted was to overthrow the cluster of reactionary little kingdoms set up by the Congress of Vienna and to form one democratic nation state. What King Frederick Wilhelm IV wanted was to conserve and to consolidate these states under his leadership.

With these dreams of a united Germany Prince Wilhelm had very little sympathy. His thoughts were all of Prussia and he did not wish to see her lose her identity by being merged into a greater, and possibly more democratic, Germany. 'In accordance with God's inscrutable decree,' he announced on one occasion, 'it seems certain that the Crown will pass to my descendants. It is therefore a sacred duty to take care that it is handed down to the heirs to the throne with undiminished rights and with the same dignity and power that I see before me today.'

But it was not to be. Hardly had these resolute sentiments been voiced than the rights of the crown faced considerable diminishing. The revolutionary whirlwind that swept through Europe in 1848 reached Berlin in March and King Frederick Wilhelm IV, losing his nerve in the face of a threatening mob, granted Prussia a constitution. Going still further, he drove through the turbulent streets of the capital sporting the revolutionary colours of national Germany and promising to identify himself with German unification. Henceforth 'Prussia merges into Germany,' he declared.

Prince Wilhelm, though disagreeing with his brother's capitulation to the wishes of the mob, was in no position to do anything about it: considered to be the personification of hated autocracy (the 'grapeshot Prince' they called him) Wilhelm had been forced to flee for his life. His portrait, flung from the windows of his palace in Unter den Linden, had been spat upon by an angry crowd. Leaving his wife and two children behind, Wilhelm made for London (the British capital was chock-a-block with royal refugees) where he was kindly received by Queen Victoria and Prince Albert.

Away from the reassuringly hidebound setting of the Prussian Court, Prince Wilhelm was revealed as being not nearly as iron-willed as had always been assumed. Lord Clarendon, later British Foreign Secretary, remarked on how often the Prince used the words '*mais*' and '*pourtant*'. I almost doubt his having the moral courage to carry out his own intentions,' noted Clarendon. It seemed that, at bottom, Prince Wilhelm's conservatism was that of the weak man who fears change rather than that of the strong one who acts from conviction.

Although Prince Wilhelm enjoyed his stay in London, he seems to have imbibed precious little of Britain's celebrated liberalism. He simply could not appreciate the fact that it was Britain's democratic institutions that had saved her from the revolutionary disorders that were still unsettling the Continent. On being allowed to return to Prussia after an absence of some months, he made it clear that, as the King's leading subject, he was obliged to accept the newly granted constitution ('The King wished it; the King's wish is sacred to me') but that his real calling in life was to uphold 'right, order and law'.

But there was no need for Prince Wilhelm to worry himself overmuch about the changed state of affairs. Once the revolutionary clamour had died down, King Frederick Wilhelm IV who was, for all his recently expressed constitutionalism, as reactionary as ever, saw to it that things continued along very much the same lines as before. The much-vaunted constitution turned out to be a watered-down version of what had been expected; with the Prussian monarch—and not the newly elected parliament—holding all effective power. This system was airily referred to as 'German constitutionalism'. Within a year of the Revolution, the little liberal flutter had died down and power had passed back into the hands of the Junkers. The fact was that respect for authority was too ingrained in the Germans; wanting freedom to be granted to them by the traditional authority, they were not prepared to press too hard for it.

King Frederick Wilhelm IV put paid to that other revolutionary aspiration as well: the desire for a unified, democratic Germany. A National Assembly, elected in the first flush following the revolution, and representative of liberals in all the states of Germany, decided to fulfil their long-cherished dream of unification. After much debate, it was agreed that the new state should exclude Austria and be led by Prussia. That settled, the Assembly offered the imperial crown of the proposed new state to King Frederick Wilhelm IV.

He refused it. Had it been offered to him by the princely rulers of the various German states, he might have accepted it; to be indebted for it to the elected representatives of the people was quite unthinkable. Henceforth, in the mind of the Prussian ruling class, the imperial crown was always associated with revolution.

In his autocratic stand, the King had the full support of his brother Wilhelm. Besides wanting to have nothing to do with so democratically inspired a project, Wilhelm had no wish to see his beloved Prussia 'merged into Germany'. However, he did object to the fact that when the King, still hankering after the re-creation of the medieval Reich, tried to put his vague

28

plans into action, he was severely slapped back into place by Austria. The ancient Hapsburgs had no intention of playing second fiddle to the upstart Hohenzollerns. It was by the Treaty of Olmütz in 1850—a treaty ensuring Austria's continued leadership of the German Confederation—that Prussia was thus humbled by Austria. The diplomatic defeat upset Prince Wilhelm profoundly. Having first thrown himself sobbing into the arms of an aide-de-camp, he declared, with rare perspicacity, that unless the leadership of Germany passed from Austria to Prussia, she would continue to languish.

However, it was under Austrian leadership that Germany lived for the following decade. They were to be the last years of Prince Wilhelm's long apprenticeship. He was in his fifties already with a grown-up son and daughter. Whatever his reputation among the German liberals might have been, among his own circle he was considered to be as worthy and gentlemanly a prince as one could hope to find. The courtliness of his manner had increased with age; his orderliness, his frugality and his piety were legendary. 'He has the noblest appearance imaginable and looks more impressive than anyone else, wrote Heinrich von Gagern to a friend; 'yet he is always simple and chivalrous, bright and amiable, though never lacking in dignity.' This assessment was echoed by Queen Victoria. 'Having lived with him for a fortnight on a very intimate footing,' Victoria once wrote to her uncle, the King of the Belgians, 'we have been able to appreciate his *real* worth fully; he is so honest and frank, and so steady of purpose and courageous.'

As such, Prince Wilhelm was in marked contrast to his brother the King, who was yearly showing more signs of what was euphemistically termed as a 'softening of the brain'. By the year 1857 the King's behaviour was so eccentric that Prince Wilhelm was obliged to act as Regent for a period of three months. In October the next year, with the King showing no signs of recovery, Wilhelm was permanently installed as Regent. 'You can understand how upset I am,' wrote the new Regent to his wife, Princess Augusta, 'and that I could only find strength and refreshment in prayer, and trusting in God's mercy. Although a weight has been lifted from many hearts, the real anxiety and trouble are only now beginning for me.' To all intents and purposes, his reign had begun.

Wilhelm's Regency lasted for a little over two years. At first, because the Regent had chosen a slightly less reactionary cabinet than his brother's, it was assumed that the Regency had ushered in a 'new era'. But Prince Wilhelm's reasons for this move were not prompted by any newly-acquired liberalism: so great had been his resentment of Prussia's humiliation at the hands of Austria at Olmütz, that he had appointed an anti-Austrian, and therefore a moderately liberal, cabinet.

If the Regency did mark the introduction of a new era, then it was an era concerned with the matter lying closest to Wilhelm's heart: the Prussian army. This meant far more to him than questions of domestic policy or schemes for a united Germany—be it the quasi-medieval Reich of his mad brother's imaginings or the federated state of the liberals' aspirations. His sole imperial ambition was to become the Commander-in-Chief of all German forces north of the River Main. To achieve this, he had to start with the Prussian army.

In order to carry out a complete reorganization of the Prussian forces, Wilhelm appointed General von Roon as his Minister of War. A military expert, a stern disciplinarian and a dyed-in-the-wool conservative, Roon was very much Prince Wilhelm's man. Like his master, Roon favoured a 'strong, active kingship' and when, on one occasion, the Regent was being advised to adopt some faintly liberal measures, Roon was quick to back up Wilhelm's own hesitations by declaring that he could not bear in 'his heart of a Prussian soldier' that the Regent should 'submit his own will to any other man's'. Unless the army were strengthened, warned Roon, Prussia would drift rapidly into 'the muddy ocean of parliamentary rule'.

This was the sort of talk that Prince Wilhelm understood. What the new Minister of War was aiming at, in fact, was to get rid of his moderately liberal colleagues in the cabinet and to pave the way for the introduction of his close associate—a man of undeniably conservative outlook who would prevent any drift to parliamentarianism—Otto von Bismarck-Schönhausen. But the time for this was not quite ripe.

2

In the year of Prince Wilhelm's assumption of the Regency, his wife, Princess Augusta, turned forty-seven. If he looked every inch a future king, she certainly did not fit popular conception of a future queen. Of majesty, of dignity, of the customary reserve of royalty, she had very little. To look at, she was more like a *femme du monde* than a princess. Notable for a porcelain-like beauty in younger days, Augusta had resolutely refused to admit its passing; 'one mass of paint; pink, white and dark' was how one visitor described her and, in her old age, the brilliance and elaborateness of her wigs was to prove a source of unending wonder. Her taste in clothes was skittish rather than stylish; she had a penchant for ribbons, laces and artificial flowers. With this decorative appearance there went—at least during the early days of her married life—a determined vivacity, or what George de Bunsen called 'a delightful, mercurial *gaieté de coeur*'. Her company, says that international busybody, Princess Lieven, was always a joy; her vitality exceptional. To more than one eye-witness, Augusta's air was that of an actress: showy, effervescent, emotional.

But there was more to Princess Augusta than met the eye. Far from being simply an ageing, painted doll with a somewhat frenetic manner, she was a woman of considerable character. She was certainly a deeper and more complex personality than her husband. Born a princess of the Grand Duchy of Weimar, her background, upbringing and outlook were utterly different from his. In almost every respect, husband and wife were poles apart. Where he was stolid, she was lively; where he was even-tempered, she was excitable; where he was unimaginative, she was sensitive; where he was slow-witted, she was intelligent. He was an unthinking conservative; she a spirited liberal.

The Court of Weimar, unlike that of Prussia, enjoyed a great deal of that romantic, scholarly and cultivated aura associated with the courts of early nineteenth-century Germany. Indeed, Weimar was looked upon as the most progressive Court on the Continent. Schiller, the Humboldt brothers and above all, Goethe, had been at home there. 'These Weimar coteries,' said one contemporary, 'were exclusive yet catholic in spirit, placid yet strenuous in their efforts to attain a wide, but essentially German culture, and carrying on their work amid the weltering chaos of intellectual and political ideas which then made up Germany....' It was thus in a *milieu* far removed from the barrack-like atmosphere of the Royal Schloss in Berlin that Augusta had grown up. And although the Princess had imbibed her share of culture, it was the general air of enlightenment at her father's Court that seems to have made the greater impression.

Open-minded and never lacking confidence. Augusta was hardly out of the schoolroom before she began airing her strongly held views. 'Princess Augusta is said to have already developed considerable strength and independence of character...' wrote the approving Wilhelm von Humboldt of her in the years before her marriage. 'Her eyes sparkle with vitality and intellect.'

This independent attitude was to characterize Augusta throughout her life. Allied to it would be another heritage of the Weimar Court: a keen awareness of royal status and a somewhat provincial obsession with royal show. In many ways, Augusta typified what has been called 'the strange mixture of intellectual grandeur and ceremonial pettiness that made up the courtly life at Weimar'. With her, progressive thinking and a taste for pageantry were always closely intertwined.

When Prince Wilhelm married Princess Augusta after his renunciation of Elisa Radziwill ('one can only really love once, but Augusta cannot and ought not to be denied respect and affection', he wrote self-righteously to his sister) he was somewhat put out to find that he had not gained the submissive, typically Prussian wife of his imaginings. If anything, he found Augusta too assertive. She tended to challenge his authority. 'If you think,' he complained to his sister, 'that I am often dissatisfied with Augusta because she is too childish, you are quite mistaken, for she is really inclined, on the contrary, to behave too little in accordance with her youth, and might be more likely to irritate me in that way. Her mental faculties are so fully developed, and her judgement is so good, that she often enters into discussions which she carries on, it is true, with a perfect grasp of the subject, but which are really outside her sphere; this naturally gives her not only a feeling of self-confidence, which encourages her to seek such discussions, but also the appearance of a *femme d'esprit,* which is not desirable for her, as she has already always been credited with having more head than heart.'

A *femme d'esprit* at the hide-bound, narrow-minded Prussian Court was a rare bird indeed. As such, Augusta was soon the object of severe criticism. Her theatrical clothes, her cultural enthusiasms, her strongly expressed views were considered unseemly; for a woman of her position, she showed a disturbing degree of professionalism in her musical and artistic endeavours. Even her literary tastes were suspect. Rather than waste her time on what were considered 'the dull dogmatics of the German schoolmen of that day', she read the French writers—Hugo, Balzac, Lamartine and Alexandre Dumas. A French reader was permanently attached to her entourage. She was far too inclined, claimed one of her many critics, 'to belittle what was German in favour of exotic literature'. Princess Augusta was too clever, it was said, by half.

To the less emotional members of the Court, her tendency towards sudden passionate friendships and violent unexplained dislikes was hardly endearing. Worst of all, however, was her involvement in public affairs; in a society where women were expected to confine their interests to the home, Augusta's political meddlings were considered scandalous indeed.

Among the hearty, insensitive and often coarse-tongued members of her husband's family, Augusta came to be looked upon as a pretentious busybody. Her unpopularity increased by the year.

Had husband and wife loved, or even liked each other, all might yet have been well. Her liveliness would have made an excellent foil for his stolidness. But there was no *rapport* between them; they lived almost separate lives. In their Berlin home—an unpretentious palace on Unter den Linden—he lived on the first floor and she on the second. At Babelsberg, their summer palace at Potsdam ('a Gothic bijou, full of furniture', noted Queen Victoria), the order was reversed: she lived on the first floor and he on the second. As he was ill at ease among her intellectual circle, and she at odds with his martial entourage, they saw as little of each other as possible. It was a cheerless relationship.

Never having known love, Augusta became increasingly cynical about it. One of her intimates reported that 'she takes no interest in anything that has to do with love, as she cannot understand it ... the heart goes for nothing'.

Theirs was not, of course, the only loveless royal marriage in Europe. Most royal couples, although ill-matched, managed to rub along somehow. What made their marriage so stormy was the widely divergent political outlook of husband and wife. And time, instead of blurring the differences between them, merely sharpened them. As he became more reactionary, so did she become more volubly liberal. The revolutionary upheavals of 1848 climaxed this diversity. They flung Augusta into what her disapproving husband called a state of 'great agitation'. On the one hand she was alarmed at the overthrow of France's constitutional monarch, King Louis Philippe and, on the other, she was an outspoken advocate for the introduction of a constitution for Prussia. So delighted was she at the granting of the constitution that the King of Hanover went so far as to call her a 'Jacobin'. The Duchess de Dino blamed Humboldt, one of Augusta's girlhood mentors, for her ardently expressed views. 'I do not assert that he is absolutely radical, but his liberalism is of a very advanced type,' wrote the Duchess, 'and at Berlin he is thought to be urging the Princess [Augusta] of Prussia along the path which she does not always follow with sufficient prudence....'

On that other great contemporary issue—the question of German unification—husband and wife were at loggerheads as well. Like all German liberals, Augusta dreamed of merging Prussia into a united, democratic Greater Germany. It was, she cried out in her impassioned way, 'an object so splendid, so necessary!'

'What must people think,' grumbled the discomforted Wilhelm, 'when they hear Augusta express herself in absolute opposition to my views?'

Feeling things deeply and lacking her husband's ability to leave well alone, Augusta never hesitated to reproach him for his intransigence. Though he was one of the most forbearing of men, he could seldom resist answering her back. They quarrelled incessantly. Hardly a day went by without some violent scene between them. Faced with his rock-like conservatism against which her arguments broke like a helpless wave, she became increasingly frustrated, embittered and neurotic. Her manner grew more feverish, more demanding, more dictatorial. It was said that 'nothing pleases, nothing satisfies her'. She flung herself into meaningless social activity; she indulged her taste for glittering ceremonial; she developed close personal relationships with women at Court. She began to absent herself from Berlin for long periods, spending weeks and sometimes months in the more sympathetic atmosphere of her brother's Court at Weimar or with her only daughter Louise, who had married the Grand Duke of Baden. There were times when, exasperated beyond endurance, Augusta resolved to turn her back on politics altogether. It was a resolve which she could not keep. 'I am weary and sick at heart,' she once complained, 'but we are in God's hands, and must leave everything to Him, otherwise only our bodies live, the soul is dead.'

Wilhelm's assumption of the Regency simply worsened the relationship between them. 'I tremble to think of all she will have to go through here [Berlin],' wrote her daughter-in-law, the Princess Royal of Great Britain, who shared her liberal views, 'her life here is as disagreeable as it can be, and it does not improve her health. If only there are no more scenes; it is so painful to witness....'

It was a vain hope. Now that her husband actually wielded power, Augusta redoubled her efforts to steer him along a more democratic course. 'Mama is influenced by such fluctuating moods,' reported her son to his mother-in-law Queen Victoria, 'that sometimes when opinions differ it is wiser to pretend to agree so as not to irritate her still further.... Papa tries to do everything to please her, but Mama does not think so ... she is too autocratic a character to put up for any length of time with not having a say in everything now.' Wilhelm's sister, the bigoted Grand Duchess of Mecklenburg-Schwerin, accused Augusta of intriguing against the state and begged her brother not to trust her. The advice was unnecessary. The more Augusta, in her full-blooded way, harried Wilhelm, the more he dug in his heels.

Yet to those who knew her well, there was an air of sadness, of nobility almost, about Augusta. Queen Victoria, in a characteristic rush of adjectives, described her as being noble-minded, wise, fair, good, right-minded and clever. 'Her position is a very difficult one,' said the Queen; 'she is too enlightened and liberal for the Prussian Court not to have enemies....'

'She knows I am sincerely and devotedly attached to her,' wrote her daughter-in-law Princess Victoria, 'and that she need not fear to be misunderstood by me, and knows that I know how much she has to bear and go through—and that I value and admire her many so truly noble and great qualities.... I know no one I pity more. She stands so alone—she has and makes so many enemies and there are so few who bear with her foibles and know what she really is. And yet you do not know how difficult it is to be her friend for she always is her own enemy!'

Politically frustrated, and denied any intellectual or emotional outlet, Augusta began to seek spiritual fulfilment. She turned to Catholicism; away from the stark, militant, unsympathetic Lutheranism of the Prussian Court to the elaborate, colourful mysticism of the Catholic Church. Although she never actually embraced the faith, she began to interest herself in Catholic affairs. Her interest once aroused, she pursued it with all the vehemence of her nature. 'A Catholic Bishop seemed to her better worth cultivating than a Superintendent-General,' grumbled one of her enemies and she was accused of favouring Catholics above Protestants for posts in her entourage. As the life of mad King Frederick Wilhelm IV drew to a close and the date of her husband's coronation drew nearer, so did Augusta begin thinking in terms of introducing Catholic ritual into the great ceremony. In this, of course, she came up against the implacable opposition of her husband. Not only did he refuse to give way to her Papist fancies but he was thinking in terms of using the coming ceremony to play up his Divinely appointed, as opposed to his constitutional, status. This simply led to further scenes.

'The disagreements (in fact quarrels) which have been going on the last few days between [Prince Wilhelm and Princess Augusta] you have no idea of,' reported Princess Victoria to her mother. 'I assure you both Fritz and I feel unwell from it—and all for the merest trifles upon which it is not worthwhile to waste two words. It is difficult to say who is in the right and who in the wrong as both are right and both are wrong. . . .'

In this bitter, life-long conflict between Wilhelm and Augusta was rooted the ideological battle which was to rage through three generations of the Hohenzollern family. And the feud was to be as much national as domestic. In some ways husband and wife represented the two opposing faces of nineteenth-century Germany: his the Prussian, reactionary and martial, hers the German, progressive and cultured. During Wilhelm's first years of power, it was still not certain which side would triumph.

3

Prince Frederick Wilhelm, of Prussia, only son of Prince Wilhelm and Princess Augusta and known to the family as Fritz, combined the best characteristics of both parents. He had his father's superb presence, good nature and gentlemanly manners, and his mother's enlightened outlook. In addition he had a gentleness and a magnanimity lacking in both his narrow-minded father and his mercurial mother. Serious-minded, well-intentioned and conscientious, yet with a commanding appearance and a talent for soldiering, Fritz seemed the *beau idéal* of the nineteenth-century liberal prince. If, on closer acquaintance, he proved to be not quite as resolute or as intellectual as he appeared, he was none the less a man of honest purpose and more than average ability.

He looked magnificent. He was tall and well-proportioned, with a mane of golden hair and eyes so wide and blue that they were said to possess 'a strange fascination'. The Empress Eugénie, consort of the Emperor Napoleon III, seeing Prince Frederick in 1857, when he was twenty-six years of age, described him as 'a tall, handsome man, almost a head taller than the Emperor; he is slim and fair with a light golden moustache—in fact a Teuton such as Tacitus described—chivalrously polite, and not without a resemblance to Hamlet'. Lord Frederic Hamilton claimed that he looked like 'the living embodiment of a German legendary hero; a Lohengrin in real life'.

Through the exertions of his mother, Fritz's education, which would otherwise have been as conventional as that of all Prussian princes, was relatively broad. As his tutor she chose the eminent and idealistic Greek scholar, Professor Ernst Curtius. Although, predictably, Augusta considered Curtius to be too indulgent with his pupil, there is no doubt that the tutor did much towards cultivating the Prince's cultural and humanitarian leanings. After turning eighteen, Fritz spent a few years at the University of Bonn. Despite the fact that his life at Bonn was more circumscribed than that of the average student, his exposure to a more democratic atmosphere helped counteract some of the formality of the Prussian Court. Bonn encouraged him to develop into a relaxed, amiable and sociable young man. It also awakened his latent liberalism. Even as early as 1849, when he was only seventeen years old, Prince Frederick had shocked the reactionary General von Gerlach by speaking out in support of the newly granted constitution. The ensuing years of study, travel and observation merely strengthened his liberal attitude.

His journey to England, to the Great Exhibition of 1851,

proved particularly significant. 'Unfortunately,' commented the London *Times*, which could never resist a dig at the autocracy of Prussia, 'his stay is too short to enable him to realize to the full the magnitude and the freedom of public life in England; nothing could probably be of greater gain to the impressionable mind of the youthful Prince than to learn from such direct observation during the period of his preparation.' But *The Times* had misjudged him. Prince Frederick did not need to be converted. The British way of life, so spectacularly epitomized under the glittering glass domes of the Exhibition Building, simply confirmed his belief in the blessings of democracy.

Despite Prince Frederick's interest in cultural and political questions, the greater part of his youth was devoted to the Prussian army. When little more than a baby, he had started his military education, and at the age of ten he had received his commission as second-lieutenant in the First Regiment of Guards. His military training continued throughout his boyhood and young manhood; during his years at Bonn University he had always spent the spring or summer on manoeuvres, and once he had completed his studies, he devoted himself almost entirely to soldiering. Yet, unlike his father, Prince Frederick never developed into one of those militant, unquestioning, dedicated Prussian officers, to whom the army was the be-all and end-all of life. He enjoyed the skill, the glamour and the *camaraderie* of soldiering, but it was never his first love.

It was during these years of early manhood that certain weaknesses in Fritz's seemingly blameless character first became apparent. He was not quite the *chevalier sans peur et sans reproche* of popular imagining. He was found to be a worrier, easily discouraged and subject to fits of deep depression. Although he had inherited his full share of Hohenzollern pride and was given to violent bursts of temper, he lacked drive and stamina. In tune with his mother's forward-looking views, his respect for authority was too ingrained for him to defy his father. Indeed, this constant friction between his parents was leaving its mark on his hyper-sensitive personality. Torn between disagreeing with his highly strung mother or his intimidating father, he tended to play for safety by not committing himself. It was a trait which Queen Victoria was quick to notice when he visited England in 1851. 'I beg of you to show confidence in your dear son,' she wrote to Princess Augusta, 'so that he may likewise show confidence in himself. I am always afraid in his case of the consequences of a moral clash, should his father strongly recommend something and his mother warn him against it. He will wish to please both, and the fear of not succeeding will make him uncertain and hesitating, and his attempts to do so will train him in falsehood—two of the greatest evils which can befall a Prince.'

False, Prince Frederick would never be, but a certain hesitancy was to plague him all his life.

'I was painfully struck by his want of confidence in himself,' wrote a friend some years later, 'which caused constant hesitation, and also made him suspicious of others, taxing him with want of ability.' The luxuriant beard which he grew in later life was known to hide a loose mouth and a weak chin.

When Fritz was twenty-four, his father appointed the fifty-four-year-old Colonel Helmuth von Moltke as his personal aide-de-camp. It was a happy choice. With the dedication and self-discipline of a military martinet, Moltke combined the cultural and intellectual interests of a scholar. As such, he was the ideal mentor and companion for the intelligent, if somewhat irresolute, young Prince. The two of them were to travel a long way together. Their first journey took them to England, in 1855, on very special business.

Prince Albert, Queen Victoria's husband, had always dreamed of some future alliance between Great Britain and a united, democratic Germany. In his conscientious and tireless fashion, Albert had been advocating this for years. His ideas had the support, not only of his adoring wife, but of their mutual uncle, King Leopold I of the Belgians, and of that astute family factotum, Baron Christian von Stockmar. This earnest Coburg coterie was convinced that if only Prussia were to be injected with a dose of British liberalism and British greatness, she would be able to lead Germany to a united, democratic and powerful future. Between them, Britain and Greater Germany could then hold the balance between reactionary Russia and fickle France. Together, these two great Teutonic nations could guide Europe—indeed the world—towards a radiantly liberal dawn.

And what better way could there be of achieving such an alliance than by linking the royal Houses of Britain and Prussia?

In the eldest children of both the British and Prussian royal families were recognized two excellent candidates for this high-minded scheme. Prince Frederick of Prussia was known to have inherited his mother's progressive views and Victoria, the Princess Royal of Great Britain, was being brought up in an undeniably liberal atmosphere. Unlike her brother Bertie, Vicky was quick-witted, industrious and eager to learn. In her, Prince Albert had the ideal pupil for his painstaking, idealistic and apparently limitless course of training. From babyhood, almost, she had had the Coburg brand of liberalism drummed into her. If Vicky were not moulded into the ideal consort for a constitutional monarch, it would certainly not be for any want of trying on the part of her father.

On a personal, as opposed to an international level, the prospect of the alliance gave no less satisfaction. Queen Victoria declared that the 'German element' was the one which she wished to be cherished and kept up in their beloved home, and Princess Augusta was no less enthusiastic. It was 'the confirmation of our dearest hopes...' she admitted to Prince Albert's brother, Duke Ernest of Coburg. 'God bless the union for these beloved children, for our family, and for our poor country....' Even Prince Wilhelm, though he might disapprove of the liberal tone of the British Court, was only too glad of the opportunity of allying relatively unimportant Prussia to all-powerful Britain.

The only drawback to the proposed match was a difference in age between the two young people. In the year 1855, Prince Frederick of Prussia turned twenty-four while Princess Victoria was some ten years younger. But the obstacle was by no means insurmountable; it was simply a question of biding one's time. In the meanwhile, it would be as well to get the matter tied up. One never knew for how long so eligible a prince might stay on the market. Fritz was duly invited to Balmoral in the autumn of 1855. There, during the course of those bracing Highland excursions and to the immense gratification of all concerned, the two young people fell in love.

Vicky, reported Fritz to his parents, 'is a pleasant mixture of childlike simplicity and virginal charm, as I like it'. She possessed 'great feeling and intelligence' and he was pleased to be able to tell them that she showed a lively interest in German art and literature. He thought that they would be well suited.

After a sleepless night (his sixth since his arrival) Fritz

40

opened his heart to the Queen and Prince Albert. Although delighted, they asked him to postpone his proposal until after the Princess's confirmation. After all, she was not yet fifteen. But love proved too powerful and one day, while the Prince and Princess were riding down Craig-na-Ban, Fritz pressed a piece of white heather into little Vicky's hand and spoke his piece. The Princess, flushed with excitement, was only too ready to accept him.

The business concluded, Prince Frederick returned to Prussia and Princess Victoria to even more intensive study. Although Prince Albert was able to assure his future son-in-law that 'from the moment you declared your love and embraced her, the child in her vanished', it was agreed that they must wait for at least two years before marrying. 'I hope the long period of waiting will not make you impatient,' added Albert.

In the meantime the two families kept in close touch. The young lovers exchanged impassioned letters; indeed, a forty-page letter from the Princess, written the day after Frederick's departure from England, caused Moltke, the Prince's aide, to exclaim dryly, 'How the news must have accumulated.'

'Dear, dear Fritz, I think of you day and night,' wrote she, while he assured her that she was now everything in the world to him. To his future father-in-law, Prince Frederick wrote on political matters. As Albert was never one to pass up the opportunity of giving advice, political or no, he answered Frederick in full. Queen Victoria was no less ready with her pen. Letters to Wilhelm, to Augusta and above all, to Fritz, poured forth in a steady stream. 'I am to tell you,' she wrote of her daughter to Prince Frederick, 'what joy it would give her just to look into your dear eyes and that she had never felt so happy before as when you kissed her! ... I would like to say that the future husband of my daughter, if he is what you are, must be almost closer to us parents than our own son!'

To her uncle, King Leopold, who was every bit as gratified to see the Coburg seed planted in yet another royal House, the Queen described Fritz as 'a dear, excellent, charming young man, whom we shall give our dear child to with perfect confidence'.

This was all very well, but not everyone shared the Queen's rapture at the proposed match. There was grumbling among the Junkers in Berlin and through their mouthpiece, the daily *Kreuz-Zeitung*, they expressed their alarm at the prospect of this alliance with liberal England. The London *Times*, for precisely opposite reasons, was just as disapproving. It could see very little advantage in this link with what it dismissed as 'a paltry German dynasty'. Queen Victoria described *The Times*'s strictures as 'insulting' and assured Augusta that Lord Palmerston had claimed that the marriage would be 'of immense importance to England and Europe'.

However, for all her optimism, the Queen did experience one nasty moment. This was when the Prussian Court let it be known that they expected the marriage ceremony to take place, as was customary for Prussian princes, in Berlin. Victoria was furious. 'The Queen *never* could consent to it...' she declared in her robust fashion, 'and the assumption of its being *too much* for a Prince Royal of Prussia to *come* over to marry the *Princess Royal of Great Britain* IN England is too *absurd*, to say the least.... Whatever may be the usual practice of Prussian Princes, it is not *every* day that one marries the eldest daughter of the Queen of England. The question therefore must be considered as settled and closed.'

And settled and closed it was. The marriage ceremony was fixed for 25 January 1858, to be held in the Chapel Royal of St James's Palace in London. The bride would be seventeen and the bridegroom twenty-six. Overcoming their reluctance, the Prussian royal family ('the three cousins will arrive,' wrote Fritz, 'then Mama, Uncle Albrecht, finally Papa, and last of all, the happiest of the happy') travelled to England. They found London crammed with royalty. Benjamin Disraeli, attending the Bridal Ball at Buckingham Palace, judged there to be as many princes present as at the Congress of Vienna. 'The Royal party did nothing but dance with each other,' he noted, 'and I thought, perhaps in consequence, looked bored. I saw the Princess [Augusta] of Prussia cram her pocket handkerchief into her mouth to stifle a yawn. The Princess Royal, however, looked bright and gay....'

The marriage ceremony was conducted, thought the diarist Charles Greville, 'with amazing *éclat*'. In a dress of white moiré silk, Honiton lace and sprays of orange blossom, the Princess scarcely reached her husband's epauletted shoulder. Queen Victoria, who felt as though she herself were being married for a second time, sobbed throughout the ceremony. When it was over and she flung herself on to the young couple, she felt so overwrought that the words simply would not come.

The four-day honeymoon was spent at Windsor and the young couple's departure for Prussia brought forth fresh floods of tears. This time not only the Queen, but her entire brood of children and indeed, the very skies, were weeping. 'It began to snow just before Vicky left,' noted the Queen, 'and continued to do so without intermission all day.'

On the night before the wedding, the Queen, in an upsurge of maternal anguish, had cried out to her hardly less distraught husband that, 'After all, it is like taking a poor lamb to be sacrificed.'

And so it turned out to be, even if in not quite the sense that the emotional Queen had meant it.

4

Few nineteenth-century princesses seemed destined for a more glorious future than did Princess Victoria. Not only was she married to a man who would one day reign over a country poised on the threshold of greatness, but she was eminently qualified for the role which she had been cast to play. Although only seventeen years of age at the time of her arrival in Berlin, she already showed signs of developing into a woman of considerable character, completely in tune with the new movements spreading through central Europe. With the year of her arrival coinciding with that of old King Frederick Wilhelm IV's final drift into madness and the assumption of the Regency by her ageing father-in-law, it was assumed that it would not be long before she held the centre of the stage. Her prospects certainly seemed brilliant.

It was true that she was not much to look at. Indeed, Queen Victoria had been afraid that her daughter might not prove attractive enough for the handsome Prince Frederick. Like her mother, she was short, although Queen Victoria refused to concede this. The Queen simply could not understand how Prussian journals could refer to the Princess as small, 'considering,' she wrote petulantly, 'that you are a good deal taller than me, and I am not a dwarf.' Walburga, Countess of Hohenthal, who had been appointed lady-in-waiting to Princess Victoria, claimed that it was the remains of the Princess's 'childish roundness' which made her appear shorter than she was. Nor did Vicky's fussy, somewhat matronly clothes help matters. Her nose was considered to be too short, her complexion too ruddy and her jaw too heavy for contemporary taste.

On the credit side, however, the Princess had a charming expression, a delightful voice and beautiful eyes; 'the iris was green like the sea on a sunny day, and the white had a peculiar shimmer which gave them a fascination that, together with a smile that showed her small and beautiful teeth, bewitched those who approached her', enthused Countess Hohenthal. Her bearing, in these early days, was modest and self-possessed.

This somewhat circumspect manner masked a lively personality. Princess Victoria was an energetic, high-spirited and intelligent young woman, with something of her father's serious-mindedness and all of her mother's enthusiasm. The American Minister in London described her as 'all life and spirit, full of frolic and fun, with an excellent head and a *heart as big as a mountain*'. To her wide-ranging interests, she brought a sense of real dedication. Whatever she did—whether it be writing a political treatise, modelling a bas-relief or studying a book on religious philosophy—she did diligently and intelligently. She had, as Prince Albert once said, 'a man's head' on her shoulders. But she had also a woman's warmth and impetuosity. Of all the princesses at the Prussian Court, she was far and away the most interesting.

She needed all her wits about her in her present situation. Her path was strewn with the most extraordinary difficulties. Berlin, as Queen Victoria's half-sister, Princess Feodore of Hohenlohe-Langenberg, reported, was 'a hotbed of envy, jealousy, intrigue and malicious knavery'. To expect a seventeen-year-old girl, no matter how bright, to negotiate such a hotbed successfully, was asking a great deal. Although the Princess had been warmly welcomed to Berlin, the pro-Russian, anti-British element remained firmly opposed to the marriage. Junker circles were reserving judgement on *die Engländerin*. They were not long in passing it.

Their chief complaint was about her persistent Englishness. 'You ask me in your letter what I think of the English marriage,' wrote Bismarck to General von Gerlach. 'I must separate the two words to give you my opinion. The "English" in it does not please me, the "marriage" might be quite good, for the Princess has the reputation of being a lady of brain and heart. If the Princess can leave the Englishwoman at home and become a Prussian, then she may be a blessing to the country. . . .'

It was sound advice but Vicky was incapable of following it. To her, England was always 'home', superior, in every possible way—be it politics or plumbing—to Prussia. It was, she assured her mother, 'my country which I shall love so passionately to my dying day, and be too proud to have belonged to ever to let myself forget'. In her unwise, if natural, attitude, the Princess received every encouragement from her parents. Even before the marriage, Prince Albert had warned his future son-in-law that 'the Princess Royal of England is expatriating herself and marrying Prince Frederick William of Prussia, but thereby she does not cease to be the Princess Royal, and with the best will in the world to become as German as possible, she can never change her nature. . . .' And to the Princess herself, he explained that she must never 'give the impression that you wish to discard your native country or let it drop'. The Queen, no less adamant, instructed her daughter to sign her name *Victoria, Princess Royal and Princess Frederick William of Prussia*, and when Vicky once suggested following some harmless Prussian custom, the Queen replied that she could 'let the German ladies do what they like, but the *English* Princess *must not*'.

That Vicky should yearn for England and English ways was understandable. For one thing she was very young. For another, she had been thrust into a *milieu* very different from that of the British royal family. On first arriving in Berlin, the newly married couple were housed in the Old Schloss, the official home of the Prussian monarchy. Although the State apartments were magnificent, the living quarters were appalling. There were no bathrooms, there was no laid-on water, there was no cupboard space. The beds were infested with bugs, the smell of the drains was overwhelming, the long-disused rooms were thick with dead bats. To reach her bedroom from her sitting-room, the Princess had to pass through the death chamber of King Frederick Wilhelm III which had been left untouched for almost twenty years. The servants were dirty, sullen and dishonest. Even when the Prince and Princess moved into their permanent home—the Kronprinzenpalais—in Unter den Linden, the domestic arrangements were far from satisfactory. Compared with Osborne and Balmoral, things were extremely primitive. There was a serious lack of what Queen

45

Victoria referred to as 'these really necessary affairs'.

Nor could the Princess take much delight in her husband's family. Old King Frederick Wilhelm IV was mad, Prince Wilhelm and Princess Augusta quarrelled continuously, the Regent's brothers and their families were the sort of idle, loud-mouthed, bickering, philistine people whom Vicky hated. The family dinners in the Old Schloss were a form of torture for her. She found the silver shoddy, the conversation indelicate, the rows unnerving. 'I confess I could not live as the rest do here,' she wrote to her father, 'in busy idleness, without rest, without work, doing no good, and at the end of the day—knocked up and tired—the next morning a headache! Often it makes me melancholy to see health and strength thrown away and existence wasted, in joyless frivolity when there is so much to be done!'

For their part, the members of her husband's family considered her to be too zealous by half. They found her priggish, pretentious and over-industrious. The ideal Prussian woman was one who confined herself to *Küche, Kinderstube, Krankenstube und Kirche*—kitchen, nursery, sickroom and church—and left intellectual pursuits to the men. Princess Victoria, with her passion for reading, discussion, painting, modelling, architecture, and her insistence on open windows, modern plumbing and long walks, did not measure up to these standards at all. When set against the empty-headed women at Court, she seemed alarmingly emancipated. Only with her mother-in-law did she develop a sympathetic relationship, and even Augusta found some of Vicky's ideas too advanced. She considered her daughter-in-law's somewhat rational approach to religion particularly unseemly. 'She is quite Renan in her ideas,' grumbled Augusta; all English princesses, she claimed, were complete atheists.

In time, the Princess's cultural and intellectual enthusiasms might have been forgiven her; it was her interest in politics that earned her the undying enmity of the ruling Junker class. She had arrived in Berlin with a strong sense of mission: it was to be through her that her adored father's progressive ideas were to be introduced into Prussian political life. For years he had been training her for this important task and she, fired by his ideals, was determined not to fail him. In the words of one of her biographers, like 'Brünnhilde to his Wotan, she was the maiden of his will'. Lest Vicky weaken in this resolve (it was an unlikely contingency) both the Queen and Prince Albert bombarded her with letters of advice. Hardly a day went by without a word from either, or both, parents. Albert's advice, if wordy, was always sound. 'To satisfy the people by means of a government that is esteemed morally and takes into account the requirements of the times is the only way to fight revolutionary aspirations,' he wrote. 'Therefore never let yourself be frightened by demagogues, as little children are by the devil, but be deeply sorry if you see popular feeling trampled under foot; and do not believe that High Society and the Army are the people.'

In reply to these lectures, Vicky would write, not only long and well-reasoned replies, but political essays and memoranda which Prince Albert, while marvelling at her good sense, would correct and criticize. One would almost have imagined, from the tone of this correspondence, that it was the Princess, and not her husband, who was one day to rule over Prussia. But then Victoria and Albert had always believed in the closest co-operation between sovereign and consort and they might have realized, even at this early stage, that their daughter had the stronger personality of the two.

Not content with this literary exchange, parents and daughter exchanged visits. Albert came to stay with the young couple in Berlin and was able to assure Queen Victoria that he had had 'long talks with both of them, singly and together, which gave me the greatest satisfaction'. The Queen herself followed soon after and the Princess made frequent journeys to England. 'Really,' wrote Vicky to her mother after one of these visits, 'there is not a thing I hear or see or do, that my first thought is not "what would dear Papa say, what would he think"!'

That Prince Albert's seeds of political wisdom had indeed fallen on fertile ground, there was no question. Lord Clarendon, on a visit to Berlin, expressed himself amazed at the 'mind, the judgement, and the foresight of the Princess Royal'. He had had, he said, 'the honour to hold a very long conversation with her Royal Highness, and has been more than ever astounded at the *statesmanlike* and comprehensive view which she takes of the policy of Prussia, both internal and foreign, and of the *duties* of a constitutional king'.

This was all very fine, but the Princess's well-considered opinions were not appreciated to anything like the same extent

47

in the country to which they applied. The men surrounding the Regent came to look upon her as, at best, meddlesome and at worst, dangerous. With each passing year she became more and more unpopular.

For this, the blame did not lie wholly with the Junkers. The Princess had certain serious defects of character and these the very defects which she could least afford in her present delicate situation. For all her brilliance, Princess Victoria lacked wisdom. 'Always clever, never wise,' was how a British statesman once summed up her personality, and one of her husband's aides complained that she had a great deal of talent but no common sense. She simply did not understand the art of handling people. She tried to win their heads, it has been said, 'rather than their hearts'. She was too dogmatic, too emotional, too tactless in her dealings with others. Aggressively honest, her frankness could be embarrassing. 'Think, think, Madam,' Professor Helmholtz once advised; 'but don't tell the entire world what you are thinking!'

She was an extremely poor judge of character. 'The Princess,' reports Walburga Hohenthal, 'often from no particular reasons, took violent fancies to people. She used at first to think them quite perfect and then came to bitter disillusion. She also took first-sight dislikes to persons, based often on a trick of manners or an idle word dropped about them in her presence, and thus she often lost friends and supporters. She was no judge of character, and never became one, because her own point of view was the only one she could see. . . .' She was incapable of making concessions or allowances or of adapting her own opinions. Once she had made up her mind, nothing would change it; with her, it was always all or nothing. Her lifelong friend, Lady Mary Ponsonby, claimed that Vicky 'had a keenly analytical mind like her father, and divided everything into three heads, turning them about so much that she often came to a wrong conclusion'.

'She was like a ship in full sail when the ballast is suddenly thrown overboard,' was how one of her ladies described her. It was no wonder that in waters as treacherous as Prussia's she should come to grief.

Among her well-wishers were those who blamed her tactless behaviour on the excessive interference of her parents. She should be left alone, they said, to make her own way; free of their constant naggings, she might be able to adapt herself to the Prussian way of life more easily. 'The Queen is really insane about the maintenance of her maternal authority (tyranny would be a more correct expression) and not recognizing that marriage justifies the smallest transfer of allegiance from herself to her son-in-law,' noted Lord Clarendon. Old Baron Stockmar, who had done everything towards encouraging the royal marriage, now felt it necessary to warn Queen Victoria against too much parental prompting. He urged 'somewhat more consideration, moderation, calm and passivity'.

Stockmar's well-meant warning, instead of stemming the flow of royal advice, merely excited the Queen into 'a towering passion'.

The one island of security in the morass of difficulties in which Vicky found herself floundering was the love between her husband and herself. Theirs had been a love match and a love match it was to remain throughout their married life. Frederick and Victoria suited each other perfectly. Both were enlightened, cultured, hardworking and conscientious and if she was the cleverer, he was perhaps the wiser. Lacking her quickness, he had the more reflective personality. His gentleness and his air of seriousness offset her impetuosity and her pig-headedness. 'She certainly was a little tyrant,' noted Walburga Hohenthal, 'and with a less chivalrous and devoted husband there might have been difficulties.' It was no wonder that, as she matured, so did she develop the more dominant personality.

Following the example of Queen Victoria and Prince Albert, Fritz and Vicky spent as much time as possible in each other's company. 'I feel that I could not do a single thing, small or great, without asking my husband's advice,' admitted the Princess to her mother; 'and he takes such pains to explain everything to me; the moments we are left alone together are the happiest in the day.'

Apart from him she was miserable. If he had to be away on military duty she would trail through his room, feeling herself to be simply another of those objects, belonging to him, which he had left behind. Once, when she visited England without him, she poured out her love in a letter written from Windsor Castle.

'I am settled in the rooms I had before my marriage,' she wrote. 'In this room I experienced the happiest moment of my life when you took me into your arms as your wife and pressed me to your heart; when I even think of that moment my heart beats madly and I have a terrible longing for you, and I think I would hug you to death if I had you here now. I find the parting unbearable ... dear God, if you only knew what you mean to me, how I would love to suffer for you and how fervently I pray God every morning and evening to let me bear all the unpleasantness, all physical and mental suffering that may be your portion, so that you may be spared. I feel quite crazy with longing for you....'

By the spring of 1858, a few months after her marriage, Vicky realized that she was pregnant. The young couple's delight at the prospect was not shared by Queen Victoria. On receipt of what she called 'the horrid news', she launched into a series of attacks on 'the shadow side' of marriage; even the poor father-to-be had cold water poured on his enthusiasm. 'I must admit, dear Fritz, that what fills you with joy, brings me sorrow and anxiety, for it is bound up with so much suffering and danger for the poor and very young mother! You men are far too selfish! You only have the advantages in such a case, whereas we poor women have to bear all the pain and suffering (of which you can have no conception). When, however, all is over satisfactorily ... I shall certainly be just as glad as you.'

And, of course, she was. On 27 January 1859, almost exactly a year after her marriage, Princess Victoria gave birth to a son. Her father-in-law, Prince Wilhelm, in his methodical fashion, had given the artillery precise orders on how the birth should be greeted. He had even anticipated the possibility of twins. The first thunder of the guns so excited him, however, that he simply rushed out of his palace into the street and, flinging customary dignity and parsimony to the winds, took a cab to the Old Schloss.

His delight—and that of all concerned—was somewhat marred by the fact that, during the course of a difficult delivery, the baby's neck had been injured. As a result the head was tilted too far to the left and, worse still, the cervical nerve plexus damaged. This rendered his left arm all but useless. This alarming fact was not discovered until three days after the baby's birth but it was hoped that time and treatment would heal it. They never did, and the effect of this withered arm on the character of the growing boy was incalculable.

He was given the names of Friedrich Wilhelm Victor Albert and, because of the plethora of Fredericks in the Hohenzollern family, he was called William. What epithet, wondered Prince Albert, would history attach to the name William? Not, he hoped, 'Rufus', nor 'the Silent', nor 'the Conqueror'; perhaps 'the Great'. In fact, the boy was to become known as Kaiser Wilhelm II or, as his mother's countrymen were one day to call him—Kaiser Bill.

'May he be a blessing and comfort to you and to his country!' wrote Queen Victoria to her daughter on the baby's second birthday. 'He may be born for great deeds and great times —be that as it may, but do you both bring him up to be fitted for his position, to be wise, sensible, courageous—liberal-minded—good and pure.'

A less appropriate set of adjectives to describe the future Kaiser Wilhelm II would have been difficult to find.

CHAPTER TWO

OTTO VON BISMARCK

1

On 2 January 1861 King Frederick Wilhelm IV died in his palace of Sans Souci at Potsdam. Prince Wilhelm, at the age of sixty-four, now ascended the throne of the Hohenzollerns, as King Wilhelm I. If there had been any doubt as to the sort of king he planned to be, it was dispelled by his speech from the throne at the opening of parliament a few days after his accession. He assured the assembled deputies that he 'never could permit the progressive development of the nation's inner political life to question or endanger the rights of the Crown or the power of Prussia'.

His coronation, on 18 October 1861, was designed to emphasize such thinking. Indeed, the fact that he was officially crowned at all was significant. Recent Prussian monarchs had dispensed with the ceremony as being too costly but the new King, determined to offset what he considered a loss of royal prestige by the granting of a constitution after the revolution of 1848, insisted on a coronation. He decided, moreover, that the ceremony be held in the chapel of Königsberg Castle, where the first Hohenzollern king had been crowned in 1701.

It was a magnificently staged affair. The Schlosskirche itself, with its slender columns, vaulted ceiling and richly canopied altar made an impressive setting. 'The *coup d'oeil* was really beautiful,' enthused Vicky, now Crown Princess of Prussia; 'the chapel is in itself lovely, with a great deal of gold about it, and all hung with red velvet and gold—the carpet, altar, thrones and canopies the same.' To the strains of a specially composed march by Meyerbeer, the procession entered the Schlosskirche and moved towards the altar through shafts of sunlight streaming in from the tall windows. The King, stiff-backed and silver haired, was trailing a long, ermine-trimmed mantle of crimson velvet. Queen Augusta, expertly enamelled and dazzlingly jew-elled, was in a white silk crinoline with a silver train. There were Knights of the Black Eagle in red velvet, *Palastdamen* in crimson and gold, an *Oberhofmeisterin* in gold and white bro-cade with green velvet, lesser ladies-in-waiting in violet and gold and blue and gold, with 'all the uniforms, and the ladies' diamonds glittering in the bright sunlight'. The regalia was carried to the altar on a gold and brocade cushion.

However, it was not for its kaleidoscopic grandeur alone that the coronation ceremony was remarkable. King Wilhelm plan-ned to imbue it with a deeper significance. Having knelt in prayer before the altar, he mounted the steps and, taking the crown in both hands, placed it upon his own head. Lest the importance of the gesture be lost on his audience, he followed it with a stirring pronouncement. 'I receive this crown from God's hand, and from no other,' he declared. It was an un-equivocal affirmation of his belief in the Divine Right of Kings. He then took up the sceptre and the sword of State and, turning, extended his arms towards the congregation. When he crowned the Queen who, according to one witness, 'looked beautiful and did all she had to do with perfect grace', there was 'hardly a dry eye in the church'. The ceremony ended in the roar of cannon, the clashing of bells and the thunderous singing of *Heil dir im Siegerkranz*.

On receiving the President and delegates of the Prussian parliament in the Castle after the ceremony, King Wilhelm again stressed his adherence to the principle of *Gottesgnaden-tum*. 'Mindful of the fact that the crown comes to me from God alone,' he announced firmly, 'I have shown that I receive it humbly from Him by being crowned in sacred precincts.'

That more enlightened opinion throughout Europe should be astonished at the Prussian King's attitude was inevitable. The London *Times* lost no time in taking him to task, and Queen Victoria admitted that 'the speech of the King has alarmed and rather distressed us'.

One of her subjects, Sir William Hardman, was more out-spoken. 'After all,' he wrote with fine British superiority, 'what can you expect from pigs but grunts, and similarly, what can you expect from a pig-headed German but that he should "be-have as such"? We had fondly hoped for better things. The Prussians have got awfully bumptious of late years.'

The first clash between Divine Right and parliamentary

democracy was not long in coming. It concerned the King's plans for the reorganization of the Prussian army. Wilhelm, backed by General von Roon, wanted the regular army strengthened, and the *Landwehr*—the middle-class reserve— weakened. He viewed this as an essential triumph of military conservatism over civilian liberalism. The Prussian parliament, who saw it in the same light, suggested a compromise plan. Refusing to accept this plan, the King dismissed his ministers and dissolved parliament.

New elections returned a still more liberal parliament, with Progressives winning a resounding victory over the Conservatives. The new parliament refused to vote any money whatsoever for the army reforms. This led to a constitutional deadlock of the most serious order. For the King to rule without a budget would mean a contravention of the constitution. It would also mean going against the recently expressed feelings of the electorate. The issue had become a simple question of whether King or parliament was more powerful in Prussia. The King professed himself disgusted at the idea of his beloved army being dictated to by a collection of Jews, Poles, Catholics and democrats. Yet he did not feel strong enough to defy parliament. He might be unyielding but he was never daring.

Faced with this crisis, the King decided to abdicate in favour of his son. When Crown Prince Frederick declined to sign his father's act of abdication (and how different the subsequent history of Germany might have been if he had) King Wilhelm played his last card. He adopted the course which the reactionary General von Roon had been urging upon him all through the crisis. He sent for Otto von Bismarck-Schönhausen to head a new government. Bismarck, at that stage Prussian Ambassador in Paris, was considered to be the only man powerful, and ruthless enough to defy parliament and carry through the reforms. He came hurrying back to Berlin and the King appointed him Minister-President.

With the accession to power of the forty-seven-year-old Otto von Bismarck, the Hohenzollern dynasty gained its greatest champion, Prussia its greatest politician and Germany its greatest statesman. At first glance, Bismarck seemed a typical representative of the class from which he sprang—the Junkers. He was tall, bull-necked, bulbous-eyed, florid-faced and energetic, with a hearty appetite, great physical stamina and a tremendous zest for life. He had a deep love of the countryside, of forests, farms and wild animals and was never happier, it seemed, than when out walking under the trees with his dogs. He might have been no more than a successful country squire. But, on closer acquaintance, it all looked a little too good to be true; it was as though Bismarck were merely acting the part of a country aristocrat. His homespun qualities seemed affected, his Junkerism exaggerated. And indeed, behind the façade of a bluff and simple country gentleman lay an extremely complex character. With the brawn inherited from his Junker father was combined the brain of his middle-class mother.

Bismarck's was a many-faceted personality. He was an intelligent, cultivated, well-spoken man of the world, witty and cynical. He could be utterly charming. Yet, for all this urbanity, he was an emotional man, with a restless manner, a high-pitched voice and eyes likely to spill over with tears. He had a violent temper. Extremely sensitive, he neither forgot nor forgave an insult. He was astute, devious, perceptive; also dynamic, ambitious and ruthless. His heart could be like stone. Above all, Bismarck had a lust for power.

Bismarck's public career had started with his election to the Prussian parliament in 1847. His well-expressed and uncompromising conservatism had soon earned him, first the attention, then the approval and finally the support of the reactionaries surrounding King Frederick Wilhelm IV. On their recommendation he had been appointed to three important posts: he had gone as Prussian Minister to the German Diet in Frankfurt, as Ambassador to St Petersburg and as Ambassador to Paris. During these years in the diplomatic service he had cemented his reputation as a harsh-tongued, hard-headed opponent of liberalism; the darling of the Junkers. Yet Bismarck was far from being a typically narrow-minded conservative. He brought a flexibility, a freshness, a certain daring to conservatism; if he was anachronistic in some ways, he was amazingly forward-looking in others. As such, he stood head and shoulders above his Junker colleagues. Indeed, he tended to treat with a thinly veiled contempt the aristocratic class to which he belonged and whose position he was dedicated to uphold. None the less, he was careful to keep in close touch with those in power; thus, when King Wilhelm's advisers needed a strong man to defy parliament during the crisis over the Army Bill, it was for Bismarck that they sent.

By his famous 'blood and iron' speech ('*Eisen und Blut*' were his words) Bismarck set the tone of future government policy. Ignoring parliamentary protests, he ruled without a budget, simply collecting and spending the taxpayers' money as he saw fit. The manner in which he chose to spend it was, of course, on army reform. The King had won the first round.

King Wilhelm was not, however, quite as elated by the turn of events as might be expected. Although he himself applauded Bismarck's strong-arm methods, his family did not. Neither Queen Augusta, nor Crown Prince Frederick and Crown Princess Victoria could be expected to approve of this cavalier treatment of the constitution. A holiday spent with the sharp-tongued Augusta at Baden-Baden soon after Bismarck's assumption of power left Wilhelm depressed and uncertain. 'I foresee exactly how this will end,' he remarked to Bismarck on his return. 'They will cut off your head, and later on mine, on the Opern Platz, beneath my windows.'

But Bismarck knew how to counter such thinking.

'Yes, we shall be dead then,' he said to the King, 'but we must die sooner or later, and can we perish more creditably? I myself in fighting for the cause of my King, Your Majesty in sealing your Divine Right with your blood? Whether it is shed on the scaffold or on the battlefield makes no difference to the fact that you would be gloriously staking your life for the rights conferred on you by the grace of God.'

At the sound of this reactionary jargon, the old King brightened perceptibly. 'He felt himself entirely in the position of the principal officer of the Prussian army,' noted the gratified Bismarck, 'for whom death at his post would be an honourable ending to the task allotted him.' It had not taken Bismarck long to get the King's measure.

From henceforth, instead of Bismarck being King Wilhelm's faithful servant, it was to be Wilhelm who would serve Bismarck's ends. By creating in the King's mind the feeling that parliament was ceaselessly contemplating bloody revolution, and that he had no defender other than himself, Bismarck kept King Wilhelm firmly in hand. The King, explained Bismarck with startling candour to a member of the parliamentary opposition, was like a horse that shied at every new object and became restive and unmanageable if handled forcefully. But he would become accustomed to it in time, he added.

Become accustomed to it he did. During the following eight and a half years, from the time of Bismarck's appointment as

Minister-President in 1862 until the proclamation of the Empire in 1871, it was Bismarck's iron guidance alone which enabled King Wilhelm to lead Prussia to greatness. The relationship between the two men was not always harmonious. Bismarck found his master mulish and unimaginative ('an officer who does his duty, well-mannered with ladies' was how he once slightingly referred to the King) while Wilhelm was sometimes appalled at Bismarck's unscrupulousness. Queen Victoria once noted that King Wilhelm had said 'with tears in his eyes, how much he felt the weight of his position'. But the simple-minded old master was no match for his astute servant; of Bismarck's virtuosity, cunning, resource and subtlety, King Wilhelm had nothing. He might be brave but, unlike Bismarck, he was never audacious.

Count Lehndorff repeats a significant story of an encounter between Wilhelm and Bismarck. The King went, early each summer, to Gastein and here, one morning, he and Bismarck had a violent disagreement on some matter of policy. They parted on the worst possible terms. Later that day Count Lehndorff accompanied Wilhelm on his customary stroll. As they walked down a narrow street, they saw Bismarck enter it at the far end. The King was horrified. 'Can't we get into a side street?' he asked anxiously. 'Here's Bismarck coming and I'm afraid he's so upset today that he will cut me.' But there was no escape. Bismarck advanced, swept off his large black hat and in his most commanding voice, asked, 'Has Your Majesty any commands for me today?'

'No, my dear Bismarck,' answered the King, 'but it would be a very great pleasure if you would take me to your favourite bench by the river, from which one can get that lovely view down the valley.' Off they went to the bench, leaving Count Lehndorff to enjoy 'the beauty of the harmony again reigning' between the two men—one of whom was called the master and the other the servant.

However, there were two things—and these the most important—on which King and Prime Minister always saw eye to eye: the need for a powerful monarchy and the need for a powerful army. In his determination to strengthen these institutions, Bismarck could count on King Wilhelm's unqualified support. Having ascertained that, Bismarck, safe behind the eminently respectable façade of the Prussian King, could manoeuvre as he pleased.

One of the first tests of Bismarck's power over the King came in the summer of 1863. The incident serves as another illustration of their tempestuous personal relationship. Austria, appreciating that something had to be done about the unsatisfactory state of the German Confederation, was determined that she, and neither Prussia nor the German people, must be the one to do it. It was important that she affirm her leadership. She therefore decided to stage a congress to which the various German princes would be invited to discuss a scheme for the reform of the Confederation. The Congress would be under the presidency of the Austrian Emperor, Franz Joseph.

The Emperor's invitation was accepted by all the German sovereigns other than King Wilhelm of Prussia. Bismarck, determined that Prussia should not dance to Austria's tune, had talked the King into refusing. But Wilhelm remained uneasy. He had no desire to insult the Emperor Franz Joseph, nor did he want to let slip this opportunity of a conservative solution to the problem of the Confederation. Thus, when the Emperor Franz Joseph sent the highly respected King Johann of Saxony to press King Wilhelm to accept the invitation, the King felt unable to refuse. Bismarck, on hearing that his master was wavering, was furious. He stormed into the King's presence and demanded that he refuse the invitation. When the King held firm Bismarck, not for the last time in his career, threatened to resign, leaving the King to face his rebellious parliament alone. The argument ended with the King flinging himself sobbing on to a chaise-longue and with the overwrought Bismarck snatching a large vase from a table and smashing it to the ground. The invitation was declined. The Congress, without the presence of the King of Prussia, was a complete failure.

The question of the German Confederation was to be solved in a distinctly more brutal fashion.

2

If Bismarck's relations with the King were not always harmonious, with the rest of the royal family they were continuously stormy. As each year passed, they became more stormy still. In the end, their violence would all but tear the royal family apart.

Queen Augusta was particularly vehement in her objections to Bismarck. In fact, she hated him. 'The truth was that their two natures were not sympathetic,' it was said; 'she was highly-strung and aesthetic—in him not even Paris and St Petersburg had been able to polish the roughness of the diamond.' But there was a great deal more to it than this. Augusta's antipathy towards Bismarck went back many years. It was rooted in the confused days that followed the Revolution of 1848. At that time, with her husband in exile in England, Augusta and her two children had been living quietly in Potsdam. Here Bismarck, furious at the apparent success of liberalism, had approached her with a plan for a counter-revolution. He had proposed that her husband abdicate his rights to the throne in favour of their eldest son, Prince Frederick, and that a conservative movement to abolish the newly granted constitution be launched in the boy's name. Augusta had been highly indignant at the suggestion. As a liberal, she had refused to have anything to do with what she considered to be a sordid reactionary intrigue. From then on, the two of them had been at daggers drawn. Bismarck was considered to be Augusta's 'deadly enemy'.

Now, a dozen years later, Augusta regarded his reappearance on the scene as nothing short of disastrous. Had he not taken control of the destinies of Prussia, she might yet have been able to nag the King into following a more liberal course. It was now hopeless. Encouraged, indeed led by Bismarck, Wilhelm could be as autocratic as he liked. The King's ranting against the constitution and the 'opposition *canaille*' met with the full approval of Bismarck and his colleagues; Augusta's arguments fell on deaf ears. But as she was never one to concede defeat, Augusta continued to do everything possible to counteract Bismarck's influence. The result was that the old King became more stubborn, she more shrill, and their domestic life more tempestuous than ever. Not until some years later, however, did the clashes between Augusta and Bismarck resound in public.

No less dedicated in their opposition to Bismarck were the Crown Prince and Princess. To this idealistic young couple, he epitomized everything they hated and were working against. During the period of political uncertainty before Bismarck's appointment, the very possibility of his gaining power had filled them with alarm. The Crown Princess had referred to him as a wretch and 'a most unprincipled and irresponsible character', while her husband, always more sensitive, had admitted to howling and sobbing after a scene with his father on the question of Bismarck's possible appointment. When the King had threatened to abdicate, Vicky had been all for her husband ascending the throne there and then. Cloaking her ambition—or at least her impatience for the introduction of a more liberal regime—in an air of disinterestedness, she had urged Fritz to accept his father's abdication.

'I see no way out and consider you should make this sacrifice for the country,' she had written. 'If you do not accept, I believe that you will regret it one day, in any case I would not wish to have the responsibility of advising against it. . . . We must not think of ourselves at this moment, the difficult times we both would have and the disagreeable duties do not count, we must think only of the country and of our children. . . .'

But the Crown Prince had not been able to bring himself to take so bold a step. He might be a liberal but his respect for the laws of succession was too ingrained. For him, no less than for his father, the considerations of the House of Hohenzollern always came first. 'It would be a very dangerous precedent for the future,' he said, 'if the Sovereign were to abdicate on account of decisions by the Chamber.' The result of his timidity was that Bismarck's accession to power worsened his position considerably; like his mother, Fritz lost almost all say in affairs of State.

'Who would have considered such devilish influence possible?' wrote the Crown Princess of Bismarck's ministry to Queen Augusta. 'One can only say, curses upon the narrow-mindedness and stupidity of the people who are now all powerful. They sow nothing but evil and unhappiness, and what the King himself will not live to reap will be left for us who are innocent of everything that is happening now. . . .'

That, indeed, was the rub. The two of them were being forced to sit by, helpless, while Bismarck built up a state along lines utterly opposed to that which they planned one day to inaugurate. 'All is going *de mal en pire*,' cried Vicky, 'that wretched Bismarck will not stop his mad career until he has plunged his King into ruin and his country into the most dangerous difficulties!' Everyone, she assured Queen Augusta, was urging the Crown Prince to come out in open opposition to the King.

One may be certain that few were urging it more passionately than she. Of the two young people, it was Princess Victoria who was the more determined in the fight against Bismarck. The death of her father, the Prince Consort, in 1861, had merely strengthened her resolve to carry out the mission which he had entrusted to her. By now her late father's ideals had become almost sacred. She missed him terribly. There was no one—not her husband, nor her mother, nor Queen Augusta —with whom she could discuss things in quite the same way. And indeed, never was she more in need of Prince Albert's guidance than during these years of Bismarck's rise to power. Mature in some ways, she was desperately immature in others. Although Prince Albert's views had been no less strongly held than hers, he had been more tolerant, more able to compromise; he had always been able to see both sides of a question. This was something which she had not yet learned. She could never appreciate that by giving way on small issues one could yet hold to larger principles. Once Prince Albert died, there was no one to teach her these lessons.

She was beginning to discover, moreover, that her husband, for all his humanitarianism, was not quite as resolute a liberal as she. Unlike her, he was not nearly so certain that his opinion was always the right one; this uncertainty often left him nervous and depressed. 'I am in no doubt about the course I should take and care very little for the opposition I meet,' the Crown Princess assured Queen Victoria, 'but with Fritz it is so different. You know how he loves his Father and what his sense of duty is towards the King and his Father—besides he is not born a free Englishman and all Prussians have not the feeling of independence and love of justice and constitutional liberty they ought to have....' She therefore felt it necessary to do everything to encourage him to stick by his liberal principles. With a persistence worthy of her late father, she urged him, day in and day out, not only to refuse to compromise but to speak out against the rising tide of autocracy. 'I keep on repeating the same thing and cannot express myself strongly enough,' she wrote to him on one occasion, 'as I am so convinced that our only duty is to make this dear country so perfect, strong and mighty by means of a liberal practical constitution and by orderly and legal methods.'

She realized, she assured him in her self-righteous fashion, that, as a Prussian prince, he had not been versed in the old liberal and constitutional conceptions, but that he had none the less made enormous strides since marrying her. 'Now I hope,' she said, 'that your knowledge of these things will steadily increase....'

And Fritz, although haunted, from time to time, by the most soul-searing doubts, always followed her advice. 'My little wife,' he wrote in his diary, 'is my most devoted adviser, my whole support, my indefatigable comforter, and no words can adequately express this. Our position is truly terrible!'

His wife was not the only one who was goading Fritz into making some sort of stand against his father's government. Liberals throughout Prussia looked to him for leadership and both Queen Victoria and King Leopold of the Belgians were urging him to play a less passive role. The Queen, using what she considered to be the strongest incentive to action, ended one particular piece of advice with the assurance that she was speaking 'in beloved Papa's name'.

The Crown Prince was receiving almost as much attention from the Junkers. His wife might find him too moderate but to them he was a dangerous liberal. Robert Morier, on the staff of the British Embassy in Berlin, reported that 'every kind of calumny spread, respecting the persons supposed to be the Prince's friends. Spies were placed over him in the shape of aides-de-camp and chamberlains, conversations were distorted and imagined....'

The first open break between father and son came about a year after Bismarck's assumption of the premiership. Bismarck abolished the freedom of the Press, thereby violating the constitution. Egged on by his excited wife, the Crown Prince wrote, first to the King and then to Bismarck, making clear his opposition to the move. This he followed up by a speech, while on a military tour of Danzig, in which he publicly dissociated himself from Bismarck's measures against the Press.

The speech created an enormous furore. The King was enraged. 'I enjoin you *never* to make such an indiscreet statement *on any occasion* in the future,' he wrote, and ordered the Crown Prince to retract what he had said. This Fritz refused to do. His defiant stand gave rise to the belief that both he and his wife were about to be arrested and imprisoned. 'We are in a dreadful position,' admitted Vicky to her mother; 'the country loudly clamouring for Fritz to come forward ... we can't sleep for excitement and worry. Fritz is quite ill with it.'

Their situation was worsened by the fact that the London *Times*, always critical of Prussia, came out in support of the Crown Prince and Princess. This made Vicky's position particularly difficult; she was prepared for a catastrophe, she said. That the King held her responsible for the fracas was only too apparent. Sending for Ernest von Stockmar, son of old Baron von Stockmar and secretary to the young couple, Wilhelm attacked him for his disloyalty to Prussia. When, by a slip of the tongue, the terrified young Stockmar referred to Vicky as 'the Princess Royal', the King lost all control. 'She is no longer the Princess Royal,' he thundered; 'she is the Crown Princess of Prussia; how dare you call her anything else?'

Poor Stockmar, overwhelmed by the whole business, fell ill and resigned. 'We are in this critical position without a secretary,' wailed Vicky, 'without a single person to give us advice, to write for us or to help us; whatever we do one way or the other is abused. . . .'

Faced with his father's fury, Crown Prince Frederick offered to resign all his civil and military offices and to retire from public life. The approving Queen Victoria encouraged her daughter and son-in-law to come and live in England until the storm had blown over. Although the King might well have accepted his son's offer, the astute Bismarck advised him against it. It would not do to make a martyr of the Crown Prince. Instead, Fritz was given a severe reprimand and the matter dropped.

But the Crown Princess was not prepared to give in so easily. Although Fritz might consider obedience to his adored father to be his first duty, she did not. 'Now I see myself bound as a good wife,' she told her mother, 'and a *really devoted* and enthusiastic Prussian (which I feel every day more that I am)— using all the influence I possess in making Fritz place his opinions and his political conscience above his filial feelings. . . . Until I find the person in whose judgement I can feel greater confidence than in my own—I shall go on with might and main trying to assist Fritz in pursuing the only road I consider right and safe.'

It was not long before she was prodding her husband into making yet another stand against that 'clever madman . . . Herr von Bismarck'. A few weeks after the Danzig affair, the Crown Prince tackled his father on the question of Bismarck's continuing unconstitutional behaviour. Immediately, King Wilhelm lost his temper. In mounting anger he railed against the entire 'infamous constitutional system'. At this the Crown Prince, to disassociate himself from all unconstitutional acts, begged to be excused from attending any future cabinet meetings.

'It is your duty as Crown Prince to take part in these sittings more than ever,' shouted the King. 'I shall deal very severely with whoever it is that puts these ideas into your head.' The shaft was aimed, of course, at the Crown Princess.

'Then I beg you to deal with *me*,' answered Fritz, 'for I am expressing my own convictions.'

After a further half-hour's fruitless wrangling, the King rose abruptly and dismissed his son. Thereupon Fritz, determined to clarify his position, reported to Bismarck that, 'the King now knows that I am a definite opponent of the Government'.

Bismarck's answer was no less to the point. 'I can only hope that your Royal Highness will one day find servants as faithful as I am to your father,' he said, and then added, 'I do not intend to be of their number.'

The battle lines had been drawn. From henceforth the Crown Prince would attend no more cabinet meetings; he would play no part in policy making. This way he hoped that none of the stigma of Bismarck's régime would rub off on him. He would remain politically unsullied. 'I regard the constitution,' he stated in a subsequent note to the King, 'as the immovable and focal point in our state and law.'

The Hohenzollern Court now split into two irreconcilable parties. On the one side stood the King and Bismarck; on the other Queen Augusta and the Crown Prince and Princess, the latter forming what Bismarck scathingly referred to as the Anglo-Coburg faction.

Despite Fritz's show of independence, he was still not sure that he was doing the right thing. The humanitarianism which had made him a liberal had also made him a devoted son, anxious not to hurt his father's feelings. In addition, there were times when he was attacked by an agonizing lack of self-confidence. 'I am in such a terrible mood,' he confessed to his wife at this time, 'that I could scratch my eyes out because I consider myself a particular species of "blockhead" (*pardonnez l'expression*). The more seriously I consider the present situation the more troubled I am about my capability of dealing at some future date with similar difficulties. . . .'

While the Crown Prince's quarrel with Bismarck was confined to domestic policies, his position, although worrying and frustrating, was not unbearable. He could simply remain aloof. It was when Bismarck embarked on his aggressive foreign policy that Fritz's dilemma increased a hundredfold.

3

Contrary to what Bismarck was to claim in later life, the unification of Germany was never one of his original ambitions. Like King Wilhelm, he feared the loss of conservative Prussian identity in a Greater German democracy. His first ambition was to make Prussia the most powerful state in Central Europe. To achieve this, he needed to oust Austria from her position as leader of Germany. What was afterwards to look like a carefully calculated, step-by-step progress to German unification was, on the part of Bismarck, a series of favourable situations, wisely grasped. Despite his celebrated shrewdness, Bismarck was an opportunist. Instead of issuing challenges, he took advantage of them. 'Man cannot create the current of events,' he would say. 'He can only float with it and steer.'

The first event in the current which was to sweep King Wilhelm to the head of a new German Empire was a war, in 1864, in which Prussia, in alliance with Austria, fought against Denmark. The quarrel concerned the duchies of Schleswig and Holstein and was a highly complicated one. 'Only three men have ever understood it,' runs Lord Palmerston's classic quip on the Schleswig-Holstein question. 'One was Prince Albert, who is dead. The second was a German professor who went mad. I am the third and I have forgotten all about it.' But however obscure the reasons for the war might have been, the results were clear enough. Little Denmark was soundly beaten, the disputed duchies went to the victors and Prussia stood revealed as being equal to, if not in fact stronger than, her Austrian ally.

Bismarck's high-handed treatment of Austria at the subsequent peace talks confirmed this revelation. Count Beust, the Saxon Minister, warned the Austrians against the growing might of Prussia. King Wilhelm's honesty, he said, was no shield against Bismarck's ambitions. 'I fear scrupulous Prussian Kings more than unscrupulous ones. The dangerous Prussian policy remains the same under the one as under the other. There is only one difference: against the unscrupulous King everybody is on his guard. But the scrupulous King inspires by his character a confidence which his acts do not justify.'

Beust was right. Within two years Prussia and Austria were at war. The campaign was incredibly swift. On 3 July 1866, three weeks after the outbreak of hostilities, the Austrians were decisively defeated at the battle of Sadowa. King Wilhelm, who had had to be coerced into taking up arms against his fellow Germans, was delighted by the victory and it was with the utmost difficulty that Bismarck (who realized that Prussia had to be magnanimous) was able to restrain him from pushing on to Vienna. 'But we—that means, of course, the King—are as easily intoxicated as we are depressed,' wrote Bismarck to his wife after the battle of Sadowa, 'and I have the thankless task of pouring water into his wine....' There was a sharp exchange between the two men and only after the customary floods of tears and shatterings of crockery did Bismarck get his way.

Austria was granted a generous peace. She lost no territory but she lost her position in Germany. The old Deutscher Bund was dissolved and all the states north of the River Main were forced into a Prussian-controlled North German Confederation. From now on Austria was to be excluded from German affairs and only four German states—the kingdoms of Bavaria and Württemberg and the grand duchies of Baden and Hesse-Darmstadt, all lying in the south between France and Austria—remained independent. By threatening three of these states with partial annexation, however, Bismarck forced them into concluding secret treaties of military alliance: if Prussia were attacked, then the Kings of Bavaria and Württemberg and the Grand Duke of Baden would place their troops under the command of King Wilhelm.

Thus, in less than four years, Bismarck had fashioned Prussia into the most powerful state in Central Europe and King Wilhelm I, as Commander-in-Chief of the forces of the North German Confederation, had almost a million men at his command. It was the most formidable army Europe had ever seen. As far as old King Wilhelm was concerned, his dearest wish had been realized. Even Bismarck, seemingly content with this magnificent achievement, could assure his wife that there was 'nothing more to be done in our lifetime'.

No such contentment reigned in the hearts of Bismarck's embittered rivals, the Crown Prince and Princess. Prussia's relentless march towards a position of European domination had thrown them into a quandary. It was a quandary faced by almost all German liberals. They approved of German unification while disapproving of the way in which it was being achieved. The hated Bismarck was fulfilling one of their most cherished ideals by the use of what they considered to be the most abhorrent of methods. As a soldier, and an enthusiastic one at that, Crown Prince Frederick was obliged to help put Bismarck's policies into practice; and Princess Victoria, once her blood was up, was no less eager for victory than he. They would have been less than human had they not taken pride in this aggrandizing of the country over which they would one day rule. Had German unification under Prussia not been the late Prince Albert's dearest wish? On the other hand, Bismarck's diplomatic machinations appalled them. Before his wars against Denmark and Austria they expressed themselves shocked at the prospect, but once the conflict was under way, they were swept along on a tide of patriotism.

The Crown Princess proved particularly changeable. No words were bad enough for the instigator of the war at one moment; at the next she was exultant at the success of the Prussian armies. Now she would be chiding her husband for softening the tone of a letter which she had drafted for him to send to Bismarck; then she would be attacking the British Press for being unsympathetic towards the Prussian cause. 'I feel so forlorn with this horrible war drawing near ...' she lamented on one occasion; on another she was thanking God for the achievements against the Austrians in 1866. 'I believe in Germany's star, or rather, in the victory of all the Good, the Great, and the Noble for which the German people have been striving for years,' she wrote.

She was increasingly torn between her pride in her native and in her adopted countries. If, in Bismarck's phrase, she had not left the Englishwoman at home, neither had she resisted becoming something of a Prussian. She had always spoken English with a German accent, and German with an English, and her brother Bertie, the Prince of Wales, was not far off the mark when he claimed that 'Vicky is always pure Prussian when she is at home, and pure English when she is in Prussia'. During the war against Denmark she raged against 'this stupid

English foreign policy'. England, she said, was making herself ridiculous by interfering in other people's affairs. 'As a German' her sense of justice rebelled at the nonsense being printed and spoken in England. Yet in the next breath almost, she could claim that when one was obliged, as she was, to live abroad, the immense superiority of England in all things was only too apparent. The very sound of the British National Anthem made her feel an inch taller.

That this ambivalence, this inconsistency, this wanting to have her cake and eat it, did nothing towards enhancing her reputation in Prussia, is understandable. Despite her bursts of patriotic fervour, she remained as unpopular as ever. She was still *die Engländerin*, and even members of the Prussian royal family accused her of being unhappy at the success of the Prussian troops. 'Our children,' she complained, 'are universally pitied for having the great misfortune of having me for their Mama with my *"unglücklichen englischen Ideen"* [unfortunate English ideas] and *"unpreussischen Gesinnungen"* [un-Prussian views].' The fact that her brother Bertie had recently married Princess Alexandra of Denmark made Vicky's attitude towards the war against Denmark distinctly suspect; nor did Bertie's open championship of Prussia's enemies—be they Denmark or Austria—do anything to ease her position. Bismarck, who hated her as heartily as she hated him (he realized that in her he had met a formidable opponent) even went so far as to warn King Wilhelm that the Crown Princess was not to be trusted with State secrets; she could so easily betray them to England. As a result, certain military dispatches were withheld from Prince Frederick as 'the Crown Princess would certainly pass on the information to her mother indirectly'. Vicky's reaction can be imagined.

Yet this was the same Princess who, on the Prussian victory over Austria, could exclaim, 'I feel that I am *now* every bit as proud of being a Prussian as of being an Englishwoman and that is saying a great deal. . . . I must say the Prussians are a superior race.'

For all this show of temperament, Princess Victoria was no virago. Removed from the hurly-burly of politics, she revealed herself as a woman of good sense and outstanding charm. Her home life was idyllic. The atmosphere of the Kronprinzenpalais in Berlin and the Neues Palais at Potsdam was lively and natural. Guests, accustomed to the formality, the friction and the philistinism of the other Prussian royal households, were always struck by the simplicity, the harmony and the air of culture pervading the Crown Prince's menage. Between the years 1859 and 1872, Princess Victoria bore her husband eight children and raised them in as unaffected a fashion as possible. They made a delightful family group: the Crown Prince with his imposing build and golden beard, the Crown Princess with her sea-green eyes and effortless grace, the children whom one witness describes as 'simply charming—so bright and lively'.

Meals at the Neues Palais were simple and wholesome. Even when entertaining, the royal couple might eat nothing more elaborate than curds and whey, veal cutlets and rice pudding. Afterwards they would retire to one of the sumptuous, somewhat French-looking salons, where the men would drink beer and the Crown Prince smoke his long pipe. 'I notice,' wrote one guest, 'that the Crown Princess always laid down her needlework to refill her husband's pipe and to bring him a fresh tankard of beer.'

In private, Vicky dressed very simply, forsaking the trimmings so dear to the hearts of both her mother and her mother-in-law; often she wore a plain ribbon to tie back her hair. With this lack of ostentation went a marked vivacity of manner; she was never idle. Her conversation, they say, was scintillating. She was interested in so many things. The playwright, Gustav zu Putlitz, spending a few weeks with the family in the summer of 1864, professed himself amazed at her talents, her knowledge and her versatility. He recognized her as a princess of more than average gifts and as 'a most wonderful woman, rich in mind, culture, energy, kindness and benevolence'. Frau zu Putlitz, who accompanied her husband on his visit to the Neues Palais the following year, was equally impressed. There seemed to be no subject—be it wild flowers, the theories of Darwin or Shakespeare's plays—on which the Princess could not express some lively and original opinion. She was never banal, never conventional. 'I know of no one who has such a fascinating way of speaking; it is a real pleasure to listen to her and to experience the charm of her peculiar personality ... there is an indescribable charm about her whole person.' Through the stuffy Court of mid-nineteenth-century Prussia, Crown Princess Victoria moved like a breath of fresh air.

While the Princess might dazzle her guests by the force and nobility of her personality, it was the Crown Prince who won their hearts. The gravity, the tranquillity and the friendliness of his manner made an immediate and lasting appeal. His warmth was irresistible. 'This was certainly the best evening that I have spent here,' reported one guest, 'and all the more welcome to me as it displayed the Crown Prince in such a favourable light, and at the same time revealed the perfect harmony of this union, in which the Crown Prince, notwithstanding the more brilliant qualities of the Princess, still preserves his simple and natural attitude and undeniable influence. Absolute sincerity is the chief characteristic of his entire nature.'

This sincerity made Fritz's attitude towards Bismarck's aggrandizing of the Prussian State more consistent than hers. Although trapped in the same dilemma as his wife, his approach to it was more reasonable, less emotional. Even if he did not grasp all the complexities of a problem, he appreciated that it *was* complicated. He never saw things in the same simple terms of right and wrong as she. He was neither as vehement in his hatred of Bismarck, nor as outraged at British disapproval, nor as elated at the Prussian victories in arms. As a soldier, he could not help taking a certain pride in his country's military successes, but he never allowed himself to be brought to her pitch of near-hysteria.

There was a further reason for his more tolerant attitude: he was longing to be an Emperor. The re-establishment of the Reich was his dearest wish. He might not approve of the methods by which it was being achieved but he could not but rejoice at the results. With his father already in his seventies, there was a strong possibility that he might be the first Kaiser of a united Germany. This was the day for which he was living; this would make the present years of waiting and frustration worthwhile.

Whereas Vicky looked upon the establishment of a Reich as the realization of the liberal dream of a united, democratic Germany, Fritz saw it in an additional light. His conception was both more imperious and more colourful. As proud as any Hohenzollern, he was ambitious for the glorification of his House. 'The Crown Prince,' wrote one of his friends, Gustav Freytag, 'was a mild and warm-hearted man, humane and altruistic. But ineradicably implanted in his innermost being was the traditional concept of his rank and caste. When on occasion he felt moved to remind others of his status, his bearing became far haughtier than that of any of his fellow princes. ... From this princely pride there grew within him the notion of a new German Kaiserdom....' With his strong streak of romanticism, he looked upon the future Empire as a continuation of the medieval Reich. The German Emperors were to be the successors of Charlemagne. Links with the old Holy Roman Empire obsessed him. He collected imperial souvenirs and redesigned imperial insignia; he tried to get the old crown jewels transferred from Vienna and the ancient throne fetched from Goslar. He planned one day to be known, not by his Prussian title of Frederick III, but in accordance with the old imperial succession—as Frederick IV of Germany. The Crown Princess, with her more progressive ideas, tried to combat this constant harking back to medieval times. It was no use.

Sometimes, of an evening, the Crown Prince would take down Bock's *German Treasures of the Holy Roman Empire*. Its illustrations of imperial insignia and its descriptions of the medieval coronation ceremony at Aachen would give him endless pleasure. 'We have got to bring this back,' he would say. 'The power of the Empire must be restored and the Imperial Crown must regain its glamour....'

4

In the year of Prussia's victory over Austria, Prince Wilhelm, eldest son of the Crown Prince and Princess, turned seven. He seems, by all accounts, to have been a delightful child—quick-witted, observant and lively. 'Willy is a dear, interesting, charming boy,' wrote his mother, 'clever, amusing, engaging—it is impossible not to spoil him a little—he is growing so handsome and his large eyes have now and then a pensive, dreamy expression, and then again they sparkle with fun and delight.'

The Crown Princess was not alone in her appreciation of the boy's personality. Prince Albert, who had lived long enough to be able to swing him, at the age of two and a half, in a large, white damask napkin, pronounced him to be a 'pretty, clever child—a compound of both parents' while Queen Victoria was for ever singing his praises. His Prussian grandparents were no less effusive. Queen Augusta made a great fuss of him and old King Wilhelm enjoyed inviting him to dine, *à deux*, in the small drawing-room which led off his study. The little boy would always remember how the two of them would sit at a rickety card table while the frugal old King, having poured two glasses of champagne, would hold the bottle up to the light and carefully mark the level of its contents. The old sovereign delighted in his grandson's company; none could resist the charm of that eager-eyed youngster. 'This little Prince Wilhelm may possibly become the best king that Prussia has had since Frederick the Great,' declared the visiting Duke of Argyll.

Yet from infancy almost, the Crown Princess had noted certain grave faults in his personality. Despite his winning ways, he was inclined to be selfish, aggressive and proud. When, at the age of four, he had been dressed in Highland costume to attend the wedding of his Uncle Bertie, the Prince of Wales, to Princess Alexandra, he had caused an uproar by first threatening his young Uncle Leopold with a dirk and by then biting him in the leg. The painter Frith, commissioned to record the wedding ceremony, admitted that of 'all of the little Turks' whom it was his unenviable task to paint, Prince Wilhelm was the worst. And while such boisterous behaviour could be dismissed as an excess of high spirits, the young Prince's arrogance was considered a more serious fault. Queen Victoria, whom the Crown Princess kept *au courant* with every detail of the boy's progress, considered this failing to be particularly serious. 'In our days,' she wrote, 'where a Prince can only maintain his position by his character—pride is *most* dangerous.'

'Bring him up simply, plainly,' she advised, 'not with that terrible Prussian pride and ambition which grieved dear Papa so much and which he always said would stand in the way of Prussia taking that lead in Germany which he ever wished her to do. Pride and ambition are not only very wrong in themselves but they alienate affection and are in every way unworthy for great Princes—and great nations.'

How much the boy's arrogance was due to his maimed left arm is difficult to say. By the time he was seven it was clear that it would never be normal. The arm had been massaged, exercised and stretched; the boy had been subjected to painful electrical treatments and had been strapped into a complicated apparatus. There had even been talk of an operation on his neck. It was all to no purpose. His left arm remained shorter, thinner and weaker than his right and although he could grip with his left hand he could not lift. He could neither dress himself nor cut up his food. Nor was the trouble confined to his arm; his whole left side seemed affected; his left ear was to trouble him throughout his life. It had been discovered that the hearing apparatus of the inner ear and the adjoining balance mechanism were faulty. The result was that he had no natural sense of balance: he had difficulty in running, climbing and jumping. He even walked awkwardly. Being an active and, apart from his disability, an extremely healthy boy, he felt his physical inadequacies very keenly. 'His tutor thinks he will feel it much more, and be unhappier about it as he grows older,' wrote his distraught mother, 'and feels himself debarred from everything which others enjoy. . . .'

In this, as far as outward appearances were concerned, the tutor was mistaken. To a very large extent, the boy overcame his handicap. In time and with admirable tenacity, he learnt to ride, to shoot, to play tennis and to swim. He taught himself to eat with a specially designed knife and fork. He never allowed himself to be looked upon as permanently maimed; in later life he seemed almost unconscious of his disability.

The effect on his character is more difficult to assess. It has been claimed that his crippled arm was responsible for crippling his entire personality. He is said to have been desperately envious of other youngsters who excelled, so effortlessly, in the very fields in which he wished, so desperately, to excel. This is supposed to have left him with a feeling of inadequacy, with a deep-rooted inferiority complex which was, in turn, compensated for by a brash, assertive manner. But such a theory is difficult to prove. Who can say that Prince Wilhelm, with two good arms, would have been any less arrogant?

Of perhaps more importance to his development was his relationship with his parents, particularly his mother.

There has persisted in Germany, for many years, the legend that the Crown Princess was a heartless mother; that she was simply not interested in her children. She is said to have been particularly harsh in her treatment of young Prince Wilhelm; 'she cherished in her heart,' says one writer, 'a secret grudge against her misshapen son'. Such accusations are wildly exaggerated. One only has to read her letters to her mother to realize the depth of her love for the boy and the extent of her distress at his deformity. That he should have to undergo such painful yet ineffective treatment was a 'torment' to her. Indeed, she might even have proved too sympathetic. Feeling desperately sorry for the boy, she always treated him with the utmost tenderness while he, being sensitive by nature, probably came to resent her obvious solicitude. It was a vicious circle. The more she pitied him, the more conscious was he made to feel of his infirmity and the more he resented her concern.

But for all this, there is probably more than a grain of truth in Wilhelm's later accusation that she did not spend enough time with her children, particularly her three eldest—Wilhelm, Charlotte and Henry. Like Queen Victoria, the Crown Princess was more of a wife than a mother. Still in her teens and early twenties during the first years of Wilhelm's life, and very much in love with her husband, she might well have neglected the children for the father. Nor, with her quick mind and intellectual interests, did she feel completely at ease in the company of the very young. She supervised the nurseries with characteristic thoroughness but to young Wilhelm the fact that she invariably sided with his governess, the grim Fräulein von Dobeneck, rendered her somewhat unsympathetic. He says that he found her remote, exacting and critical.

Her bitter grief at the death of her third son, the two-year-old Sigismund, made him realize, he afterwards claimed, that she did not love him nearly as much as she had loved his dead brother. In this he was correct: Sigismund had been her favourite child. The baby's death, which occurred when Wilhelm was seven and while the Crown Prince was away fighting the Austrians, plunged her into the deepest grief. 'Oh *how* I loved that little thing, from the first moments of its birth, it was more to me than its brothers and sisters...' she admitted to her mother. 'He was so clever, much more than either of the others, and I thought he was going to be like Papa. Fritz and I idolized him....'

In the fashion of the day Vicky converted the dead child's room into a shrine. Many years later Lady Macdonell, visiting the Neues Palais, was allowed to peep into the undisturbed room. 'I saw a cradle,' she writes, 'and in it a baby boy, beautiful to look upon, but it was only the waxen image of the former occupant, Prince Sigismund, who had died when the Crown Prince went to the war of 1866. How pathetic it was to note the silver rattle and ball lying as though flung aside by the little hand, the toys which had amused his baby's mind arranged all about the cradle, his little shoes waiting, always waiting—at the side.'

It was no wonder that in the face of this emotional, brilliant and busy mother Prince Wilhelm sometimes felt inadequate. Many years later he described her as 'a woman of unwearied energy, she was passionate, impulsive, argumentative, and had an undeniable love of power'.

At the age of seven Wilhelm was handed over to a tutor. In spite of their modern ideas, the royal couple chose an old-fashioned martinet to educate their son. George Hintzpeter was a harsh, unsmiling disciplinarian, determined to instil in his pupil the virtues of hard work, self-control and self-sacrifice. As 'joyless as the personality of this dry, pedantic man, with his gaunt meagre figure and parchment face, grown up in the shadows of Calvinism, was his educational system,' remembered Wilhelm, 'joyless the youth through which I was guided by the "hard hand" of the "Spartan idealist" '.

Lessons started at six in the morning and continued for twelve gruelling hours. Occasional periods were given over to tours of museums, galleries or factories and to rigorous physical exercises. It was the stern Hintzpeter who taught Wilhelm to ride. For a boy with no sense of balance, it was a frightening prospect. 'Therefore the tutor, using a moral authority over his pupil that by now was absolute, set the weeping Prince on his horse without stirrups and compelled him to go through the various paces,' runs an account of these riding lessons. 'He fell off continually; every time, despite his prayers and tears, he was lifted up and set upon its back again. After weeks of torture, the difficult task was accomplished: he had got his balance.'

Some relief from this cheerless existence was afforded by family outings. Each summer the Court moved from Berlin, which Wilhelm described as 'a sea of stone buildings', to Potsdam where life was less arduous for the young Prince. His father would take him to Sans Souci to show him where Frederick the Great had once lived; there would be picnics in the woods, boating on the river and visits to the royal farm at Bornstedt. His mother had laid out an intimate English garden in the grounds of the Neues Palais and it became the scene of many animated family gatherings. There were holidays in the South of France or in Italy. Here the Crown Princess loved to bustle round the marble masons' yards. 'What a people!' she would exclaim of the Italians. 'They are born artists. They know intuitively how to do things. The old Roman culture is still alive in these people.'

One visit which Prince Wilhelm was never to forget was to the naval base at Wilhelmshaven. Here, for the first time, he saw the fleet of Prussian ironclads lying at anchor in the road-stead. Standing beside his father on the deck of a paddle-steamer, he stared up, 'with beating heart', at the ships loom-ing above him. 'The closer we came, the more powerful was the impression made upon me by the *König Wilhelm,* then prob-ably the largest ironclad in the world,' he wrote. 'When we anchored near her I gazed speechless upon this mighty ship towering far above us.'

He was unable to get to sleep that night, he says, for the sight of the ships 'left me no rest and recurred again and again to my mind's eye'. It was on that glittery afternoon at Wil-helmshaven, perhaps, that his passion for the navy was born.

Of all the family holidays, Prince Wilhelm enjoyed his visits to Queen Victoria best. The Queen was devoted to her eldest grandchild ('a clever, dear good little child, the great favourite of my beloved Angel') and young Wilhelm, unlike her own children, always felt thoroughly at home with her. He had only the happiest memories of his childhood visits to his grand-mother. 'The Queen was always particularly kind to me from the very first,' he wrote, 'she was a real grandmother, and our relations to one another were never changed or dimmed to the end of her life. I was allowed to play with the same toys and in the same places as did formerly my English uncles and aunts when they were my age. And by the same token we could go and drink tea and make butter and cream cheese in the little kitchen fitted out for them in the dairy at Frogmore, which was in Windsor Park. At Osborne I could play with the same old iron cannon on a model redoubt where my uncles had played when they were boys. And I remember a lottery organized for us children at Windsor of which the winning prize was ar-ranged by my grandmother to be a huge English cake. . . .'

One hilarious conversation always remained in his memory. It took place during a family luncheon at Osborne soon after the sailing-frigate *Eurydice* had sunk off Portsmouth. The ship had since been salvaged and towed in and the Queen had invited Admiral Foley to luncheon so that she might hear his account of the incident. 'After she had exhausted this melancholy subject,' remembered Wilhelm, 'my grandmother, in order to give the conversation a more cheerful turn, inquired after his sister, whom she knew well, whereon the Admiral, who was hard of hearing and still pursuing his train of thought about the *Eurydice,* replied in his stentorian voice: "Well, Ma'am, I am going to have her turned over and take a good look at her bottom and have it well scraped." The effect of this answer was stupendous. My grandmother put down her knife and fork, hid her face in her handkerchief and shook and heaved with laughter until the tears rolled down her face.'

CHAPTER THREE

THE FRANCO-PRUSSIAN WAR

1

On the last day of the year 1866, old King Wilhelm sat down to pen his customary 'testamentary memorandum'. He believed, he wrote, that with the defeat of Austria and the unification of all the states north of the River Main into a North German Confederation, the work which God had given him to do had been accomplished. He hoped that he would be allowed to reign over the Confederation in peace and quiet and that he would be able to leave it as a legacy for his son. 'May God's grace now continue to help him build up and consolidate the newly united Germany, of which the foundation has just been laid.'

Bismarck, with his achievements rewarded by the title of Count, was not nearly so certain that God's mission had been accomplished. Nor had he any intention of leaving the consolidation of what had been achieved to either God or his rival, Crown Prince Frederick. It was Bismarck's daring that had led to Prussia's victory over Austria; he must now make certain that the control of the new North German Confederation remained in conservative Prussian hands. It must not be tainted with the Crown Prince and Princess's reforming ideas.

His first task was to give the Confederation a constitution. It was not that Bismarck was any more enamoured of constitutionalism than was King Wilhelm; it was simply that he realized that he must make some gesture towards the trends of the age. Just as he was harnessing that other *bête noire* of his fellow conservatives—nationalism—so must he harness democracy.

The result was a highly complicated constitution which seemed to promise everything and gave, in fact, almost nothing. The King of Prussia became President of the North German Confederation. The various other German princes remained on their thrones and their states were represented in a federal council known as the Bundesrat. This Bundesrat was controlled by a Chancellor chosen by the most important state —Prussia. The Chancellor, quite naturally, was Bismarck. This princely Bundesrat took care of conservative opinion. As a sop to liberal opinion, there was the Reichstag. This was a parliament elected by universal suffrage. The introduction of universal suffrage was so dazzling a concession that it blinded a great many people to the fact that the Reichstag was all but powerless. Such legislation as the Reichstag was allowed to pass required the consent of the Bundesrat which was, of course, controlled by the Prussian Chancellor—Bismarck. If a majority in the Reichstag—be it Conservative, National Liberal or Progressive—disagreed with the Chancellor, then it was the Reichstag, and not the Chancellor, that had to be changed. The Chancellor was not responsible to the Reichstag. Thirdly, there remained the old Prussian parliament, headed by its Minister-President. And this Minister-President was none other than Count Otto von Bismarck.

What the entire, confused and cumbersome hotch-potch amounted to was that all effective power remained in the hands of the Prussian Chancellor, who was answerable only to the King of Prussia. As Bismarck remarked in a frank aside to a Saxon minister, what he was trying to do was 'to destroy parliamentarianism with parliamentarianism'. The very diffuseness and intricacy of the constitution allowed him to indulge in his favourite game—the maintaining of power by the playing off of the various forces in Germany against each other; all this to the advantage, not only of Prussia, but of the autocratic Prussian monarchy.

'The main disadvantage...' wrote Karl Marx from London after the establishment of the North German Confederation, 'is the inevitable swamping of Germany by the Prussian spirit.'

It was an inevitability, however, which not all Germany was willing to concede. The four, largely Catholic, states lying south of the River Main—Bavaria, Württemberg, Baden and Hesse-Darmstadt—were not at all sure that they wanted to be swamped by the Prussian spirit. What would be needed to overcome their reluctance and bring them into the fold was some issue, other than a religious one, which would lead to an upsurge of German nationalism. Only in a flush of defiant patriotism would these four states identify themselves with the Prussian-dominated North German Confederation. To create such a mood, Germany must be supplied with an enemy.

It was not necessary to look very far. One nation only stood between Prussia and the domination of the Continent of Europe —France. It was the France of the Emperor Napoleon III: the showy, vainglorious France of the Second Empire. Ever since the Prussian victory over Austria at Sadowa, war between France and Prussia had become almost inevitable. Europe was too small to contain two such aggressively patriotic nations— the one declining, the other burgeoning—as France and Prussia. And then, to the majority of Germans, France, unlike Austria, was the traditional enemy. The conservatives had never forgotten Napoleon I's invasion of their country (King Wilhelm himself had fought against France in 1814) and liberals regarded Napoleon III as the epitome of the despotism they hated. Mutually antipathetic, the two nations were bound to come to blows sooner or later.

Yet Bismarck would have been content to stop short of war. If, by means of some sort of diplomatic crisis with France, he could stampede the South German states into the Prussian fold, that would suit him very well. 'I had to try one way after the other—the most dangerous last,' he had said of the clash between Prussia and Austria; it was no less true of his dealings with France. But if Germany could not be unified by any way other than war, he would certainly not flinch from going to battle. By the end of the 1860s, with the powerful Prussian army at his command, Bismarck was prepared for some incident which could be used to complete German unification, either by diplomacy or war.

It came in the summer of 1870. By championing the candidature of a Hohenzollern Prince for the vacant Spanish throne, the Chancellor provoked France into demanding that King Wilhelm give a guarantee that the Hohenzollern would never accept the crown of Spain. This the King refused to do. Bismarck published a shortened and therefore more abrupt-sounding version of the King's refusal and France, insulted before all the world, declared war. By 19 July 1870, King Wilhelm, who throughout the bewildering, ten-day crisis had done everything to keep the peace, found his country at war with France. Completely unaware of the fact that it was his Chancellor's manoeuvrings and not French aggression that had led to hostilities,

Wilhelm made ready to defend his country. On the last day of July, as nominal Commander-in-Chief, the King left Berlin for the French frontier. With him, in a state of high gratification, went Count von Bismarck.

He had every reason to be pleased. There had been moments, during the crisis, when Bismarck had thought that his scheme might not work. Not only had he had to contend with the timidity of the King and the vacillations of the Hohenzollern Prince himself, but his old rival, Queen Augusta, had been untiring in her efforts to preserve peace. At first Augusta had rather fancied the idea of a Hohenzollern on the throne of Spain but once she had realized that such a prospect might lead to war, she had changed her mind. With her strong French and Catholic sympathies and her innate humanitarianism, she had not been able to face the thought of a war against France. Hurrying to Bad Ems from nearby Coblenz, she had done her utmost to get her husband to force the withdrawal of the Hohenzollern Prince. She is even rumoured to have flung herself to her knees before the hardly less anguished Wilhelm. Her histrionics had been to no purpose. Between Bismarck's machinations and inflamed French public opinion, peace had not had a chance. Once hostilities had actually broke out, moreover, the impetuous Augusta was caught up in the wave of German nationalism.

For Bismarck, things were evolving perfectly. The South German states, bound by treaty to come to Prussia's aid if she were attacked, placed their armies under the command of King Wilhelm. A victorious campaign was bound to knit the combined German armies, and ultimately the states, closer still. On 4 August they invaded France. Although the French fought with great *élan*, they were no match for the superbly organized Prussians. In less than a month after the invasion, the Emperor Napoleon III surrendered at Sedan. The German army, continuing the war against the Republic which had been proclaimed after the Emperor's surrender, marched on to Paris. By the end of September 1870, the French capital was in a state of siege. Although the struggle was to drag on for another five months, the war was as good as won.

Bismarck could now turn his attention to that other, more important matter: the unification of all Germany under Prussia.

The attitude of the Crown Prince and Princess Frederick towards the outbreak of the Franco-Prussian War was distinctly less equivocal than it had been towards the wars against Denmark and Austria. Like the King, they were unaware of the fact that it was Bismarck who had trapped France into declaring war. They considered Prussia to be the victim of French aggression. That theirs was a just and righteous cause, they had no doubt. Carlyle's contrasting of 'noble, patient, deep, pious and solid Germany' with 'vapouring, vainglorious, gesticulating, quarrelsome, restless and oversensitive France', summed up their own attitude exactly. Their Fatherland had been unfairly attacked and there seemed to them a strong possibility that it might be overrun, defeated and laid waste. Like all the world, with the possible exception of Napoleon III and the Prussian High Command, they believed the French army to be invincible.

The Crown Princess was particularly passionate in her denunciation of the enemy; indeed, throughout the seven-month-long struggle her patriotism was of so feverish a quality as to be almost hysterical. She was never more German than now. 'We have been shamefully forced into this war, and the feeling of indignation against such an act of crying injustice has risen in two days to such a pitch that you will hardly believe it,' she assured Queen Victoria soon after the outbreak of hostilities. 'There is a universal cry "To arms", to resist an enemy who so wantonly assaults us.' To her eyes there was something infinitely moving, almost holy, about the unquestioning way in which the German people were preparing to defend their country. To her, they seemed 'the noble army of martyrs indeed'.

With this view of the righteousness of the Prussian cause Queen Victoria was in full agreement. 'Words are too weak to say *all* I feel for you or what I think of my neighbours!' she wrote. 'We must be neutral *as long as* we can, but no one here conceals their opinion as to the extreme *iniquity* of the war, and the unjustifiable conduct of the French! Still, *more publicly*, we cannot say; but the feeling of the people and the country is *all* with you, which it was not *before*. And need I say what I *feel*? ...'

But whatever the Queen's feelings might be, England remained neutral. This was something which the Crown Princess found difficult to forgive. England, she claimed, should have joined Russia, Austria and Italy in threatening to take up arms against France; as it was, Britain's neutrality was proving of inestimable value to 'the aggressor'. She suspected Lord Granville, the British Foreign Minister, of siding with the French and when it was reported that her brother, the Prince of Wales, had publicly expressed to the Austrian Ambassador the hope that Austria would join France in defeating Prussia, she was furious. 'The King and everyone are horrified at Bertie's speech which is quoted everywhere,' she said. She had been obliged, indeed delighted, to contradict it as 'energetically' as possible. She was quite sure, she wrote on another occasion, that Bertie must envy Fritz who, in command of one of the three German armies, was leading a 'trying, but such a useful life'. She had rather see him serve his country, she added maliciously, than sit by her side.

And, as the Prussians moved from one victory to the next and the fear of a French invasion receded, so did Vicky's tone become more and more patronizing. 'Ever since the Emperor's health has been failing,' she sighed, 'the prestige of his genius has been waning and he has made one blunder after another. It is a melancholy history.' She would hate, she assured her mother, to be in the position of the French Emperor and Empress. Napoleon III's capitulation at Sedan filled her with elation. In page after page she poured out her reactions to this momentous victory. Such a downfall was meant to teach deep lessons, she declared. 'May we all learn what frivolity, conceit and immorality lead to! The French people have trusted in their own excellence, have completely deceived themselves.'

For victorious Germany she had nothing but praise. 'Our poverty, our dull towns, our plodding, hardworking *serious* life, has made us strong and determined; is wholesome for us,' she claimed.

But no matter how ardent her championship of the Prussian cause, she was still distrusted by her adopted countrymen. This, very largely, was Bismarck's doing. He never let slip an opportunity of inflaming public opinion against her. Not that opinion—particularly among the Junkers—needed much encouragement. Nothing Vicky said or did could convince the Prussians that she was wholeheartedly on their side. Her jubilation at the German victories was taken with a pinch of salt and her tireless hospital work went unremarked and unappreciated by those in power. 'I never make a plan that is not crossed by the King and Queen and they invariably disapprove of what I do,' she complained.

Being an Englishwoman, she was suspected of siding with those of her countrymen who favoured France. And as, with the mounting Prussian victories, British public opinion swung towards France, so, in turn, did German public opinion become increasingly anti-British. 'How I suffer from all this I cannot say, as of course I cannot hear a word said against England—and I give it back (I fear not always gently) when I hear sharp words.' In fact, she was caught in her old dilemma. When Queen Victoria, opening parliament, expressed some mildly worded sympathy for France, Vicky was roundly attacked by an excited Queen Augusta. And when Crown Prince Frederick hesitated to sanction a German bombardment of besieged Paris, he was said to be acting under instructions from his wife. The Queen of England had forbidden any bombardment of Paris, said Bismarck, and as the Crown Prince was known to be under the thumb of his wife, no bombardment was being allowed to take place. The Crown Princess had pounded a table, claimed the Chancellor, exclaiming that 'Paris shall not be bombarded!'

Yet, whatever the Crown Princess's difficulties, she at least had the satisfaction of believing wholeheartedly in the rightness of the German cause. Her enemies might not credit it, but she felt confident that all Prussia's actions were fully justified. Even when the postponed bombardment of Paris did take place and the world expressed its horror at such brutality, she found an excuse for it. 'The bombardment is too dreadful to be thought of, and yet I know it cannot be helped,' she said. 'The French should have thought of all the risks they were running in case theirs should not be the winning side when they forced the war!'

With the Crown Prince it was different. Although he too, at the outbreak of the war, had assumed Prussia's cause to be just and had unhesitatingly taken command of the Third Army, he no longer felt quite so easy. Even before leaving for the front, he was reported to be looking ill and nervous, and Vicky admitted that he was quite often in tears. As a commander he acquitted himself well and earned a considerable military reputation. Yet he gained small satisfaction from his achievements on the battlefield. Was it not strange, he one day confided to his diary, that he 'who would prefer to earn recognition for works of peace, should be called upon to win such bloodstained laurels?'

The increasing arrogance of the victorious German armies alarmed him. So too, did the loss of sympathy of the hitherto friendly European nations. He was particularly upset by British disapproval. 'The longer the war lasts,' he wrote in his diary on the last day of 1870, 'the better it will be for the French and the worse for us ... We are no longer regarded as the innocents who have been attacked, but rather as the arrogant victors. We are considered capable of every evil, distrust of us increases more and more. That is not the result of this war alone—it is the theory of blood and iron, invented and acted upon by Bismarck, which has brought us to this pitch. He has made us great and powerful, but he has robbed us of our friends, of the sympathies of the world, and of our conscience. . . .'

3

With the victorious German army laying siege to Paris in that winter of 1870–71, the time was considered opportune for the final unification of Germany. The flame of German nationalistic feeling, kindled by the French declaration of war and fanned by a succession of victories, was now a roaring fire; in it, before it cooled, must be forged the new German State.

The scheme was by no means a generally acceptable one. The great mass of the German people might be ready for unification but several important individuals were not. Of the rulers of those four states still to be incorporated into a Greater Germany—Bavaria, Württemberg, Baden and Hesse-Darmstadt—only King Wilhelm's son-in-law, the Grand Duke of Baden, was not actually averse to unification. The King of Württemberg and the Grand Duke of Hesse were anti-Prussian and Ludwig II, the eccentric King of Bavaria, was too obsessed with the glory of his own House of Wittelsbach to want to play second fiddle to the Hohenzollerns. But chief among the opponents to the scheme was the man who would head the proposed new state—King Wilhelm I of Prussia.

King Wilhelm had several objections. For one thing, there was his ineradicable aversion to change. Strongly conservative and wholly unimaginative, he was wary of the projected Empire in which he would be expected to head a conglomeration of states rather than what up to now had virtually been an aggrandized Prussia. Might this not lead to a weakening of his hold? For another thing, he hated the idea of Prussia losing its identity in a Greater Germany and of his having to exchange his proud title—King of Prussia—for the amorphous-sounding name of German Emperor. He had no desire, he once said graphically, to trade 'the splendid crown of Prussia for the crown of filth'. But his main objection was the long-standing one to the political flavour of the proposed new state. For so long German unification had been synonymous with German liberalism: liberals had always dreamed of the day when a newly-proclaimed Kaiser would reign over a united, democratic Germany. King Wilhelm certainly did not want to give the impression that he was making this particular dream come true.

It was, of course, precisely this aspect of the scheme which appealed to the Crown Prince. What he longed for was the united Germany envisaged by such men as that high-minded Coburg triumvirate, the Prince Consort, King Leopold of the Belgians and Baron Stockmar. 'Would to God that a free German Empire ...' he wrote in his diary, 'could arise which would march in the forefront of civilization in the true sense of the word, which would develop all the noble ideals of the modern world and turn them to account, so that Germany would be the means of humanizing the world, ennobling its manners and customs...' In alliance with those other constitutional monarchies—Great Britain, Holland and Belgium—Germany would form a bulwark against republican France and autocratic Russia and thus secure peace for years to come. With his father, the King, already in his seventies, Fritz assumed that the old man would enjoy the honour of being Kaiser for a few years only. 'But on me and mine devolves the task of setting our hands in true German fashion to build the mighty edifice on principles in conformity with modern times and free from prejudice.'

The Crown Prince had less idealistic motives as well. He was determined that the Hohenzollerns must become Kaisers. When Gustav Freytag suggested that the King of Prussia take the title 'Duke of Germany' or 'Commander-in-Chief' of the new federation, Fritz cut him short. 'No,' he said hotly, 'he must be Emperor.' The Crown Prince then went on to tell Freytag of his feeling of humiliation during the visit of his father and himself to the Great Exhibition of Paris in 1867. 'When the visit of the Emperor of Russia was announced, Napoleon III sent someone along to inquire which order of precedence he, my father, wished to see observed, as Napoleon intended to arrange everything according to the preference of the King of Prussia. My father replied: "The Emperor must take precedence." That ... no Hohenzollern is ever to say again; it must never be true again of a Hohenzollern.'

Thus, while the King would have preferred to be no more than the leading German sovereign, and Bismarck might have been content with a Prussian dominated confederation, the Crown Prince wanted nothing less than an Empire. No one at Versailles was more anxious for the proclamation of the new Reich than he; in fact, Bismarck went so far as to say that the Crown Prince would die of 'Kaiserwahnsinn'—Emperor-madness. Although the Chancellor, in later life, would never admit it, it was Crown Prince Frederick's tireless promptings that finally forced him into taking action.

For Bismarck, the matter was by no means simple. In his determination to prevent the new Reich from being identified with liberalism he faced a considerable dilemma. It was the democratic Reichstag that supported the idea of unification and the rulers of the various South German states that resisted it. In Bavaria, for instance, the most reluctant of the states, the discomforted Bismarck found himself being indebted to the National Liberal Party for whipping up enthusiasm for the idea of unity. Therefore, to avoid any flirtation with democracy (which the King would certainly never countenance) Bismarck set about coercing the South German sovereigns into accepting the scheme for unification. Only if these princes offered the imperial crown to King Wilhelm would he consider accepting it.

In October 1870 the representatives of the four South German states were invited to Versailles, where the German army was head-quartered, to negotiate on the future of Germany. By shrewdly playing off one state against another, Bismarck obtained the agreement of the delegates of Württemberg, Baden and Hesse-Darmstadt to the new Empire, but nothing could induce Bavaria to join. A letter from the Duke of Baden, asking King Ludwig II of Bavaria to acquire 'immortal glory' by inviting the Prussian King to become German Emperor, went unanswered. On this, the King of Württemberg, who had never been anxious to join, ordered his delegates not to sign unless Bavaria signed. 'I really am ashamed of the German princes,' wrote Fritz, 'who cannot and will not learn anything and whose mean character makes them unable to do their duty towards the great common Fatherland.'

When the disappointed Crown Prince suggested to Bismarck that the reluctant Kings be compelled to join, Bismarck would not hear of it. It was not, of course, that the Prussian Chancellor was averse to the use of threats; it was that he feared that the Crown Prince wanted to use the Reichstag to coerce the princes into signing an agreement. This would never do. The new Reich must be the creation of the autocratic Chancellor, not of the democratic Reichstag. Now, with Württemberg hesitating to join unless Bavaria joined, and with King Ludwig of Bavaria refusing to join, there seemed to be no way out of the impasse.

As usual, Bismarck found one. He bribed King Ludwig II. This bizarre monarch, with his luxurious tastes and his passion for architectural fantasies, was deeply in debt. Indeed, he was facing financial disaster. It is said that by offering him the sum of £15,000 a year, Bismarck induced him to agree to Bavaria joining the Empire. And not only to agree, but to write a letter to King Wilhelm inviting him to become Emperor. Bismarck drafted the letter, Ludwig II copied it and signed it, and it was handed back to a gratified Bismarck to present to his master.

So far, so good. However, the greatest obstacle still remained: King Wilhelm had yet to be convinced of the desirability of becoming an Emperor. At first he would not hear of it. When, towards the end of September 1870, the impatient Fritz had broached the subject, the King had treated the matter lightly, saying that he could see no prospect of it at all. During the October and November negotiations with the delegates of the South German states, the Crown Prince again raised the matter. The King cut him short. 'This great change in Germany falls into my lap, as it were, against my will and against my wish,' he grumbled. 'I, with my inherently Prussian heart, am to live to see the name which has achieved and created such greatness give place to another, which was violently hostile to the Prussian name for a whole century. Once more the fates conspire against me, and force me into something to which I can only agree with a heavy heart. . . .'

Eventually, his resistance was worn down. He agreed to accept the crown from the princes on the condition that the Reichstag had no hand in the proceedings. But just after this, the Reichstag, having amended the constitution to convert the Confederation into a Reich, decided to send a deputation to the King. It would ask him to accept the imperial crown. When Wilhelm heard of the arrival of the parliamentary deputation, he was furious. The address to be delivered to him had been drafted by Eduard Lasker, a member of the National Liberal Party and one of the most ardent champions of German unification. 'Why, then I am indeed indebted to Herr Lasker for an Imperial Crown!' was Wilhelm's sarcastic comment. With that he refused to receive the deputation. Once more the long-suffering Bismarck, anxious to avoid a public scandal, had to talk his master round. It was explained that the deputation was not offering him the crown, merely begging him to accept it from the princes. Wilhelm, as always, gave in and received the deputation, but only after all the princes of Germany had joined King Ludwig II in his request.

There remained one more hurdle to be cleared before the proclamation, set for 18 January 1871. This was the question of the exact imperial title. At first Wilhelm, still anxious to safeguard his Prussian title, wanted to be known as 'King of Prussia, elected Emperor of Germany'. When this was refused, he decided on 'Emperor of Germany'. The refractory Bavarian delegates, on the other hand, favoured 'German Emperor'. This seemingly unimportant detail led to endless squabbles, culminating in a violent scene between the King, the Crown Prince and Bismarck on the afternoon before the proclamation.

Bismarck, anxious to placate the Bavarians, insisted on 'German Emperor', as this, unlike 'Emperor of Germany', had no territorial connotation. Wilhelm, equally stubborn, would not hear of it. At one stage during the afternoon the old King burst into tears, claiming that he wanted to have nothing to do with any 'mock imperial title' and accusing his son of being 'heart and soul with the new state of affairs', whereas he cared not one jot for them, wanting only to remain King of Prussia and nothing else. The meeting ended with the King, in a white-hot fury, turning his back on Bismarck and refusing to discuss the following day's ceremony any further. Fritz, so upset by the scene, was obliged to hurry back to his quarters to take something to steady his shattered nerves.

'This imperial confinement was a difficult one,' complained Bismarck in characteristically colourful fashion to his wife, 'and Kings have at such times strange desires, like women ... As *accoucheur*, I sometimes felt the urgent desire to be a bombshell and to explode, that the whole building would fall to pieces.'

Instead of exploding, Bismarck managed things more subtly. On the morning of the great ceremony, the Chancellor waylaid the Duke of Baden as the brilliantly uniformed throng was ascending the staircase to the Galerie des Glaces. To the Duke of Baden had been assigned the honour of being the first to hail the new Emperor after the proclamation and by now Bismarck had worked out a compromise solution to this problem of the imperial title. The Duke of Baden was to hail the Emperor with these words: 'Long live his Imperial Majesty, Kaiser Wilhelm!' This way, he would be called neither German Emperor nor Emperor of Germany.

And that is what the Duke of Baden, to the new Kaiser's intense fury, cried out. So it was that when the Emperor stepped down from the dais to make his way through the acclaiming throng, and passed by the man who had made possible this day's triumphant ceremony, he had no word to say to him. Indeed, Wilhelm refused to shake Bismarck's proffered hand.

'I have just come back from the Palace after completing the Imperial deed!' wrote the Emperor to the Empress Augusta later that day. 'I cannot tell you how depressed I have felt for the last few days, partly on account of the heavy responsibility I must now accept, partly and chiefly on account of the grief it is for me to see the Prussian title supplanted! I was so cross at the end of a conference ... yesterday that I was on the point of abdicating and making everything over to Fritz! It was only after earnest prayer that I recovered self-control and strength! God grant that as many hopes and expectations as are desirable may be fulfilled through me! There shall be no lack of honest intention on my part.'

PART TWO

KAISER WILHELM I

CHAPTER FOUR

THE SECOND REICH

1

Kaiser Wilhelm I made his official entry into his capital on 16 June 1871. It was indeed a triumphant entry for he returned, not only as a brand new Emperor of a brand new state, but as an all-conquering hero. Ten days after the new Reich had been proclaimed at Versailles, the French had asked for an armistice. A month later they had accepted the German peace terms. These were extremely harsh. The Reich annexed the French province of Alsace and most of Lorraine, and France had to pay an indemnity of five thousand million francs. Until this was paid, France was to be partially occupied. In addition, the conquerors had staged a victory march down the Champs Elysées and a massive review at Longchamps. That the once invincible French, the warrior race of Europe, had been well and truly humbled, there was no doubt; nor was there any question that Germany was now the leading military power on the Continent. For centuries, until the German victory in the Franco-Prussian War, France had been mistress of Europe and Paris the capital of the civilized world; now, quite suddenly, Germany stood predominant and the centre of European gravity swung from Paris to Berlin. And there, for the duration of the Second Reich, it would remain.

Yet, unsuspected by the vast majority of jubilant Germans, there lay buried, in the exultant beginnings of the new Empire, the seeds of its destruction. Born out of military victory, the Second Reich was convinced that continued militarism was the only sure way of safeguarding its new standing in Europe. German militarism, linked to German nationalism, became haloed in glory and the German military caste, looked upon as the most important in its society, became increasingly arrogant. Power for the sake of power was the creed of the new

Germany. The French writer, Ernest Renan, in an open letter published after the Franco-Prussian War, claimed that whereas previous victorious races had always had something to offer to the world—their art, their civilization or their faith—Germany offered nothing except brute force.

The old Germany, the Germany of Goethe, of the classical and romantic writers, of small universities and cultural provincial cities, was buried beneath the pompous militarism of the Reich. The new standards were all materialistic. Germany was fast developing into an industrial giant, second only to the United States of America. Friedrich Nietzsche, regretting the passing of this old Germany, complained of the price of Germany's coming to power: 'Power makes people stupid ...' he wrote; 'the Germans—once they were called the nation of thinkers—do they think at all today? The Germans are bored by intellect, politics swallow up all their interest in really intellectual matters. *Deutschland, Deutschland über alles,* I fear, was the end of German philosophy....'

The Crown Princess echoed these sentiments when she cried out that what she had wanted was for Germany to become, not a great *Militärstaat* but a *Kulturstaat*.

In addition to the cultural and political sterility threatening the state from within, was the danger from conquered France. The French, noting the self-confident swagger with which the Germans each year celebrated their great victory, were determined to wipe out the stain of defeat. The annexation of Alsace-Lorraine was an act of plunder which they refused to forget. In the Place de la Concorde in Paris, the statue representing Strasbourg, capital of Alsace, was draped in black as a constant reminder of the national humiliation. The French were resolved, not only on winning back Alsace-Lorraine, but on having their revenge. *Revanche* became a national obsession and a second war between the two countries almost inevitable.

But for the moment, nothing disturbed the self-satisfaction of the Reich. There was too much to be done. For one thing, the country must have a capital worthy of its new imperial status. Berlin must be transformed from a dull provincial city into a world metropolis. For years the Berliners had envied the assured imperial air of Franz Joseph's Vienna and the magnificence of Napoleon III's Paris; now they were determined to make their capital into a triumphant *Kaiserstadt*.

To this end, the Berliners were giving themselves over to a

frenzy of rebuilding. The city's notorious open drains were being covered over, the cobbles were being replaced by asphalt, unpretentious eighteenth-century buildings were giving way to mile upon mile of stucco façades decorated, it was said, with 'porcelain plaques, glass mosaics, and other incongruous details dear to the garish soul of the Berliner'. New quarters were springing up; new processional ways were being laid out. In half a dozen years the population increased to one million; by the turn of the century it had almost doubled. 'This is a fine city...' wrote Disraeli of Berlin in the 1870s. 'Its public buildings and palaces and hotels are much finer than anything we have, and its streets have an air of architectural splendour....'

Yet it remained an upstart city; a new, brash, grandiose, Hohenzollern city, with none of the charm and personality of towns such as Dresden or Munich. Its atmosphere was stridently militaristic. Almost every Platz sported a colossal group of statuary honouring military achievements. On the Potsdamer Platz towered *Victory*, flanked by smaller figures representing the captured fortresses of Metz and Strasbourg. In the Lustgarten, a helmeted and ample-bosomed *Germania* kept company with statues of the newly-acquired provinces of Alsace and Lorraine. On the Schloss-Brücke, marble groups represented episodes in the life of a victorious warrior. Soaring above the great boulevard running from the Brandenburg Gate to the Charlottenburg Palace was the *Siegessäule*—a two hundred and ten foot high red granite column crowned by a winged Goddess of Victory. If imperial Paris had been a monument to French civilization, imperial Berlin was to be a monument to Prussian militarism.

It was thus into a city already blossoming into a *Weltstadt* that the victorious troops came marching on that June morning in 1871. It was a day of brilliant sunshine. At the head of the procession rode the old Kaiser, followed by his son the Crown Prince Frederick and his nephew, Prince Frederick Charles, each carrying a newly-won Field Marshal's baton. Behind jogged Bismarck (forgiven now and created Prince), Generals von Moltke and von Roon, and over thirty ostentatiously uniformed, if politically emasculated, German princes. At the Brandenburg Gate stood a bevy of maidens, all dressed in white, to welcome the procession. The Emperor sat his horse while one of the maidens recited an interminable poem in his honour and then the procession swung on down Unter den

Linden. The entire, ruler-straight length of this great thorough-fare had been lined with captured French guns, and the whole route of the procession was decorated with banners, garlands, Venetian masts, portraits and triumphal arches. Flags waved, handkerchiefs fluttered and cheer upon deafening cheer drowned the clash of the military bands. Three German prin-ces fainted in the sweltering sunshine but the seventy-four-year-old Kaiser remained firmly in the saddle. Nothing stimulated him as much as a parade and here, surely, was a parade that confirmed his newly-won status, not only as the most powerful military commander of the day but as the most important sov-ereign on the Continent of Europe.

The majority of his subjects certainly regarded him as such. Already, throughout the new Reich, the glorification of the Kaiser's person had begun. Children in schools and students at university were being taught to adulate him. Encouraged by writers such as Heinrich von Treitschke, whose massive *History of Germany in the Nineteenth Century* praised the Ho-henzollerns to the skies, the cult of Emperor-worship gathered strength. Devotion to the Kaiser became synonymous with German patriotism; to follow blindly the 'policy of the Em-peror' was to be a good German; to oppose it was to be a *Reichsfeind*. Referred to, quite unself-consciously, as *der Aller-höchsteselber*—the All-Highest, the Emperor became almost indistinguishable from God.

A charming but significant illustration of this deification of the Hohenzollerns is the story of a visit by the Crown Prince Frederick to some village school.

'To what kingdom does this belong?' asked the Prince of a little girl, touching one of his medals.

'To the mineral kingdom,' she answered promptly.

'And this?' he asked, pointing to a flower.

'To the vegetable kingdom,' she replied.

'And I myself,' continued the Prince, 'to what kingdom do I belong?'

'To the kingdom of Heaven,' breathed the little girl.

And not only did the Emperor appear all-important; his position was every bit as powerful as it appeared. He was, or was in a position to be, a dictator pure and simple. His will was absolute. In theory he was the leading sovereign of a col-lection of sovereigns and Prussia the leading state in a federa-tion of states; in practice, the Prussian Kaiser ruled all Germany. Bismarck's constitution for the North German Confederation, which had vouchsafed the Prussian King this position of power, had simply been extended to embrace the entire Reich.

One needed to be a man of considerable strength of character to withstand the effects of this combination of near-hysterical adulation and unbridled power. Luckily, Kaiser Wilhelm was such a man. Or rather, as that perceptive journalist, Maximilian Harden once put it, 'he has been endowed with that wholesome limitation that alone begets firmness of will'.

The London *Times* was more trenchant. Wilhelm I, it maintained, was 'gifted in a high degree with the chief characteristic of his subjects—a capacity for plodding; he accomplished by method tasks which would have fretted the patience of a genius'.

An additional curb on any tendency towards conceit was Wilhelm's piety. It was exceptional. 'Do not extol me in your address,' he had said to the Court chaplain before the proclamation at Versailles, 'for I have been but an instrument in the hand of God.' This piety was obvious, not only in his lengthy prayers and regular church attendance but in his public speeches and his war dispatches. His telegrams from the front were said to read like 'King David's psalms of thanksgiving for triumphs over the Philistines'.

Success never went to Kaiser Wilhelm's head. Of the pride, the arrogance, the overweening vanity of his grandson, the future Kaiser Wilhelm II, he revealed not a trace. Indeed, he had frequently to be reminded that he was now an Emperor. Even four years after the inauguration of the Empire, he once spoke to a guest of some violets which 'the Queen' had picked in the palace gardens that morning. At this the Crown Prince, who was as punctilious about the new title as his father was casual, quickly intervened. 'Yes,' he said firmly, 'the *Empress* told me about them.' 'When did you see the Queen?' retorted the old sovereign.

His way of life remained almost completely unchanged. It was as unpretentious as it had always been. Although his capital was being aggrandized, the Kaiser himself remained in the same palace Palais which he had occupied since his marriage. Despite the fact that his palace was regarded as being 'commonplace and ugly' and its furnishings distinctly shabby, he preferred it to the official palace, the Old Schloss which, for all its inconveniences, was unquestionably more grandiose.

The Kaiser slept on an iron camp-bed covered with a simple white quilt, in a bleak, narrow room whose only window looked out on the palace courtyard. On the wall above his head hung a wooden crucifix; in one corner of the room stood a case containing his orders, in another, a stand for swords. With the exception of a painting of his mother, Queen Louise, at her lying-in-state, all the pictures in his bedroom were of Prussian or Russian uniforms. Wilhelm rose early; even in winter he was up before daylight. Adjoining his bedroom was his dressing-room. There was no bath in this room; whenever the Emperor wanted a bath, he would have a wooden tub brought over from the Hotel de Rome. This would then be rolled back across the street by a manservant. In matters of dress he was always very particular though never extravagant. His valet, Eysel, would coax a few long, thin strands of silver hair from above one ear, across his domed forehead, to above the other. This the Kaiser would call his 'Chinese pigtail'. He was always extremely polite to his servants.

Wilhelm would spend most of the morning in his study. Advancing age and enhanced status made him no less frugal in his habits. He wasted nothing. He would always make use of old envelopes, gumming them up and re-addressing them. Once, during the siege of Paris, while out walking with his staff, he disappeared behind some bushes; on re-emerging, he explained that he had been eating a piece of chocolate which he had had in his pocket for weeks. There had not been enough of it, he announced solemnly, to share.

Having attended to his correspondence (he always wiped his pens very carefully before putting them away) he would grant audiences or confer with his ministers. Each noon, after buttoning his coat and pinning on his orders, he would cross to the corner window of his study and from there watch the changing of the guard in the forecourt below. The sight of 'Old Wilhelm', standing to attention at the corner window of the palace, was one of the most famous in Berlin for almost three decades.

On most days he lunched off a tray balanced on one corner of a bookshelf and was usually indifferent to what he ate. In the afternoon he would go for a drive in the Tiergarten and, at what one guest understandably calls the 'unholy hour of 5 p.m.', he went down to dinner. If he were not entertaining in the evening, he would go to the theatre, always being careful, reports his valet, not to wear his 'good trousers'. After the theatre, he would join the Empress at tea.

His tastes were conventional, his outlook prosaic and his conversation banal. He loved battle pictures, light comedies, martial music and the conversation of pretty young women. On examining the newly unveiled Leipzig war memorial, he complained about the figure representing Baden. 'Now you know Baden?' he asked the sculptor. 'My son-in-law's is such a rich country; why have you clothed the Baden lady so scantily here? She has not even got stockings on!'

Princess Louise of Schleswig-Holstein gives another example of his artlessness. One of the innumerable Hohenzollern princesses, talking to the Kaiser on the morning after her wedding night, complained that the eagle adorning the canopy above the marriage bed had crashed down on to her bridegroom's busy back. 'Good God!' exclaimed Wilhelm. 'Does Alexis always sleep on his stomach?'

Yet there was no denying the magnificence of the Kaiser's appearance or the cordiality of his manner. Lord Frederic Hamilton, seeing him for the first time during these early days of the Second Reich, claimed that, 'this splendid-looking old man may not have been an intellectual giant, but he certainly looked an Emperor, every inch of him'. So tall, so upright, so correctly dressed, he was dignified without ever looking pompous. On State occasions he bore himself superbly; at informal affairs he was unfailingly courteous. The Empress Augusta's evening parties, which often suffered from the hostess's feverish determination to keep things moving, were usually saved by the arrival of the Emperor. He would come in, straight from the theatre and, by the tranquillity of his manner, ease away all traces of strain. Throughout the serving of the curious choice of refreshments—the tea, the cakes, the wine, the oranges and the ices—he would delight the company with his *bonhomie*. 'The old gentleman is always the same——' wrote one of the guests, 'kindly, cheerful, taking part in all the conversation, and delightfully informal.'

On nights such as this, it was difficult to believe that he was the most powerful monarch in Western Europe.

But, of course, it was not he who wielded the power. It was Bismarck. The Imperial Chancellor was the real dictator of the

Second Reich and the arbiter of the Continent. It was not to the tune of the autocratic sovereign of Germany that the statesmen of Europe danced, but to that of his autocratic Chancellor. The first two decades of the Second Reich were the Age, not of Wilhelm I, but of Bismarck. No matter how stubbornly the Emperor might resist his Chancellor's proposals, Bismarck now, as always, got his way. There might be harsh words, there might be sulks, there might be tears, but there was never a complete break.

In any case, it was only where military matters were concerned that the Emperor was likely to dig in his heels. Wilhelm was still obsessed with the making of the army quite free of parliamentary control (it was the Reichstag that had to vote the military budgets) and the concern of himself and his military cabinet only. As Bismarck was just as anxious for the restriction of parliamentary control, yet did not want the military cabinet—which was independent of him—to become too powerful either, he had always to play one side off against the other.

The always simmering controversy came to the boil in the year 1874 when the Reichstag refused to give up its right to vote the military budget each year. Bismarck allowed the *impasse*, between the Emperor and his generals on the one hand, and the Reichstag on the other, to continue until it reached danger point. Then, in his masterly way, he effected a compromise. The Emperor would have personal control of the army, but for seven years only. With this, Wilhelm had to be content.

Even during clashes like this, the Kaiser never seriously considered dismissing his Chancellor. Nor did Bismarck, for all his grumblings about his master's ingratitude, even seriously consider leaving him. Indeed, for most of the time, the two men were fully conscious of what each owed the other. Bismarck had an ingrained reverence for the monarchy; Wilhelm a healthy respect for his Chancellor's strength of character. 'It was almost touching to watch the great Chancellor speaking to the old sovereign,' reported one eye-witness of a meeting between the two men, 'the respect in his countenance and the expression of his eyes had something peculiar I never remembered having seen in them before.... I doubt if many observed what to me was its most curious part, the homage Bismarck's eyes paid to the sovereign, without whom he could never have become the great man he had risen to be, whom in his inmost soul he respected as much as he loved, and to whom he had given all the admiration, all the affection, his stern heart was capable of feeling.'

The Kaiser was just as appreciative. 'As usual,' he once wrote to Bismarck on the latter's birthday, 'I offer you my heartiest congratulations on the anniversary of the day on which the Almighty in His wisdom and grace gave you to the world and —to me! !'

2

If Kaiser Wilhelm I was sometimes inclined to forget his new imperial status, the Empress Augusta was never guilty of the same lapse. Fully conscious of her new role, she played it for all it was worth. She had always loved pomp; now she could indulge that love to the full.

Augusta was just sixty in the year that she became an Empress and advancing age had done nothing towards mellowing her personality. Denied the opportunity of playing an active political part, she flung herself into a round of ceaseless, and purposeless, social activity. With her be-ribboned dresses, rouged cheeks and chestnut-coloured wigs, she was as frenetic as the Emperor was dignified. The Empress could 'stand more fatigue, excitement and knocking about than anyone I know', reported the Crown Princess to Queen Victoria. 'She has more physical power and stronger nerves than anybody. She wears everyone out who belongs to her Household, Gentlemen and all. She never sits down indoors, for fourteen or fifteen consecutive hours—she is never without talking, loud and long on exciting topics to dozens of different persons ... she walks, eats, dresses and writes in the most tremendous hurry, she has parties every night, she is never alone—she never takes up a book or a paper because she has no time, she reads the newspapers aloud at breakfast, she pays visits innumerable, she inspects all public establishments, she gives audiences unceasing—in fact, only the thought of what she does all day long makes me quite giddy....'

With so feverish a personality as its hostess, it was no wonder that the German Imperial Court became notable, not so much for its brilliance as for its busyness. There was hardly an evening during the season on which the Empress did not entertain or was not, in turn, entertained. Most frequent were her *soirées de la Bonbonnière'*—informal parties to which five or six people would be invited and at which the Empress, in her often indiscreet fashion, held forth unabated. Her grandson, Prince Wilhelm, claimed that although the Empress could give the impression of formality, 'in a small circle, and especially *tête-à-tête*, she was warm and affectionate, and lovingly demonstrative'.

Her 'Thursdays', held during Lent, were larger and more formal gatherings to which the entire royal family, the *corps diplomatique* and various members of society were invited. Despite the hostess's vitality, these occasions seem to have been distinguished chiefly by their dullness. The guests would form the customary circle, within which the imperial pair would move, with agonizing slowness, exchanging a few banalities with each guest. This was a standard royal procedure at which Augusta is said to have been especially adept; as a girl she had been trained to *cercle* by walking around a lawn and addressing a few polite phrases to each shrub or tree as she passed.

'After waiting for nearly an hour,' wrote Constance de Rothschild of one of these imperial receptions, 'we all stood up a little stiffer and straighter and were aware of a magnificent apparition gliding down towards us. It was the Empress.... Her Majesty, dressed in white, was literally covered with jewels and wore plaits and curls waving down to her waist and encircled by emeralds and diamonds. She was rouged up to her eyes, and when she stood in front of us and began to talk she looked like an actress—or rather, like a painted doll. She is certainly handsome, but has no charm and no nature and goes about with a continual smile which does not go up to her eyes. She has a marvellous figure and moves beautifully.'

This lengthy Thursday circling was followed, complains another guest, first by a 'still longer concert' and then by a supper at which the menu never varied. It was always salmon with mayonnaise, cold chicken and ices. Princess Frederick Charles, sharp-tongued wife of the Kaiser's nephew, used to claim that a barrelful of mayonnaise was whipped up each autumn and made to last out the season.

More impressive were the State dinners, followed by a Court or a ball. These were held in the Old Schloss, whose rooms were said to be among the most sumptuous in Europe. A select company would sit down to eat at five in the afternoon at a vast table decorated, says one guest, with 'rows of gigantic silver dish-covers, each surmounted by a Prussian eagle, with nothing under them, running down the middle of the table'. After dinner the imperial party moved through a succession of magnificently furnished rooms, filled with guests, until they reached the Throne Room. This flamboyantly decorated hall, with its painted ceiling, its glittering chandeliers, its tapestried panels and its wealth of rococo detail, was said to be without equal in Europe. 'The whole of the wall surface was gilded— carvings, mouldings and pilasters forming one unbroken sheet of gold ...' enthused one witness. 'When the Throne Room was lighted up at night, the glowing colours of the Gobelin tapestry and the sheen of the great expanses of gold and silver produced an effect of immense splendour.'

The State balls took place in the White Hall of the Old Schloss. Here, in contrast to the kaleidoscopic brilliance of the Throne Room, the decoration was entirely white and silver, and served as an excellent foil for the dresses and uniforms of the dancers. The sight of the imperial *cortège* entering the ballroom was claimed to be 'one of the finest spectacles in the world'. Only one thing was likely to mar the majesty of the occasion. An inlay, in the shape of a crowned Prussian eagle, decorated the centre of the dance floor and was kept in a state of high polish. It was consequently as slippery as ice. If, in his exuberance, an officer set foot on it and crashed to the floor, he would be banned from all Court balls for a year.

Every year the imperial couple gave a less grandiose but more select ball in their own palace. To be invited to this ball in the Kaiser's palace was the height of social ambition; one could then number oneself, not among the first ten thousand, but among the first thousand in the Reich. 'Nothing could be plainer than their scale,' reported one of the honoured few, 'but the great charm of them consisted in the kind way in which the royal hosts received their guests and bade them welcome. It was on these occasions that the proverbial amiability of the Emperor was seen to its fullest advantage, and it was at them that he displayed the gallantry which had made of him in his youth one of the most fascinating personages in Europe.'

When the Empress was not entertaining, she would be paying calls or granting audiences. Her arrival at some household was usually enough to send the gentlemen scurrying to safety, leaving the ladies to cope with their demanding guest. Her audiences were no less unnerving. Princess Catherine Radziwill, whose husband's aunt had been Elisa Radziwill, the old Kaiser's first love, tells of her formal presentation to the Empress. Despite the fact that it took place at eleven in the morning, Augusta was dressed in the most elaborate, and juvenile, manner possible. Her dress was of pale cream satin, lavishly trimmed, and round her ageing throat hung ropes of magnificent pearls. Atop her wig, 'composed of innumerable curls, the colour of which would have been sufficient to cast doubts as to its genuineness', she wore a concoction of lace and pink ribbons. 'That strange get-up did not produce a favourable impression,' reports the Princess; nor did the manner in which the Empress rattled off her formal speech of welcome. Only when Augusta fell to gossiping with the Princess's sister-in-law did she appear more natural.

Although the Empress was never extravagant, she found her husband's frugality extremely trying. Only under pressure would he sanction the buying of any new articles for the royal household. There was a certain tea service which Augusta hated: it was in white porcelain, decorated with entwined grass-green and bright blue ribbons, and had once belonged to the Kaiser's mother, Queen Louise. Under no circumstances would the Emperor allow his wife to replace it with something more restrained. Prompted by her maid, the ill-natured Frau von Neundorff, the Empress decided on a way of getting rid of the offending service. Already suffering from the shaking palsy which was to become more pronounced with age, she put her affliction to good use. Every time she passed a cup to a guest she dropped it; this way she rid herself of a dozen cups and saucers. As she was about to order a new set, the Kaiser presented her with an exact replica of the old one. He had had it copied by the Royal Porcelain factory in Berlin.

Augusta's love of scandal, or what was called her 'taste for intrigue', quite often landed her in trouble. Her nightly *soirées de la Bonbonnière* seethed with gossip and her hearers could not always be trusted to keep their mouths shut. This same Princess Radziwill, who proved to be as malicious as she was observant, remembered what she had heard during those evening parties and later published it, under the pseudonym of Count Paul Vassili, in a book entitled *La Société de Berlin*. In this notorious and widely read book, Princess Radziwill held the entire imperial Court up to ridicule, aiming some of her deadliest shafts at the Empress. Augusta was revealed to the world as being 'intriguing, false and affected' and without the slightest notion of dignity or propriety. The publication of the book caused an uproar at Court and led to the dismissal of the Empress's reader, the blameless M. Auguste Gérard, on the grounds that, as a Frenchman and an intimate, he must have been the anonymous author of the scurrilous attack.

Such squalls blew over; it was the Empress's feud with Bismarck which raged unabated. Had her passion for intrigue confined itself to the day-to-day life of the Court, the Chancellor would have ignored her. What he could not ignore was her continued involvement in affairs of State. She never stopped trying to influence her husband against him. 'When, overnight, some matter or other has been arranged,' complained the Chancellor, 'at the breakfast table next morning everything is turned upside-down.... If only the Emperor were a widower!'

Lady Russell, wife of the British Ambassador in Berlin, reported to Queen Victoria that 'Prince Bismarck often expresses his hatred for the Empress in such strong language that my husband is placed in a very difficult position'; while the Empress boasted that she had only twice spoken to Bismarck in the course of three years.

Their quarrel reached its height during the *Kulturkampf*— the grandiloquently termed 'conflict of civilizations'—which all but tore Germany apart during the first few years of the Empire.

The *Kulturkampf* was Germany's version of that general nineteenth-century problem—the conflict between the State and the Roman Catholic Church. To liberals this *Kulturkampf* was looked upon as a war between enlightenment and obscurantism; to Catholics it was a defence of the rights of the Church; to Bismarck it was an opportunity to break the Church's power. As it was the National Liberal Party in the Reichstag that opposed the Church and the newly formed Centre Party that defended it, Bismarck was forced into a somewhat uncomfortable alliance with the National Liberals. With their support, he passed a series of harsh laws against the clergy. In this long struggle, he came up against the implacable opposition of the Empress.

Someone once called the Empress Augusta a *'personnage d'opposition'*. It was a telling assessment. Her policies, as Bismarck once pointed out, were determined more 'by special dislikes than by any positive aims'. Now, in her hatred of Bismarck, she was quite ready to desert the liberal line she had hitherto pursued and to fling herself heart and soul into the Catholic cause. 'To be Catholic was at that time regarded as a mark of distinction in Berlin, especially if one was not actually Catholic,' writes Emil Ludwig. 'The Empress herself stood at the head of this vogue.' With the passing years, moreover, Augusta's interest in the Roman Catholic Church had deepened; she could thus give her taste for Catholicism and her detestation of Bismarck full play. It has been claimed that the *Kulturkampf* would never have been so prolonged had it not been for the encouragement given by 'the Catholic party at Court', at whose core, of course, was the Empress.

Bismarck, for his part, was just as violent in his denunciation of Augusta as she was of him. In his speeches to the Reichstag he would allude to 'inexperienced diplomatists' and to the 'drawing room influences of highly placed personages'. He would go to almost any lengths to spite her. His treatment of Count von Arnim was a case in point.

Count von Arnim was the German Ambassador in Paris during the early 1870s. Bismarck who, according to his own boast, always expected his ambassadors 'to fall into line like soldiers', considered Arnim to be far too independent for his liking. Not only did the Ambassador's sympathy with the French monarchists run counter to Bismarck's scheme for keeping republican France isolated in monarchist Europe, but in his support for a royal restoration in France, Arnim had the ear of the Kaiser. Still worse, by Bismarck's reckoning, was Arnim's outspoken opposition to the *Kulturkampf*. In this, of course, the Ambassador had the ear of the Empress. Worst of all, however, was the rumour that Count von Arnim, being thus in favour at Court, was about to succeed Bismarck as Chancellor. To the achievement of this end, the Empress was suspected of using her still considerable influence.

Bismarck lost no time in organizing his rival's downfall. He had him spied upon and, having uncovered some trifling error, insisted on his recall from Paris and his dismissal from the diplomatic service. 'You are plotting with the Empress and will not stop intriguing until you sit at this very desk where I am sitting now,' he bellowed at the unfortunate Arnim. 'And then you will see,' he added in typically Bismarckian fashion, 'even that isn't worth a damn!'

Not content with Arnim's dismissal, the vindictive Chancellor had the Empress's favourite arrested and flung into prison on a trivial charge of not having handed over certain documents which the ex-Ambassador regarded as his own property. The trial caused a sensation. Arnim, found guilty, was forced into exile, and a subsequent pamphlet, in which he defended himself, earned him a fresh prosecution and the outrageous sentence of five years' penal servitude *in absentia*.

That the blow was aimed at Arnim's ardent champion, the Empress Augusta, there could be no doubt.

It was not long after this that Bismarck, increasingly annoyed at the Empress's interference ('The Emperor is old and lets himself be influenced by her more and more,' he grumbled) and feeling somewhat dispirited, decided to put matters to the test. He handed in his resignation. 'He is going,' noted Moritz Busch, one of Bismarck's toadies, in his diary; 'it is not a question of leave, but of resignation peremptorily demanded. The reason: Augusta, who influences her husband, plots with Queen Victoria ... and stirs up the Papists.'

Bismarck, expecting a shocked refusal on the part of the Emperor to accept his resignation, was somewhat discomfited to find that ten days elapsed before he received any answer. 'How I wish with all my heart,' wrote the Crown Princess to Queen Victoria, 'that his time [would] come to a close during the Emperor's reign or at this present moment.... I should consider it a Godsend. I fear it is too good to come to me, and Bismarck too fond of power ever to give it up—often as he may threaten with the intention of doing so.'

Augusta, of course, was beside herself with excitement. 'Bismarck,' she announced to the British Ambassador, 'must be taught to obey his sovereign.'

But it was not to be. The Emperor could not bring himself to part from his Chancellor. He wrote to him, saying that he hoped he would continue to serve his country for many years to come.

'The sensation produced by this letter was immense,' reports the ubiquitous Princess Radziwill. 'The Empress, quite disgusted, started for Coblenz the next day....'

On 1 September 1874, Prince Wilhelm, now fifteen years old, was confirmed. The ceremony took place in the Friedenskirche at Potsdam and was treated as an occasion of great significance by the assembled Hohenzollerns. For the young prince himself, it must have been a nerve-racking ordeal. He was positioned alone on a dais, facing two rows of chairs on which, in sombre black, were ranged the Emperor, the Empress and the entire Prussian royal family. Behind them, a vast congregation filled the nave to overflowing. Among the royal guests, as representatives of the boy's grandmother—Queen Victoria—were the Prince and Princess of Wales.

Young Wilhelm seems to have acquitted himself remarkably well. Looking back on that day in later life, he claimed, with a characteristic lack of modesty, that although Dr Persius, who had prepared him for confirmation, had proved wanting, his own meditations had resulted in 'a really elevating initiation'. And Hintzpeter, the boy's tutor, allowing his reverence for the ruling family full play, observed that 'the Prince was to be free so to adapt the Christian faith himself to his own individuality that it might become the standard on which he could model his life'.

The Prince read his *Glaubensbekenntnis* in a steady voice and then, without the slightest hesitation, answered the forty questions put to him by the Court chaplain. The theological inquisition done with, the chaplain launched into what the Crown Princess described as 'three *long* addresses which might have been better shorter'. The sermons finally over, the chaplain served communion to Prince Wilhelm, his parents and the Prince of Wales. Bertie, who had undergone a similar trial in St George's Chapel at Windsor some years before, dutifully assured his mother that he was 'much struck with the solemnity and simplicity of the service'. The Emperor and Empress professed themselves deeply moved, the Crown Princess was lavish in her praise, and even Prince Wilhelm's younger brothers and sisters, overcome by either emotion or exhaustion, cried throughout the service.

'My confirmation fortified me and invested me with new strength,' noted Wilhelm a few days later, 'and I look to the future with firm conviction and trust in God.'

Though disappointed at not being able to attend the ceremony herself, Queen Victoria had made sure that her grandson would not forget her on this great occasion. Among her many gifts, spread out in Bertie's sitting-room at the Neues Palais, was a bible in which she had inscribed an appropriately uplifting message ('All you said I thought so very true,' commented Bertie piously) and a portrait of the late Prince Consort. One can appreciate what the Crown Princess meant when she assured her mother that Prince Wilhelm had been 'surprised at suddenly becoming the possessor of so large and beautiful a picture of dear Papa!'

The Prince's confirmation marked the close of one phase of his life. Two days after the ceremony he and his younger brother Henry were packed off to school at Cassel and the Prince's boyhood could be said to be at an end. From now on he would be coming home for holidays only. His departure thus marked, as his sentimental mother put it, 'a sort of break up'.

The Crown Princess was not dissatisfied with his progress to date. As he had matured, so had she begun to pay more and more attention to his education. Between them, she and Hintzpeter stuffed him with more information than he could possibly absorb. 'I watch over him myself, over every detail, even the minutest, of his education...' reported Vicky to her mother; upon which the Queen, realizing, perhaps, that her own son Bertie was a poor advertisement for the advantages of tight parental control, shrewdly observed that 'too great care, too much constant watching, leads to the very dangers hereafter which one wishes to avoid'.

However, during these first fifteen years of Prince Wilhelm's life, his virtues seemed to have outweighed his failings. His parents might find him a shade assertive or a trifle oversensitive, but, by and large, they had no cause for anxiety. They were certainly not as critical of him as he afterwards claimed them to have been. The Crown Prince, who had been obliged to spend long periods away on active service, sometimes worried about whether or not the boy was being raised in the right atmosphere (he feared the reactionary tone of the Court) but he felt confident that because of the 'simple, natural, cordial relations' between parents and son, young Wilhelm would always look upon them as his best friends. The Crown Princess, always less prey to self-doubt, was certain of it.

'I am sure you would be pleased with William if you were to see him——' she wrote to her mother on one occasion, 'he has Bertie's pleasant, amiable ways—and can be very winning. He is not possessed of brilliant abilities, nor any strength of character or talents, but he is a dear boy, and I hope and trust will grow up a useful man. He has an excellent tutor, I never saw or knew a better, and all the care that can be bestowed on mind and body is taken of him. I am happy to say that between him and me there is a bond of love and confidence, which I feel sure nothing can destroy. He has very strong health and would be a pretty boy were it not for that wretched unhappy arm which shows more and more, spoils his face (for it is on one side), his carriage, walk and figure, makes him awkward in all his movements, and gives him a feeling of shyness, as he feels his complete dependence, not being able to do a single thing for himself. It is a great additional difficulty in his education, and is not without its effect on his character. To me it remains an inexpressible source of sorrow! I think he will be very good-looking when he grows up, and he is already a universal favourite, as he is so lively and generally intelligent. He is a mixture of all our brothers—there is very little of his Papa, or the family of Prussia, about him.'

Vicky, in this generous assessment of her son's personality, had made no mention of his imperiousness; yet it was a characteristic which was beginning to alarm the boy's tutor. Thus far Hintzpeter's efforts to inculcate his pupil with a sense of modesty had been unsuccessful. It was he, therefore, who suggested to the Crown Princess that Prince Wilhelm be sent to a State-run grammar school; only by mixing with boys of humbler birth, but superior brain would Wilhelm be cured of his arrogance. Vicky, at first somewhat put out by this revolutionary suggestion, finally agreed to it. She announced that Wilhelm would go to the Gymnasium at Cassel.

The old Emperor was horrified at the idea. It would hardly do, argued the Kaiser, for a Prince who would one day rule by Divine Right, to pit himself, publicly, against others who might well prove more intelligent than he. With this reasoning young Wilhelm was inclined to agree. Already suffering from a sense of inferiority, he dreaded what he afterwards called rendering himself 'defenceless to the world's criticism'. In later years, he made mention of his objections to the scheme with a revealing candour: 'to learn with strange boys in a public school was to compete with them and—to come out lower in the list!' For one with his blend of self-importance and sensitivity, the thought of such competition was intolerable.

But the Crown Princess held firm and Wilhelm, accompanied by his younger brother Henry, set out for Cassel. In accordance with Hintzpeter's peculiar mixture of Spartan and medieval ideas, the young Princes were forced to hike to Cassel like 'travelling students'. But neither this, nor the relatively democratic atmosphere of the Gymnasium itself, was able to conquer Wilhelm's conceit. Indeed, the reverence with which his fellow students always treated their future ruler simply encouraged it. Nor did the two and a half years which he spent at Cassel awaken his interest in learning. He was kept hard at work but Hintzpeter complained that he was both lazy and incapable of sustained concentration on any one subject. This was to be one of his chief failings in later life: he simply could not fix his attention on any one thing for long.

It was at this time too, that another of the boy's less commendable characteristics began to manifest itself. This was his tendency to attract attention to himself by outrageous exaggeration. Queen Sophie of Holland, meeting him in the year that he went to Cassel, had some shrewd comments to make on his personality. 'The eldest is fifteen years old—is an ugly likeness of the Prince of Wales,' she wrote. 'He has a strange propensity to lying, inventing whole stories, which have no shadow of truth.... He has a lame arm—incurable—and they say he feels his infirmity deeply, but he is not awkward. In every sense he will be a strange specimen of a Sovereign, perhaps the more warlike, because nature did not fit him for a soldier.'

The Queen went on to say that 'the Princess's favourites are the younger ones, and the eldest feel it. She governs the Crown Prince, but this may change, when he sits upon the throne.'

An aspect of school life which seems to have struck Prince Wilhelm unfavourably was the emphasis placed on learning at the expense of the nurturing of what he called 'the German spirit'. The things to which he thrilled—the military triumphs of the Franco-Prussian War, the proclamation of the Reich, the awakening of a militant nationalism—seemed to mean very little to his fellow students. He complained that the German school curriculum, unlike the British, did nothing towards fostering nationalism; it produced no *conscious* Germans. At schools such as Eton, he afterwards maintained, 'the young Britons had learned much less Latin and Greek, but they were inspired with the idea of making Great Britain still greater and stronger. They dreamed of new colonial conquests, of exploring unknown regions, of expanding British trade, and of acting as pioneers for their Fatherland with the slogan "my country—right or wrong".'

Prince Wilhelm left the Gymnasium in January 1877. He was to spend the next six months in the army before going on—like his father before him—to the University at Bonn. A few weeks after leaving Cassel he celebrated his eighteenth birthday. On the occasion of this coming of age he solemnly noted that, just as he had dedicated himself to God at his confirmation, so did he now dedicate himself to his military career. This burgeoning sense of his own importance was further illustrated by the fracas over a suitable decoration from Queen Victoria to mark the occasion. She had offered him the Grand Companionship of the Bath but he demanded of his mother that he be given a still higher decoration—the Order of the Garter. He explained that the Emperors of Russia and Austria and the King of Italy had already bestowed their highest orders on him; why then should he be content with less from the Queen of England? The Crown Princess pleaded on his behalf ('while Willy would be satisfied with the Bath, the nation expects the Garter', she was forced to argue) and the Queen granted his wish.

If his years at the Gymnasium had done nothing towards curbing Prince Wilhelm's lordliness, his time at Bonn increased it to an almost unbelievable degree. Housed in a mansion, attended by aides and treated with the utmost deference, he began to develop along lines quite different from those visualized by his progressively minded parents. Each time he returned home on holiday, his rudeness, his conceit and, above all, his reactionary ideas, seemed more pronounced. He did not even appear to have inherited his parents' cultural enthusiasms. The Crown Princess complained that he did not 'care to look at anything, took no interest whatever in works of art, and did not in the least admire beautiful scenery and would not look at a Guide Book'. This might have been an exaggeration, dashed off in a moment of exasperation, but there can be no doubt that she was very upset by the way her son was shaping. The relationship between the two of them was worsening by the year; their differences of opinion were becoming increasingly bitter.

One of the troubles was that mother and son were so very much alike. It was the old story of a mother and child having similar personalities and opposing views. Both were clever, didactic and domineering. Neither would see the other's point of view. The more forcefully she aired her opinions, the more violently he contradicted them. Queen Victoria, who was often caught in the crossfire between mother and son, sometimes suspected that, for all her grandson's insolence, the fault was not entirely on his side. 'Alice,' she wrote of her second daughter to the Empress Augusta, 'has grown so mature, so reasonable; one can say anything to her, which is unfortunately not the case in another quarter!'

Vicky had hoped, so ardently, to mould her son in the image of her adored father whereas his heroes were his grandfather and Prince Bismarck. The liberalism which formed the cornerstone of her philosophy was becoming anathema to him. The louder she preached it, the more she set him against it. How much his views were simply a reaction to her self-righteous nagging one cannot know; his reign was certainly to be conducted along lines quite different from those laid down by her. The militarism of his grandfather's entourage was much more to his taste. The boy had grown up during the years of Prussia's surge to greatness; one of his most exciting memories was of that swaggering cavalcade of victorious troops through Berlin after the Franco-Prussian War. His country's greatness had been achieved, not by a spread of progressive ideas, but by military conquest—by blood and iron. Whereas his father's generation had been inspired by the revolutionary ideals of 1848, his had been dazzled by the less complex, but more spectacular, military triumphs of 1864–71. There seemed to him something depressingly old-fashioned about his parents' political philosophy. It was not what he looked upon as their mealy-mouthed liberalism that had transformed Germany into the most important nation on the Continent. Quite obviously, their ideas counted for very little in the present scheme of things; they were simply ignored by Bismarck and the ruling élite. Fretfully, they were obliged to sit on the sidelines, growing older and more impatient by the year. That Wilhelm himself would one day reign over this mighty Empire was due, not to any rigid adherence to their constitutional principles, but to the triumph of German arms. Might was what mattered.

CHAPTER FIVE

THE MAELSTROM

1

On the afternoon of Sunday, 2 June 1878, as the Kaiser's calèche went bowling along Unter den Linden towards the Brandenburg Gate, a sudden sound of gunfire shattered the summer air. A shotgun had been fired at the carriage from a second floor window of No. 18. The Emperor, in the act of waving acknowledgement to the cheers of the Sunday afternoon strollers, was peppered with shot. He was hit in the back, the neck and the right arm, with some of the shot ripping through his helmet and grazing his forehead. Streaming blood, he was driven back to his palace at breakneck speed and carried up to his rooms. Over thirty grains of shot were removed from his body. Throughout the incident the eighty-one-year-old Emperor remained remarkably composed but the loss of blood had considerably weakened him and it was doubted that he would last the night. Telegrams were sent to the Empress at Baden and to the Crown Prince and Princess, who were visiting England. All night long an anxious crowd packed the streets around the palace; only the Platz directly in front of the building was kept empty to ensure that no noise disturbed the monarch. Not until morning did the crowd learn that the Emperor, though weak, was still alive.

The would-be assassin was a Dr Karl Nobiling. A well-educated member of a wealthy middle-class family, Nobiling seems to have had no political connections. His motives for the attempted killing remained obscure, for at the moment of his arrest he tried to shoot himself and died of his self-inflicted wounds before he could be properly questioned. Like so many assassins, he might have harboured some private grudge against his victim or he may simply have been in search of fame or self-justification.

Bismarck was at his country place when the news of the attempted assassination was brought to him. Tiedemann, his confidential assistant and secretary, having read the news first, hurried out into the park in search of the Chancellor. He found him strolling across the fields in the bright sunlight, his dogs gambolling at his heels. He was obviously in the best of moods. When Tiedemann warned his master that some important telegrams had arrived, Bismarck smilingly asked if they were so urgent that they had to be dealt with in the open air. 'Unfortunately, they are,' answered his secretary. 'The Emperor has again been fired at and this time he has been hit. His Majesty has been seriously wounded.'

Bismarck stopped dead. Patently agitated and breathing heavily, he drove his walking-stick hard into the earth. Tiedemann, expecting to be pressed for news of the Emperor's condition or for details of the attempt, was amazed to hear the Chancellor's first reaction.

'Now we can dissolve the Reichstag!' cried the gratified Bismarck.

This was the chance for which he had been waiting. For some time now Bismarck had been anxious to change the composition of the Reichstag. He wanted, not only to get rid of the small but dynamic Social Democratic Party, but to break the power of his recent allies, the National Liberals—still the strongest party in the House. His association with the National Liberals had never been a natural one; now that he had had their help in breaking the power of the Catholics, he was ready to ditch them.

Having decided that the time was ripe for discrediting liberalism, Bismarck raised the cry that the life of Germany's beloved Emperor had been endangered by the spread of new political ideas. He blamed the socialists by name and the liberals by inference. Legislation must be passed to suppress the Social Democrat opposition but, as an earlier attempt on Bismarck's part to introduce such legislation had been opposed by the National Liberals, the Reichstag must be dissolved and new elections held. By playing up the 'Social Peril' for all— and rather more than—it was worth, and by tarring the Social Democrats and National Liberals with the same brush, Bismarck hoped that fewer National Liberal candidates would be elected. Bismarck's Press launched an all-out attack on the National Liberals, blaming the shooting of the Emperor on their refusal to vote for Bismarck's first anti-Socialist bill. Precisely how the passing of this bill would have prevented Dr Nobiling, who had no connection with either the National Liberal or the Social Democratic parties, from firing at the Kaiser, no one bothered either to explain or to question. The suggestion that the Kaiser's life would be in permanent danger without suppression of the 'Social Peril' was enough. The voters must be panicked into supporting Bismarck.

This was always his way. By keeping things in a state of crisis, by implying that the Fatherland was somehow in danger, Bismarck kept himself in power. In his early days he had held the support of Wilhelm I by keeping the struggle between King and constitution on the boil. He had achieved the unification of Germany by whipping up national feelings against Denmark, Austria and France. After the establishment of the Reich he had played up the dangers of Catholicism. In the mid-1870s he had fabricated a war threat from France. Now, ostensibly to save the Kaiser, and the Reich, from the menace of Socialism, the Reichstag must be dissolved, the Social Democratic Party suppressed and the National Liberals weakened.

But Bismarck faced one problem, and this a very serious one: Crown Prince Frederick.

Immediately on hearing of the attempted assassination, the Crown Prince and Princess had come hurrying back from England. Their moment, surely, had arrived; their long apprenticeship was about to end. It was unlikely that the eighty-one-year-old Kaiser would recover from so serious an attack. Even if he did, his convalescence would probably be a long one, leaving him permanently disabled. Was history about to repeat itself? Wilhelm I, after years of waiting, had become Regent for an incapacitated monarch; would the same thing happen to his son, the Crown Prince? Wilhelm's assumption of the Regency had ushered in a short-lived 'new era'; would Frederick's Regency introduce a more permanent era of enlightenment? Whatever happened, the Crown Prince was about to come, at last, into his own. One cannot know his innermost thoughts, but it must have been with a characteristic blend of trepidation and dedication that Crown Prince Frederick prepared to assume the Regency.

As for Vicky, she must have felt an even stronger sense of fulfilment. Free of any of her husband's inhibitions, she could finally bring all her talents into full play. The long-delayed schemes of her father, Prince Albert, were about to be launched.

As usual, Bismarck was one step ahead of them. Realizing that the Crown Prince would not only refuse to be panicked into dissolving the Reichstag but that he would attempt to inaugurate a more progressive policy, the Chancellor was ready to clip his wings. As soon as it was apparent that the Kaiser was not going to die, Bismarck acted. He arranged for the Crown Prince to be appointed, not as Regent, but as the Emperor's deputy only. This way he would be obliged to carry out his father's policy. With this arrangement, the Kaiser was in complete agreement. 'Gentlemen,' murmured the old man to the ministers assembled about his sickbed, 'go to my son now. You know exactly what I wish and expect done, and I insist upon the government of the country continuing to be carried on in accordance with my views, and everything remaining as it is, and hold you responsible for this.'

Crown Prince Frederick's hands had been tied. He was to be allowed no scope whatsoever; his duties were to be purely honorary. And as his father's health gradually improved, so did his hopes fade and his position become more and more frustrating. 'It is not easy,' he admitted in a letter to Prince Charles of Rumania, 'to exercise the rights and bear all the burdens of a monarch to the best of one's ability and conscience without taking the sole responsibility.'

He was thus obliged to sit by, helpless, while Bismarck went ahead with his plans. The Reichstag was dissolved and new elections held. Although neither the Social Democrats nor the National Liberals lost as much support as Bismarck had hoped, enough of the newly elected deputies favoured the passing of a law against 'the dangerous activities of the Social Democrats'. This allowed Bismarck to move, with accustomed ruthlessness, against the entire Social Democratic organization, while the reduction of the former sizeable National Liberal majority allowed him to resort to his old game of playing off one party against the other with even more effectiveness than usual.

Not content with having cut the ground from under the Crown Prince's feet, Bismarck continued his fulminations against him and his wife. 'They are preparing for treason,' he once exclaimed. 'They have not a trace of German feeling, they have lost their footing in the heart of the people, they foment

117

discord among the members of the family.' When Moritz Busch, whom Bismarck used for ensuring that his views were published in the Press, once sent a newspaper a comment by the Crown Prince, the Chancellor was furious. 'I told you to publish what I say,' he thundered, 'not what that fool the Crown Prince said!'

'Well,' answered Busch deftly, 'may I publish that?'

If Fritz's duties were mainly social, he at least had the opportunity of exercising them to the full during his period of office. The summer of 1878 saw the meeting of the Congress of Berlin. This Congress, under the Presidency of Bismarck, had been convoked mainly to settle the state of unrest in the Balkans and to keep the peace between the Great Powers most directly concerned—Great Britain, Russia and Austria. Germany was not especially interested in Balkan affairs; in fact, the Near Eastern crisis gave rise to two of Bismarck's most memorable phrases—one was that affairs in the Balkans were 'not worth the bones of a Pomeranian grenadier', and the other that Germany wished only to play the part of the 'honest broker' in the forthcoming Congress.

The Congress of Berlin was a month-long, magnificently staged affair. It opened in the newly decorated hall of the Radziwill Palace, the splendours of which, noted one of the delegates, made a perfect setting for 'all the golden coats and glittering stars that filled it'. From then on it was a ceaseless round of meetings, banquets, balls and receptions, with as much business being conducted behind the scenes as around the conference tables. Champagne flowed like water. The Congress emphasized, if emphasis were needed, that Berlin had replaced Paris and Vienna as the leading Continental city.

Over all the many formal ceremonies connected with the Congress presided the Crown Prince and Princess. The Empress Augusta, despite her *penchant* for such affairs, had decided to withdraw from public duties during her husband's convalescence. Prince Frederick played his part with dignity and aplomb, impressing everyone with the magnificence of his appearance and the simplicity of his manner. Disraeli, the British Prime Minister, was particularly taken with the Crown Prince. 'Nothing in the world is more natural and cordial than he is,' noted Disraeli, 'and with good sense and, among his senses, a sense of humour.' In his present situation—revealed to all the world as little more than Bismarck's puppet—Fritz certainly needed a sense of humour.

As a hostess, the Crown Princess was equally accomplished. Her smallness, her quickness and her vivacity served as an excellent foil for her tall and slow-moving husband. The British Prime Minister pronounced her to be 'most animated and entertaining'. She seemed, he noted with just a touch of exasperation, 'to know everything'. Their palace at Potsdam ('a Paradise of Rococo', wrote Disraeli) was the scene of many brilliant gatherings during the course of that summer. One blustery Sunday afternoon they took a party of delegates in the royal steamer along the River Havel to visit the palace of Sans Souci. They had hardly set off, with the band playing bravely, when a violent squall struck the steamer, all but capsizing it. 'If the Congress is drowned,' said a laconic delegate, 'that would be one solution to our problems.' At Sans Souci the men in the party were ushered into a vast room, lined with wash-hand basins but boasting only one 'porcelain receptacle', very necessary after the long journey. 'Europe collected around that,' noted Prince Hohenlohe solemnly.

The Congress seems to have been conducted efficiently and to the satisfaction of at least some of the delegates. For this, Bismarck received a great deal of praise. But just how honest his broking had been was made evident in a startlingly candid report to the Crown Prince after it was all over. 'It would be a triumph for our statesmanship,' he wrote, 'if we succeeded in keeping the Eastern ulcer open and thus jarred the harmony of the other Great Powers in order to secure our own peace.'

By the autumn of 1878 the Kaiser had recovered sufficiently to make his first public appearance since the attempted assassination. He attended a military review: 'I am profoundly grateful to God for having enabled me to recover sufficiently to appear before my beloved troops again today although still a semi-invalid,' he wired to his sister. 'I was much affected.' By the beginning of December he was well enough to resume the business of government.

He returned to Berlin early that month. As his carriage drove through the Brandenburg Gate and down that same Unter den Linden in which, six months before, the assassination attempt had taken place, he was greeted by a vast and sympathetic crowd. The fact that their reaction was somewhat restrained could be blamed on the excessive vigilance of the police who, apprehensive of another attack, eyed even the way-ing of pocket handkerchiefs with suspicion.

No such restraint marked the Kaiser's second public appearance. That evening he took his seat, as quietly and as unostentatiously as usual, in his box at the Opera. His entrance caused an uproar. 'With one spontaneous movement,' wrote a member of the audience, 'the whole house rose to its feet, and a manifestation, the like of which I am sure I shall never witness again, took place. The crowd simply yelled, without stopping, for something like a quarter of an hour; women frantically waved their handkerchiefs, their shawls, everything they could find or lay their hands upon. Men threw their hats and their caps into the air; one wild acclamation filled the whole of the building. The Emperor came to the front of the box, and for a few moments stood quite still, looking at the excited mass of humanity acclaiming him. He made a sign with his hand as if he wished to speak; but the shouts became louder and louder, until at last, as if unable to bear it any longer, he withdrew to the back of the box; but as he did so, one could see his hand with its white glove pass over his cheek, as if he wiped away a tear.'

And the Crown Prince? What was to become of him now? There was a widely held belief that, in recognition of the way in which he had deputized for his father for six months, he would be granted a more responsible position. The belief was groundless. On the day after Fritz had stepped down there appeared, in all the newspapers, a letter of thanks from the Kaiser, complimenting his son on the exemplary manner in which he had fulfilled his duties. Nothing more. There was no mention of any possible future employment. The Emperor was ready to resume all his tasks. At the age of eighty-one, he seemed as strong as ever. Indeed, the shock appeared to have revitalized him. There was no reason why he could not go on living for several more years.

Crown Prince Frederick was obliged to resume his circumscribed life. He was now almost fifty.

2

The Empress Elizabeth of Austria, in her self-dramatizing fashion, once claimed that there was a moment, in every human life, in which one 'inwardly died'. If there was any truth in this assertion, then the winter of 1878-9 was such a moment for the Crown Princess of Germany. Until that time, whatever the trials and disappointments of her public life, her private life had been relatively happy. Even the friction between herself and her eldest son had not yet reached dangerous proportions. Her most notable characteristics were still her vitality, her gaiety and her spontaneous charm. Whatever she did, she did with gusto. Whether painting in Venice, playing hostess to journalists or studying the theories of Karl Marx (he always spoke of her, she was told, with 'due respect and propriety'). she radiated enthusiasm. At the wedding of her eldest daughter, Charlotte, to Prince Bernhard of Saxe-Meiningen, early in 1878, she was said to be looking 'blooming'.

But that winter, when the Crown Princess had just turned thirty-eight, she suffered two personal tragedies. In December her sister Alice, Grand Duchess of Hesse, died of diphtheria. The two of them had been very close and, in letter after letter to her equally bereaved mother, Vicky poured out her grief. 'I cannot realize it, it is too awful, too cruel, too terrible...' she cried out. 'Oh that God would give wings to our souls to soar into the regions of calmness and peace above.'

Then, while still mourning the loss of her sister, her fourth and (after the death of little Sigismund) her favourite son, the eleven-year-old Waldemar, died suddenly, also of diphtheria. He seems, by all accounts, to have been an exceptional child; even Prince Frederick Charles, who seldom saw eye-to-eye with his cousin the Crown Prince, had to admit that Prince Waldemar was the most delightful boy that he had ever known. His death prostrated the Crown Princess. Almost ten years later, when the break between herself and her eldest son was all but irreparable, she was still bemoaning the death of her adored Waldemar. 'The dream of my life,' she sighed to Queen Victoria, 'was to have a son who should be something of what our beloved Papa was, a real grandson of his, in soul and intellect, a grandson of yours. Waldie gave me hopes of this—his nature was full of promise from the first, and I saw it with such pride and pleasure, and thought I could one day be of use to him! He is gone!' And in the still darker days that lay ahead, when almost her entire family was to turn against her, she would cry out that if only Waldemar were still alive, he would have stood by her; 'he was so staunch and affectionate'.

Walburger Hohental, now Lady Paget, meeting the Crown

Princess soon soon after Waldemar's death, claimed that 'she was in despair and said that the two clever ones had been taken, and the stupid ones left: "good boys" she said, "but nothing in them" '.

Even in this extremity of grief, the Crown Princess was not spared the barbs of her political enemies. A minister of the sect known as the Orthodox Protestants maintained that Prince Waldemar's death had been God's way of forcing humility on the Crown Princess's proud unfeeling heart. His opinion found its way into print and was read by the anguished mother.

The truth was that Vicky's somewhat rational religious views had always scandalized orthodox Christians. Having grown to maturity during a period of religious and intellectual ferment (these were the years of *Ecce Homo*, Renan's *Vie de Jésus* and Darwin's *Origin of Species*) she had not the same blind, unquestioning approach to Christianity. Her opinions and especially the candour with which she aired them, alarmed friends and enemies alike. Prince Hohenlohe, in conversation with her on the subject of personal bereavement, claimed that 'she thinks in many ways as I myself do, and expresses her opinion very frankly. I am only afraid that she does the same to others, which is not wise. It may be that Christian consolation does not suffice one, but it is better to keep this to oneself and think it over. Plato's dialogues and the ancient tragedies she finds very consolatory. Much that she said was true. But she is too incautious and hasty in her verdicts upon things which are, after all, worthy of reverence.'

It was during this period too, that Vicky seems to have come to a full realization of the worthlessness of her present way of life. The impotence of her husband's position during the Kaiser's recent convalescence probably emphasized this. Brimful of energy, burning for an opportunity of proving herself useful, longing to express her full personality, she was forced to lead an utterly unproductive existence. 'To be friends with the present regime is impossible,' she complained to her mother, 'and yet to be in opposition is a thing as impossible. I always feel like a fly struggling in a very tangled web, and a feeling of weariness and depression, often of disgust and hopelessness, takes possession of me....' She would soon be forty; was the whole of her life to be spent in this frustrating fashion? Was she already past her prime?

'The Crown Princess was never the same after that winter

which transformed her into a Mater Dolorosa,' claims one of her admirers, 'and that childlike capacity for enjoyment, which had constituted one of her principal charms, left her, never to return.' Fritz, writing to Prince Charles of Rumania, admitted that with that season's sorrows, their life had lost what little joy had remained to them.

However, they were not allowed to mourn long. Just over two months after Waldemar's death, the Emperor and Empress celebrated their Golden Wedding and the Crown Prince and Princess were obliged to attend the festivities. The eighty-two-year-old Kaiser, with his simple tastes, was dreading the occasion, but the Empress Augusta threw herself into it heart and soul. She could hardly contain her excitement; the celebration afforded her exactly the sort of glittering ceremonial she adored. Although already suffering from the internal illness which would eventually confine her to a wheel-chair, she summoned up all her energies in order to play her part with accustomed verve. She chose, for the great day, a dress of cloth of gold, encrusted with diamonds, and over her brilliant orange wig she wore a gold-spangled veil. As, on the arm of her stiff-backed and uniformed consort, she entered the chapel of the Old Schloss for the first of the day's ceremonies, she was said to be looking 'wonderfully young' for her age. The service lasted for several hours, much to the exasperation of the congregation who had been denied the luxury of seats. Prince Bismarck, bored beyond endurance, scandalized his near neighbours by chatting animatedly to a pretty young princess throughout the sermon.

If, in the years following that tragic winter, the Crown Princess became less cheerful, she was certainly no less spirited. She still pursued what the rest of the Hohenzollerns considered to be her unorthodox activities and still held, and voiced, her advanced views. She read widely. A visiting Englishman was astonished to discover that she regularly took, not only the *Quarterly*, the *Edinburgh*, the *Fortnightly* and the *Saturday*, but the *Journal of Mining and Metallurgy*. Because of her cultural enthusiasms, the Neues Palais was nicknamed 'The Palace of the Medicis' and the Prussian nobility never ceased to be affronted by the fact that such things as the number of quarterings, by which they set so much store, meant nothing to her when drawing up her guest lists. She simply invited whoever she thought would be interesting.

Her concern for such unaristocratic matters as prison reform, social welfare, nursing and sanitation continued unabated; she scandalized the anti-semitic ruling class by accepting the honorary chairmanship of a newly founded orphanage for Jewish girls. Her ideas were incredibly advanced for her time, her class and the country in which she lived. 'The rule of Communism is every bit as bad as that of Absolutism,' she declared, 'but both are death to order, peace, safety and quiet and Liberty!' She scoffed at Bismarck who, in his arrogant fashion, assumed that as Britain was democratically governed, she was fast 'drifting towards a Republic or Communism'.

Her life became infinitely more difficult when, in 1879, the twenty-year-old Prince Wilhelm returned from Bonn to Potsdam to resume his military career. Among the swaggering, self-confident, superbly uniformed officers of the First Regiment of Guards his dawning militarism was given every encouragement. He was flattered, listened to and fawned upon until his conceit knew no bounds. To return from these agreeably martial surroungs, to the cultured and enlightened atmosphere of his parents' home in which his reactionary opinions were given short shrift, was always deeply humiliating. There were innumerable scenes. The Crown Prince, regarding his son as little more than a self-opinionated young pup, might hold his tongue, but the Crown Princess was not nearly so long-suffering. Hardly a day went by without some violent flare-up between them. She castigated young Wilhelm for being vain and selfish and for holding 'the most superficial rubbishy political views—rank retrograde and chauvinist nonsense'. When he aired the currently fashionable anti-British sentiments of his fellow officers, she slapped him down pretty sharply. And of course, the more she sang the praises of all things English, the more she rubbed him up the wrong way. It was an impossible situation.

'The old Napoleon,' Vicky had written to her mother on one occasion, 'said "heureux sont les phlegmatiques intelligents", how true that is, and what would I give for a little of it.' But, with both mother and son being anything but phlegmatic, feeling between them became increasingly bitter.

Separation was the only way out of the dilemma and in the young man's twenty-first year the means presented itself. He became engaged to be married. The bride-to-be was Princess Auguste Viktoria, daughter of Duke Frederick of Schleswig-

Holstein-Sonderburg-Augustenburg, one-time claimant to the duchies over which Bismarck had gone to war against Denmark in 1864. Known as Dona, the Princess seemed an eminently suitable choice. She was pretty, even-tempered and mild-mannered. Although not without a certain physical dignity which would stand her in good stead on public occasions, her interests were confined to the home. She would be precisely the sort of submissive, church-going, child-bearing *Hausfrau* of which the Prussians approved. Unlike Prince Wilhelm's mother and grandmother—the Empress Augusta—Dona would never involve herself in affairs of State nor try to influence her husband's policies. Of the impetuosity, the dogmatism, the wilfulness of the Empress Augusta and the Crown Princess, she had nothing. Nor did she have their quickness or their democratic views.

As such, Dona suited, not only Prince Wilhelm, but the old Kaiser and Bismarck very well. They had had enough of brilliant and strong-minded consorts. The Chancellor, who was beginning to look favourably on the autocratically mannered Prince Wilhelm, hoped that the 'cow from Holstein', as he called Dona, would freshen up the Hohenzollern blood. The Crown Prince and Princess too, were satisfied with the choice. 'We had a great esteem and affection for her father, who had great confidence in us and with whom we were so intimate,' Vicky explained, years later, to Queen Victoria. 'I then hoped and thought she might be grateful and affectionate to me and show me confidence...' There was some grumbling in Court circles at the relatively modest background of the Princess but Dona's sweet smile, good manners and distinguished appearance soon disarmed all criticism. She was dispatched to Windsor for Queen Victoria's approval and the Queen pronounced her to be 'gentle and amiable and sweet'.

The couple were married on 27 February 1881. Both were twenty-two years of age. Flocks of white doves greeted Dona as she passed through the Brandenburg Gate but it was said that Wilhelm, in command of the troops awaiting her arrival in the courtyard of the Old Schloss, was 'commanding with such enthusiasm that her entry seemed to be a matter of secondary interest in his eyes'.

The wedding ceremony was followed by first, the traditional torchlight procession in the White Hall in which over a hundred royalties made an agonizingly slow circuit of the guests, then by a vast State banquet and finally by a performance of Gluck's *Armida*. These various and protracted ceremonies exhausted everyone other than the old Emperor and Empress. 'My parents-in-law are wonderful and never tired,' noted Vicky with just a hint of asperity; 'standing, heat, toilettes, talking, nothing seems to knock them up.' Dona, with her look of 'innocent happiness', charmed guests and crowds alike and even Prince Wilhelm professed himself much moved. The Crown Princess, always dewy-eyed on occasions like this, expressed her anguish at the fact that her son had left his old rooms for the last time. Dismissing her regrets as 'absurd sentimentality', Prince Wilhelm assured his mother that in whatever place or house or room he lived, it was all the same to him.

It was no wonder that, remembering their troubled years together, she could sigh, 'This son has never been really mine. . . .'

3

One of the results of the deliberations of the Berlin Congress was the creation of the new state of Bulgaria. Having created it, the Great Powers, in lordly contemporary fashion, nominated a foreign prince to rule over it. Their choice was the twenty-two-year-old Prince Alexander of Battenberg. In choosing him, they precipitated the most violent clash—both political and domestic—that had yet afflicted the Hohenzollern family.

Prince Alexander, known to his family as Sandro, was the second son of Prince Alexander of Hesse. The father, having contracted a morganatic marriage with a former lady-in-waiting to his sister, the Empress of Russia, was obliged to forfeit Hessian rank for his sons and to give them the name of Battenberg. He thus became the progenitor of a family which was destined to rise to a position of world prominence. Sandro, like his three brothers, was clever, capable and exceptionally handsome. His dark good looks, combined with the romanticism of his father's morganatic marriage, gave him a decidedly glamorous aura; this was offset by the respectability of his close relationship, not only to the Tsar of Russia, but to the Queen of England. For his father's brother, the Grand Duke of Hesse, had married Queen Victoria's daughter, Alice. Strengthening this British connection was the fact that Sandro's eldest brother Louis had taken British nationality and joined the Royal Navy. In time, both Louis and another brother, Henry, would marry into the Queen's family. Thus, while stuffier royal families tended to look down their noses at the colourful Battenberg princes, more tolerant royalties welcomed them for the charm, the intelligence and for what Queen Victoria called the 'fresh blood' they brought into the ruling Houses of Europe.

With newly created Bulgaria being looked upon as a Russian dependency, it had been the Tsar who encouraged Alexander of Battenberg's candidature. He had assumed that, as the Tsarina's nephew, this young Prince would dance to Russia's tune. This, indeed, was what Britain feared. However, it was not long after Sandro's acceptance that his uncle, the Grand Duke of Hesse, assured Queen Victoria that Sandro 'is not Russian in heart and that he is not inclined to act as Russia's tool'. This the Queen was able to see for herself when the Prince, making a tour of various European Courts before taking up his new duties, visited her at Balmoral. She was delighted with him. Not only was he the tall, dashing-looking sort of young man that she liked, but the fact that he had always been a particular favourite with her daughter Alice, Grand Duchess of Hesse, endeared him to her. 'He is not at all Russian,' she decided, 'but has *was natürlich ist* [as is only natural] a personal attachment for the Czar.'

Even this attachment was not nearly as strong as Victoria imagined. In fact, Sandro had hardly arrived in Bulgaria before he began proving himself to be anything but the Tsar's catspaw. Anxious to make Bulgaria completely independent of Russian influence, he lost no opportunity of flouting the Tsar's wishes. As a result, he was applauded by Russia's enemies and castigated by her friends.

Sandro's stand split the Berlin Court into two irreconcilable camps. On the one hand the Kaiser and Bismarck disapproved strongly of his show of independence. The Chancellor, who was working towards an alliance between the Emperors of Germany, Austria and Russia (it materialized in 1881) was determined that nothing should upset relations with the Tsar. On the other hand, the Crown Prince and Princess, both violently anti-Russian, supported Sandro.

The Crown Prince was particularly passionate in her championship. 'Few people in the world,' she was to write to Lady

Ponsonby at a later stage of Sandro's stormy career, 'have gone through what Prince Alexander has had to struggle with in *every* shape and form. My admiration for him increases every day. As a patriot, a soldier, and a statesman, he has shown an energy, patience, perseverance, modesty and moderation such as one has rarely seen and which one can only find in the perfect gentleman.... He *deserves* to be successful and happy. May he be so!'

Outpourings such as this were not prompted solely by the Crown Princess's hatred of Russian autocracy. The position was further complicated by the fact that she was championing Sandro for more personal reasons. The Crown Princess's second daughter, Victoria, called Moretta by her family, was in love with young Prince Alexander. And Moretta's mother had thrown herself, with all the vehemence of her nature, into the promoting of the match.

In this she came up against the implacable opposition of the Hohenzollern family. The Emperor, backed up to the hilt by Bismarck, would not hear of it. The Chancellor claimed to see it all as a deep-laid plot on the part of Queen Victoria to encourage a permanent estrangement between Germany and Russia. The Queen would not rest, he assured Moritz Busch, until she had achieved this political aim. 'In family matters she is not accustomed to contradiction,' he said, and, in the event of her visiting Berlin in the near future, she 'would immediately bring the parson with her in her travelling bag and the bridegroom in her trunk and the marriage would come off at once'.

That Bismarck should convince the Emperor of the inadvisability of the match was to be expected; what appalled the Crown Princess was that her mother-in-law, her eldest son, and even her normally compliant husband disapproved of the romance. Prince Wilhelm's objections were, of course, the same as Bismarck's: the Tsar must not be offended. And not only did the Prince identify himself with the Chancellor's pro-Russian policy but he welcomed yet another chance of opposing his mother. With a rudeness that had increased a hundredfold since marriage had given him independence, Prince Wilhelm made clear his distaste for the proposed alliance.

The Empress Augusta objected on the grounds of birth. As a minor German princeling, born of a morganatic union, Sandro was not nearly good enough for the grand-daughter of the

German Emperor. It was said that Augusta, in her disapproval, refused to speak to, or even look at, poor Moretta.

With his mother's outmoded thinking, Crown Prince Frederick was inclined to agree. 'My own dear husband (like the Empress) attaches too great an importance to etiquette...' complained Vicky. But one suspects that Fritz was merely anxious to avoid yet another family row. 'Ever since I discovered how much Moretta had familiarized herself with the monstrous idea, it has been a weight on my mind,' he admitted to his wife. When the Crown Princess sprang to her daughter's defence, he backed down. If only, he sighed, the girl would not rush them, and Sandro would keep away, they might, in time, be able to see their way more clearly.

But Sandro could not keep away. It was not that he was so desperately in love with Moretta as that he needed a well-connected wife to strengthen his position in trouble-fraught Bulgaria. Besides this, his life in Sofia would be both enriched and enlivened by the presence of a good-looking and cultivated consort. Arriving in Berlin on a visit, he was egged on by the Crown Princess to tackle the Kaiser about the match. The old monarch would not hear of it. There was a violent scene between them which ended in Sandro threatening to quit Bulgaria for ever and the Kaiser assuring him that it would not bother him in the least if he did. Bismarck handled the young man with more cynicism. Sandro's best plan, advised the Chancellor smoothly, would be to marry some millionairess; one could rule in the East only by bribery, and bribery cost money. When the Crown Princess heard the result of Sandro's interviews, she dug in her heels still further. In defiance of the Kaiser's wishes, she arranged a secret meeting between the two young people and talked her husband into giving a banquet in Sandro's honour. Raising his glass, the Crown Prince toasted Prince Alexander as 'the pioneer of Germany in the East'. He took the precaution, however, of keeping his voice low.

Vicky had at least one formidable ally—her mother, Queen Victoria. The Queen was enchanted with the Battenbergs. So pronounced was her championship of the handsome Battenberg princes that it became known as 'Court Battenbergism'. Not only did the Queen encourage Sandro's romance with Moretta (during a house-party at Darmstadt she saw to it that the young couple were thrown together as much as possible) but she sanctioned two Battenberg marriages into her own

129

family. In April 1884, her grand-daughter, Princess Victoria of Hesse, married Louis, the eldest of the Battenberg princes and, just over a year later, the Queen's youngest daughter, Princess Beatrice, married Henry, the third brother.

This marriage strained relations between the British and German royal families to near breaking-point. The Hohenzollerns were incensed by the match. The Austrian Ambassador to Berlin reported that 'even the Crown Prince is annoyed about it and makes no attempt to hide his displeasure'. Both Fritz and the Empress Augusta wrote to Queen Victoria expressing their reservations. Victoria was furious. How *dare* they address her in that tone? How *could* they refer to Prince Henry as not being '*Geblüt*'—pure bred—as though he were an animal? And did the Empress Augusta forget that her own daughter, the Duchess of Baden, had married the grandson of 'a very bad woman', whose children had none the less been acknowledged as Princes of Baden? It would never do to inquire too deeply into the history of the royal families of Europe; one would discover many 'black spots'.

When the Queen heard that young Prince Wilhelm and his wife Dona had also expressed their disapproval, her anger blazed forth afresh. It was extraordinarily impertinent and insolent of Wilhelm, she declared; 'as for Dona, poor little insignificant Princess ... I have no words'.

'If the Queen of England thinks a person good enough for her daughter,' she quoted Lord Granville as saying, 'what have other people got to say?'

But no matter how many Battenberg princes married into Queen Victoria's family, the Emperor Wilhelm saw no reason why any should marry into his. In March 1885, he informed Sandro that he would never countenance a match between him and Moretta.

His refusal seemed to confirm the spate of rumours that had been circulating in Sofia. Some claimed that the Kaiser had found out that Prince Alexander had contracted a venereal disease; others that the Prince's 'Turkish tastes'—his imperviousness to women—had led to the Tsar's hasty recall of two of Sandro's young Russian aides-de-camp. Whatever the rumours, the fact remained that while old Kaiser Wilhelm was alive, Sandro had very little hope of marrying Moretta.

The Crown Princess refused to accept the situation. 'I love a fight and am not intimidated,' she declared. Indeed, one cannot help suspecting that there was something more to her almost hysterical advocacy of Sandro than her dislike of Russia or her concern for her daughter's happiness. She was far too obsessed by the matter. For year after year, in page after page —to her mother, to her friends, to her political allies, to Sandro himself—she poured out her feelings. Her hatred of Bismarck was probably one reason: the more he objected to the match, the more she insisted on it. Her time of life might have been another: she was in her mid-forties at this stage and, for a woman of her passionate nature, denied any satisfactory outlet, this was a difficult period. She might even have been infatuated by Sandro. So young, so virile, so swashbuckling, he was a marked contrast to her own cautious and mild-mannered husband. 'How I envy you seeing Sandro!' she exclaimed in a letter to her mother on one occasion. 'I am so glad to hear you think him looking well.... Being in Scotland is sure to do his spirits good.'

Bismarck, in his coarse way, once mentioned this aspect of the affair. 'She's a wild woman,' he said of the Crown Princess. 'When I look at her picture, I am filled with horror at the uncurbed sensuousness which glows in her eyes. She is in love with Battenburg and wants to have him near her....'

In the autumn of 1885 a popular rising on Bulgaria's borders added more territory to Sandro's domain. The achievement brought him an ecstatic, twenty-eight-page letter from the Crown Princess. A few weeks later his tempestuous career was further enlivened by a Serbian invasion of his country. Much to the Tsar's displeasure, the Serbian army was decisively beaten. The Bulgarian victory sent both Vicky and her mother into transports of delight, although Victoria suspected that Russia would not be prepared to countenance 'dear brave' Sandro's show of independence much longer.

Fully alive to this danger, Sandro realized that it was more important than ever that his position be stabilized by his marriage to the Kaiser's grand-daughter. 'If only I knew [Moretta] were to be allowed to be Princess of this country,' he confided to his brother Louis, 'then everything would be all right. Everything I would do to improve my country, to safeguard my position in this country, would be for her, that would give me immense strength, courage and endurance. But is it possible that Bismarck would ever agree to this in view of the hatred that Emperor Alexander bears me?'

The answer was no. Bismarck had no intention of allowing the marriage, and the hatred of the Emperor Alexander for Sandro was brought home only too clearly in the summer of 1886. On 21 August, Sandro was kidnapped by a group of Russian officers and shipped down the Danube. A week later a popular movement in his favour led to his return but by now the Prince had had enough of the vagaries of Bulgarian politics. He had lost the taste for power. Convinced that nothing would ever soften Russia's attitude towards him, he abdicated.

The crisis, which lasted for two weeks and rapidly assumed international proportions, raised the Crown Princess to the highest pitch of indignation. She could hardly contain herself. She raved against those 'treacherous, abominable conspirators in Bulgaria' and attacked the 'insolence and barefaced audacity' of the Russian government for its part in the 'shameful dastardly plot against Sandro'. Queen Victoria was no less incensed. 'I am so excited—I can think of nothing else!' she wrote. 'The feeling in England against Russia is very strong.'

However, feeling was not quite as strong as she would have liked and her Prime Minister, Lord Salisbury, decided that military intervention on the part of Britain was out of the question. Nor was any other Great Power prepared to move against Russia in support of Sandro. When the British Ambassador asked Bismarck what the German attitude would be in the event of a civil war breaking out in Bulgaria and of Russia occupying the country in defiance of the Treaty of Berlin, the Chancellor replied, unequivocally, that Germany would fold her arms.

Once Vicky had finished lashing out at the infamy of the Russians, she comforted herself by declaring that Sandro's exit had been 'an honourable one for him and his people and he [could] lay down his crown of thorns with a clear conscience, proudly aware of having done his duty'.

She had no intention, however, of giving up her particular struggle: she was still determined that Moretta should marry Sandro. It would compensate him, she said, for all his sufferings and would it not mean her child's whole happiness? Queen Victoria, displaying more realism, tactfully suggested that an engagement without any hope of eventual marriage would not be quite fair on Sandro.

To rule in Sandro's stead, the Bulgarian Assembly chose the young Prince Ferdinand of Saxe-Coburg, one of Queen Victoria's many Coburg cousins. That Prince Ferdinand would replace Sandro in Moretta's heart as well was unlikely. Very much the darling of his mother, King Louis Philippe's strong-minded daughter Clementine, Ferdinand was a quite different proposition from his brave and dashing predecessor. Queen Victoria considered him to be 'totally unfit—delicate, eccentric, effeminate'. Lady Walburga Paget was more explicit. 'His affectations are innumerable,' she wrote. 'He wears bracelets and powders his face. He sleeps in pink surah nightgowns, trimmed with Valenciennes lace. His constitution is so delicate and his nerves so finely strung, that he only consults ladies' doctors. What an effect such a man will produce, after the handsome chivalrous Alexander, I don't know; but he is bent upon it. At all events, he will not arouse any jealousies.'

Lady Paget was wrong. Prince Ferdinand roused a host of jealousies. Before many weeks had passed he was obliged to appeal to Crown Prince Frederick for moral support. 'My family and most of my friends have disowned me, the whole of Europe is furious with me. Why?' he wrote petulantly. He went on to list his troubles and ended the letter with the plea that it was 'for your eyes alone, read it, destroy it, and should you have an opportunity of putting in an effective word for our cause, accept herewith the thanks of the Bulgarians and their ruler'.

The Crown Prince could do no more for him than he had been able to do for Sandro. Yet, for all his flutterings, Ferdinand was to prove surprisingly durable; there was considerable tenacity, it seemed, behind that scented façade. Prince Ferdinand reigned in Bulgaria for over thirty years.

In December 1886 the exiled Sandro visited Queen Victoria at Windsor. It was an emotional meeting. The young Prince seemed so sad, so gentle, so calm and so wise. Victoria thought him as 'wonderfully handsome' as ever and with a dignity and a lack of rancour worthy of the late Prince Consort. He still hoped, Sandro assured the sympathetic Queen, to marry Moretta one day.

In this, the suitor was to prove himself rather less constant than the girl or her mother.

4

'In view of the immaturity as well as the inexperience of my eldest son, together with his tendency towards overbearingness and self-conceit,' wrote Crown Prince Frederick to Bismarck in the autumn of 1886, 'I cannot but frankly regard it as dangerous to allow him at present to take any part in foreign affairs.'

The Crown Prince was endeavouring to dissuade the Chancellor from carrying out his latest scheme: that of allowing young Prince Wilhelm to enter the Foreign Office to gain experience in international affairs. For the Crown Prince, who had never been allowed the slightest say in affairs of State, Bismarck's latest project was particularly galling. On the rare occasions that he had asked Bismarck for any information, he had usually been fobbed off with the excuse that the Chancellor was too busy to attend to him. His latest intervention received exactly the same offhand treatment. It was the Emperor's wish, explained the Chancellor blandly, that Prince Wilhelm should acquaint himself with foreign affairs. And, continued Bismarck, as the Crown Prince no doubt realized, parental authority must always yield to monarchical authority in the affairs of the Hohenzollern family.

So Wilhelm duly entered the Foreign Office, in which, once the first flush of self-importance had worn off, he spent less and less time. He was usually ready, noted a contemporary, 'for anything exciting, but [had] no liking for continuous work, for real knowledge'. This, as far as Bismarck was concerned, was unimportant. The Chancellor had achieved his aim. He had ingratiated himself with Prince Wilhelm, and the Crown Prince had once more been slighted.

More and more during the past few years had Bismarck pursued these tactics. He saw, in this bombastic young man, a tool to be fashioned to his own purpose. Unlike the Crown Prince, young Wilhelm was completely in accord with Bismarck's ideas. Indeed, he had nothing but admiration for the Chancellor's strong-arm methods. 'Bismarck was the idol in my temple,' he declared in later years, 'and I worshipped him.' He was thoroughly at home in the Chancellor's family circle. Always attended by the great man's son, the wily Count Herbert Bismarck (whom the father later made Secretary of State for Foreign Affairs), Prince and Chancellor would spend gratifying hours in each other's company. Having eaten a gigantic meal in the Chancellor's haphazardly furnished dining-room, the Prince would listen enthralled to the old man's stream of bold and irreverent talk. 'For you,' wrote the admiring young man to Bismarck on one occasion, 'I would let my limbs be hewn off piecemeal rather than undertake anything which would be disagreeable to you or cause you difficulties. . . .'

The Chancellor could hardly ask for better than that. Such hero-worship on the part of the future heir to the throne was invaluable. Bismarck made full use of it to isolate the Crown Prince and Princess still further. And Wilhelm, of course, was only too ready to fall in with the Chancellor's plans. Bismarck sang the young man's praises to the Emperor, and the old monarch, only too relieved to know that his wife's and his son's liberalism had not been passed on to the third generation, took the Prince into his confidence. Unbeknown to his father, young Wilhelm and Bismarck exchanged letters on affairs of State and the Prince even went so far as to receive various foreign ambassadors.

Nor was Bismarck the only one backing Wilhelm rather than his father. There were other, less powerful, but more insidious, champions. One was Baron von Holstein, a discreet and influential official at the Foreign Office, who gave the young Prince the benefit of his considerable experience. Another was Count von Waldersee, a political general who favoured an autocratic, as opposed to a constitutional, monarchy, and who was working for an increase in the powers of the Head of the Kaiser's military cabinet at the expense of the Minister of War. His hints about 'dispersing parliament with a handful of guards' sounded sweet indeed to the swollen-headed Wilhelm. Although men such as these might not see eye to eye with Bismarck on all points, they heartily approved of his elevation of the young Prince.

In the spring of 1884 the Crown Prince had been dumbfounded to hear that his son was being sent to St Petersburg to represent the Kaiser at the coming of age of the Tsarevitch. Here was a slap in the face indeed. It should have been Prince Frederick's task to go to St Petersburg but by Bismarck's entrusting of the mission to Prince Wilhelm, the Crown Prince once more stood revealed as a man of little account.

However, Bismarck's move was not entirely malicious. It had a sound political motive. In 1881 he had succeeded in organizing the Three Emperors' Alliance—a treaty of neutrality signed by the Emperors of Russia, Germany and Austria. With Russia and Austria always at loggerheads in the Balkans, Bismarck hoped that this alliance would save him from having to choose between the two of them. German Austria was the Reich's natural ally, but for Bismarck, friendship with Russia was equally important. The treaty, designed to last for three years only, was renewed in 1884 for a further three years. 'We clearly need a triple alliance as a dyke against the flood-tide of anarchy,' declared the gratified Tsar Alexander III. It was in order to consolidate this success that Prince Wilhelm was sent to Russia. Bismarck could hardly have expected the liberally minded and anti-Russian Crown Prince to have been anything like as suitable an envoy to the despotic Tsar.

Prince Wilhelm relished his errand to the full. He propounded to the Tsar, not only his support for the Three Emperors' Alliance, but his views on the inadvisability of the match between his sister and Prince Alexander. Warming to his task, he warned the Tsar against the machinations of the Prince of Wales who, he said, was stirring up British feelings against Russia. His listener, he claimed smugly, was deeply impressed by this valuable information. Once back in Berlin, the Prince backed up his warnings by letter. The Tsar was on no account to trust Prince Wilhelm's English relations. Nor was he to pay any attention to the opinions of the Crown Prince. 'You know him,' wrote Prince Wilhelm of his father, 'he loves being contrary and is under my mother's thumb, and she, in turn, is guided by the Queen of England, and makes him see everything through English eyes.' He went on to assure the Tsar that the Kaiser, Bismarck and he were of one mind, and that he regarded the consolidation of the Three Emperors' Alliance as his highest duty.

A year later, in 1885, Bismarck once more passed over the Crown Prince in favour of his son. The Emperors of Germany and Austria met formally at Gastein and the Chancellor arranged for Prince Wilhelm to attend the conversations. Hardly was this meeting over before the young man was dispatched once more to Russia with a mission to Tsar Alexander III. The news horrified his parents. 'I need hardly say,' wrote the Crown Princess to Queen Victoria, 'that it would make endless mischief and do endless harm. William is as blind and green, wrong-headed and violent on politics as can be.'

Wilhelm, giving his version of the incident in his memoirs, writes of his 'violent shock' at being told that his father was once again being ignored in favour of himself. 'That was a hard path for me!' he protests. 'I told myself that my father would be very deeply hurt, and that he would be bound to assume that I had tried by an intrigue to set myself in his place. I resolved, therefore, to beg [Bismarck] to set me aside and to turn to my father. The Chancellor, however, cut all my arguments short by pointing out that the Emperor had issued his commands and that it was for me to obey. The formal responsibility for this step, he said, was borne by His Majesty, and that morally neither he, the Chancellor, nor I, even as regards my father, had any responsibility whatever. So whether I liked it or not, I had to undertake the ticklish commission.'

It was no wonder that Baron von Holstein could claim that 'the relations between the three generations of our royal family are remarkable, not to say comic. The Kaiser ignores the Crown Prince completely and so far as possible never informs him on anything. The Crown Prince, in turn, ignores Prince Wilhelm in the same way.'

Prince Wilhelm's second visit to the Tsar was not nearly as successful as the first. When Wilhelm, in his lordly fashion, began assuring Alexander III that if—in defiance of Britain— he wished to occupy Constantinople, Germany would raise no objection, the Tsar cut him short. If, countered Alexander dryly, he wished to take Constantinople, he would do so without Prince Bismarck's permission. Prince Wilhelm himself he dismissed as 'un garçon mal élevé et de mauvaise foi'.

Yet, on closer observation, Prince Wilhelm was more than just a loud-mouthed, empty-headed and conceited young man. His was a complicated nature. His sense of inferiority, linked with his exceptional egotism, made him long for recognition. For one thing, he was determined to shine in the field in which —because of his bad arm—it was most difficult for him to shine: the physical. He had a good brain but he was anxious to prove himself as a man of action. He wanted to be known for his soldierly, rather than his intellectual prowess. He yearned to be heroic, larger than life, a worthy representative of the glorious military traditions of his House. He must be admired for his energy, his militarism, his masculinity.

It was this that forced him to persevere until he had excelled in even so exacting a career as the cavalry. 'Never,' wrote

Hintzpeter after a particularly impressive display of horsemanship by the Prince, 'was a young man enrolled in the Prussian army who seemed so physically unfitted to become a keen and brilliant cavalry-officer. The few who could estimate the significance of this victory of moral force over bodily infirmity felt justified in their proudest hopes for this royal personage.' This was why Wilhelm developed a tough and hearty manner; why his talk was so wild and bombastic; why, in his professed loathing for his mother's liberal outlook, he could even declare that, on his father's accession to the throne, it might be necessary to arrest her. If the Crown Prince were suddenly to become Kaiser, noted the apprehensive Count von Waldersee, there would be nothing for it but 'to station the Prince in some remote garrison'.

But there were still more layers to that complex personality. Despite his air of masculinity, women held little emotional appeal for Prince Wilhelm. His marriage seems to have been successful enough. His wife Dona, uncritical and uncomplicated, adored him and regularly presented him with yet another child. She bore him seven in all, six of whom were sons. Once, when his mother asked him if he would not have preferred a daughter, Wilhelm replied that 'girls were useless creatures, he did not want one and far preferred to be without'. In a rare show of spirit, Dona once said, 'I don't want to be looked upon exclusively as a means of propagating the royal race but under Count Bismarck's teachings, the Prince seems to have forgotten that I possess any of the qualities of a woman besides that of child-bearing.' Dona was right. There was very little to their relationship other than this. No companionship existed between husband and wife; he scarcely bothered to conceal his boredom with her. At home—the Marmor Palais at Potsdam—he ignored her other than to remark, usually unfavourably, on her clothes. While he entertained guests with a flow of jocular and sometimes *risqué* talk, she would sit in her daringly *décolleté* and lavishly trimmed dresses, knitting shapeless little woollen caps for orphans.

'Clothes and children are her chief conversation and the only things she thoroughly understands...' wrote the sharp-tongued Princess Daisy of Pless. 'For a woman in that position I have never met *anyone* so devoid of any individual thought or agility of brain and understanding. She is just like a good, quiet, soft cow that has calves and eats grass slowly and ruminates. I looked right into her eyes to see if I could see anything behind them, even pleasure or sadness, but they might have been glass.'

Despite its malice, the picture is hardly overdrawn. Dona was simply a pious, provincial, unimaginative *Hausfrau*. As such, she was hardly likely to hold the interest of so restless, neurotic and mercurial a man as her husband. Yet for all this, his name was never linked with that of another woman. The time would come when he would appreciate feminine sympathy and understanding, but romantically, women meant nothing to him. He was much happier in the company of men. This might be explained, in part, by the customs of his time and his class. In the militarily dominated society of the Second Reich, in which women were generally regarded as inferior beings, male friendships abounded. Women were useful for breeding, child-rearing and housekeeping but for true companionship one looked to one's fellow officers. Such friendships were not necessarily homosexual; they simply helped to uphold the mystique and feed the vanity of the officers of the more élite regiments. Prince Wilhelm was simply following the fashion of the day.

However, it was obvious that in his addiction to masculine society, Prince Wilhelm was looking for something more than mere *camaraderie*. Active, assured and aggressive he might sometimes appear, but at other times a more passive, sensitive and sentimental side of his nature was revealed. There was 'a great deal of the woman' in Prince Wilhelm, claimed the Princess of Pless. Along with the militarism of his Hohenzollern grandfather, he had inherited much of the artistic, poetic and idealistic temperament of his maternal grandfather, the Prince Consort. This romanticism needed an outlet. What better way than in one of those ardent, self-conscious, quasi-mystical friendships so prevalent among the officers of the Gardes du Corps? In 1886, when Wilhelm was twenty-seven, he met the thirty-nine-year-old Count Philip von Eulenburg. Into their friendship he poured all the long-suppressed sentimentality of his nature.

Eulenburg was a diplomat—a handsome, subtle, polished, witty dilettante with a taste for music, poetry, painting and, it was rumoured, young men. He could sing, he could mimic, he could compose 'nordic ballads and roseate songs of sentiment', he could tell anecdotes in his slow, seductive voice, he could, by the exercise of his considerable charm, create an atmosphere of heady, hot-house romanticism. Side by side on the piano stool would sit the Prince and his bewitching companion, Wilhelm turning the pages while Eulenburg played and sang; his performances, claimed the older man, drove the younger into 'almost feverish raptures'. When the two of them met in some forest glade at shooting parties, Wilhelm would greet his friend with quotations from Eulenburg's own verses. 'I have had many a ravished listener to my performances,' noted Eulenburg blandly, 'but hardly ever have I inspired such ravishment as in Prince Wilhelm.... I can understand that the young Prince should have felt as if looking deep into a cup filled with a draught whose ingredients were delightful to his palate.'

They were indeed. Whenever Eulenburg 'set foot in our Potsdam home,' admitted Wilhelm, 'it was as if the common day was flooded with sunshine'. Whether or not Wilhelm shared, or knew anything about, Count von Eulenburg's rumoured homosexuality (which was subsequently to be blazoned in the world's Press) one does not know. Given their long intimacy, it is unlikely that he was unaware of it. Of more importance, however, was Eulenburg's political influence on the younger man. Once it was known that Eulenburg had become the favourite, the official world lost no time in harnessing his services. The astute Count was quite prepared for them to be harnessed. Yet, for the most part, Eulenburg's influence was a good one. Sensible, warm-hearted and worldly, he was one of the few people able to speak frankly to Wilhelm and to curb his verbal extravagance. What the Crown Princess, in her hectoring way, had never been able to do, Eulenburg could sometimes accomplish in his more relaxed and feminine fashion. He alone could appeal to the Prince's better, softer and more sentimental side; he was the first, as Emil Ludwig put it, 'to open the gates of the garden of Romance to the young man who had been forced into the part of a hard-bitten Prussian Prince, and now was taking leave of an adolescence poor alike in love and in the dreams of youth'.

CHAPTER SIX

CROWN PRINCE FREDERICK

1

Crown Prince Frederick turned fifty-five in the autumn of 1886. Although still an imposing-looking man, the long years of his apprenticeship—of frustrations, slights and disappointments, of unfulfilled hopes and enforced inactivity—were beginning to leave their mark. He had lost weight, he looked pale, he seemed tired. He was suffering, he would sigh, from '*Weltschmerz*'—world-weariness. The Crown Princess claimed that although 'I have a great deal of fight left in me and do not lose heart ... poor Fritz [is] often in bitter despair and sees all *en noir*'. He simply did not have the will to pit himself against Bismarck any longer. In earlier days he had argued back, had spoken out against the Chancellor's despotic methods, had tried to prevent the monarchy from associating itself with the country's most reactionary elements. It had never made a scrap of difference. Now he had to be content to sit quiet and bide his time. It was a humiliating position.

'We may try to make *ourselves* as *small* as we can,' reported Vicky, 'we are *never* small enough for certain people, and there are many who do not scruple to say that William is much more to their taste than we are, and that it would be far more convenient if we were to disappear completely! So it *would be for them, there is no doubt*, but I hardly *think* it would be for the *good* of Germany ... we are not active and *blind partisans* of the present system, therefore they must *needs try* to make *out* that we are enemies, in order to have an excuse for attacking us!! ... The ingratitude to Fritz is very great, as he surely has done enough for his country—that *is* however appreciated in Germany at large though not by the clique at Berlin!'

Yet the Crown Prince never lost faith in those broad liberal principles which formed the basis of his creed and which he planned to put into practice on ascending the throne. A lesser man might have thrown in his lot with Bismarck's seemingly successful regime; Fritz refused to be dazzled by tactics which he knew could bring only short-term advantages. All he could do was to remain as detached as possible and to keep himself informed on everything that was happening in the country. To this end he interested himself in men of every shade of political opinion and read all opposition papers. A Court official, new to the Crown Prince's Household, was horrified to find that his master subscribed to the radical *Volks-Zeitung*. 'But Your Royal Highness,' protested the official, 'it is a regular revolutionary paper!'

'Never mind, my friend,' answered the Crown Prince, 'I know full well what the Government thinks; I wish to know what other people think as well.'

As far as he was able, Fritz never let slip even some slight opportunity of putting his principles into practice. Once, when a Jewess, Fräulein von Bleichröder, was attending her first Court ball and faced the possibility of being ignored by the violently anti-Semitic young men, the Crown Prince detailed two of the more enlightened officers to dance with her. 'The Crown Prince,' writes one of them, Count Bernstorff, 'was well aware that I, like him, regarded anti-Semitism as a stain on the escutcheon of German culture....'

To escape from the politically stifling atmosphere of the Court, Prince Frederick steeped himself in cultural activities. He was passionately interested in history and archaeology; it was largely due to his initiative that the successful excavations of Pergamon and Olympia was undertaken by Germany. His descriptions of the ruins and monuments of the Near East have a lyrical quality. Both he and his wife adored Italy and they usually managed to spend a few weeks there each year. In Rome and Florence and Venice they were enthusiastic and indefatigable sightseers; in villages such as Portofino they lived a life of idyllic simplicity. There were, of course, official journeys as well, though Queen Victoria noted that whereas Bismarck always sent young Prince Wilhelm on the important missions, he reserved the purely formal and less pleasant journeys for the Crown Prince. Prince Frederick was sent to Russia to attend the funeral of the murdered Tsar Alexander II when there was a strong possibility that the Nihilists would try and eliminate all the royalties assembled for the occasion. A few years later he was dispatched to equally turbulent Spain to visit King Alfonso XII and, on his return journey, was ordered to Rome to call on both the Pope and his rival, the King of Italy. For a Protestant Prince, this was a difficult commission. The Crown Prince handled the situation, as always, with great tact and dignity and managed to delight Pontiff and monarch. The Romans were greatly taken with his impressive appearance and greeted him with enthusiastic cries of '*Che bel uomo, che simpatica figura, che bel soldato.*'

Of considerable comfort to the Crown Prince and Princess during these years was the presence of their three youngest daughters—Victoria, Sophie and Margaretha, known in the family as Moretta, Sossie and Mossy. These three good-looking girls, with their tightly curled poodle fringes, their slender necks and their tiny waists, were devoted to their parents; not even when Moretta's romance with Sandro was at its most turbulent, did it cause any friction between her parents and herself. The loyalty of these daughters was in marked contrast to the attitudes of the three eldest children—Wilhelm, Charlotte and Henry. To Prince Frederick, the lack of sympathy between his elder son and himself was a source of deep concern. He took the situation, said his wife, 'profoundly *au tragique*'. Wilhelm always accused his father of hating him while the Crown Prince looked upon his son as 'impossible'—simply the unthinking tool of Bismarck. Wilhelm, wrote Vicky bitterly, 'fancies himself consequently of enormous importance and that he is of more use to the country than his Papa, who in his eyes does not keep up the Prussian tradition enough....'

Princess Charlotte, their second child, by now married to Prince Bernhard of Saxe-Meiningen, was hardly less of a trial. Vivacious and amusing, but frivolous, flippant and indiscreet, Princess Charlotte was very much in the Bismarck camp. So was the third child, the still unmarried Prince Henry. From being a 'careless, unlettered youth', he had developed into an objectionable young man, completely under the influence of his elder brother. With each passing year these two self-opinionated princes seemed to be counting for more and more and their father for less and less.

But there was nothing that even the all-powerful Bismarck —however much he might detest the Crown Prince's liberalism —could do about the imperial succession. With the Emperor almost ninety and Prince Frederick only fifty-five and in seemingly good health, Bismarck could not help feeling apprehensive about the future. He would have to do something to safeguard himself. His self-erected position of power depended on either of two institutions: the monarchy or the Reichstag. While he had the support of the Kaiser, he could afford to ignore parliament; if he were to lose the Emperor's championship, then he must be certain of a sympathetic majority in the Reichstag. This, at present, he did not have.

In the year 1880 the old majority party—his one-time ally the National Liberal Party—had split into two, and its left wing had since amalgamated with the Progressive Party, together forming the *Freisinnige Partei*. Whenever this newly-formed *Freisinnige* Party voted with the Centre and the Social Democrat parties, they formed a majority hostile to Bismarck. What the Chancellor found particularly alarming was the fact that the *Freisinnige* Party was considered to be the Crown Prince's party. It was rumoured that Prince Frederick had wired his congratulations on the formation of the party; he had certainly hailed it as 'a new cure for our unsettled parliamentary conditions and for my future government a possibility of being based upon a liberal majority'. It seemed certain that, on his accession to the throne, he would choose his cabinet from among its leaders. Not much imagination was needed to appreciate that with a liberal Emperor, a liberal cabinet and an opposition majority in the Reichstag, Bismarck's days would be numbered. Thus, as there was nothing that the Chancellor could do to get rid of the future liberal Emperor, he had to do everything in his power to get rid of a future liberal cabinet—or what he derisively called a 'Gladstone Ministry'. There was nothing for it but to weaken the *Freisinnige* Party.

He set about it in his usual fashion. First he had to find an excuse for the dissolution of the Reichstag; then he had to panic the voters into electing more conservative deputies. As military matters were always guaranteed to cause parliamentary turmoil and arouse patriotic fervour, he turned to these. He introduced a new Army Bill to the Reichstag. It proposed an increase in the strength of the army which was to hold good for seven years. He knew that the *Freisinnige* Party would never agree to this: one of the principles on which the party had been founded was that they would not vote an Army Bill lasting longer than three years. Therefore, although they passed

144

Bismarck's new bill, they voted it for three years only. As soon as this result was announced, Bismarck rose to his feet, drew from his portfolio an imperial order and read out the dissolution of the Reichstag. He had won the first round.

For the election which followed, he again employed customary tactics. He whipped up a threat of foreign invasion. Fortunately for him, the French War Minister of the time was General Boulanger—cardboard idol of those Frenchmen determined on *revanche* against Germany for the humiliations of the Franco-Prussian War. By creating the impression that Boulanger was about to launch an attack on the Reich and that the acceptance of the seven-year Army Bill (which the *Freisinnigen* had rejected) was the only way to prevent it, Bismarck stampeded the voters into repudiating the 'Crown Prince's Party'. The results, as always, were as expected. The *Freisinnige* Party lost half its seats and the National Liberals emerged triumphant. As the National Liberals had long since shed their left wing, they were now very much a party after Bismarck's own heart; 'pompous submissiveness' was how Ludwig Bamberger, one of its erstwhile members, summed up the spirit of National Liberalism.

Bismarck had won. He would now be supported by a majority in the Reichstag. If the old Kaiser were to die, his successor would have to face a united Chancellor and Reichstag. 'The Crown Prince,' wrote Bamberger, 'is now compelled to do what Bismarck wants.'

Bismarck's gain, once more, meant Germany's loss. By his clipping of Prince Frederick's wings Bismarck had robbed the country of the services of the one man who might have been able to set it along a different course. With the implementation of his democratic, humane and, above all, sensible ideas, the Crown Prince might have saved the Second Reich from disaster. Whether or not he would have proved strong enough to introduce the necessary changes one does not know. Did he have the required drive? Those who knew him intimately were inclined to doubt it. It was said that on being photographed or painted he adopted a firmness of expression quite alien to his true nature. This might have applied to his political abilities as well. Queen Victoria described him as 'straightforward and honest and kind-hearted but rather weak and to a certain extent obstinate, not *conceited* but absurdly proud, as all his family are....' And there was some truth, of course, in the accusation that he was dominated by his wife. 'You have only to look what she's made of him,' claimed his Private Secretary, Colonel Sommerfeld. 'But for her he'd be the average man, very arrogant, good-tempered, of mediocre gifts and with a good deal of common sense. But *now* he's not a man at all, he has no ideas of his own, unless she allows him. He's a mere cipher. "Ask my wife" or "Have you discussed the matter with the Crown Princess?" and there's no more to be said.'

But that Prince Frederick, for all his weaknesses, was a man of honest intention, there is no doubt. And, with his strong sense of duty, he might yet have overcome these weaknesses. To some, he seemed a paragon of all the virtues. *Ein sittenreiner Mann*—a thoroughly moral man—is what a great many of his countrymen called him. Princess Catherine Radziwill, to whose lips malice always sprang more easily than praise, had nothing but good to say of him. It would have been difficult, she once claimed, to find a more lovable personality than his; 'he was everything that is noble, everything that is good; to listen to him was to grow better, to be near him was to get away from all the pettiness of the world, from all the fret, the evil, the injustice of so-called society. His mind was noble, his nature was true, his heart was kind. He had known disappointment and sorrow, had measured the ingratitude of mankind, had been confronted by some of the most serious problems of life, and had never failed in any of his duties. His was an heroic existence ... he had but few faults in him, and these were mostly of a kind which would have been called qualities in anyone else. A dutiful son, an admirable husband and father, a faithful friend, a good man. ...'

In the winter of 1886, this same Princess Radziwill, about to spend some months in Egypt, went to the Kronprinzenpalais to take leave of the Crown Prince and Princess. The Prince had recently recovered from an attack of measles but, apart from having lost some weight, he looked his usual imposing self. The only reminder of his recent illness, he assured his guest, was a slight soreness in his throat.

2

In March 1887 Kaiser Wilhelm I celebrated his ninetieth birthday. 'Ninety years,' he wrote to Bismarck; 'a lifetime, and what a long span! When I look back upon it all, it seems inconceivable that I could have lived through and achieved so much. During the time that still remains to me, it will continue to be my aim as hitherto to promote the welfare and safety of my people.'

He was still surprisingly active. As stubborn as ever, he refused to give in to his undeniably failing powers. After five hours' sleep, he would be up at six in the morning and by seven he could be seen standing on the pavement outside his palace, often in the dark and wet of a winter's day, to take the salute as the guard went tramping by. He never bothered about his own comfort. To the very end of his days he slept on his hard iron camp-bed and travelled in a rattling old saloon carriage without rubber tyres. At receptions he was as punctilious and courteous as ever although it was not always easy for his guests to follow the conversation. For one thing he was almost completely deaf and for another, he had been, it was said, 'indifferently handled by his dentist'. The result was that it was not only difficult to hear what he was saying but one was never even sure what language he was speaking. If one detected a Teutonic guttural, explains Lord Frederic Hamilton, one bowed, hoped for the best and murmured '*Zu Befehl, Majestät*'. If, on the other hand, one caught the sound of a nasal 'n', one ventured a tentative '*Parfaitement, Sire*'.

'Still,' continues Lord Frederic, 'the impression remains of a kindly and very dignified old gentleman, filling his part admirably.'

During one evening's *cercle*, the Emperor stopped in front of one of his own gentlemen-in-waiting, Baron Reischach, and addressed him as though he were a complete stranger.

'I am Reischach, your Majesty,' whispered the embarrassed young man.

Unperturbed, Wilhelm continued his formal pleasantries.

Again, and with more emphasis, Reischach whispered his name.

'But you are not *my* Reischach,' answered the Emperor.

On being assured that he was, Wilhelm pronounced him 'unconscionably rejuvenated since your marriage', and passed on.

His good manners remained exceptional. When that rough-hewn old Boer, President Kruger of the Transvaal, scandalized the company by drinking the water from his finger-bowl while lunching at Court, the Kaiser gamely drained his own finger-bowl.

Lady Randolph Churchill, taking tea with the Kaiser in his palace, was impressed, not only by his old-world manner and his gaiety, but by his enormous appetite. 'It was a mystery to me how he survived what he ate and drank ...' she reported. 'He began with poached eggs, and went on to potted meats and various strange German dishes, added many cups of strong tea, and ended with strawberries, ices and sweet, tepid champagne.'

The Kaiser attributed his longevity to the fact that he had always eaten a lobster salad at midnight.

It was away from the ostentation of Court life that the Emperor was at his happiest. Winters he was obliged to spend in Berlin but in the spring, summer and autumn he could relax as he moved, with unvarying regularity, around the Empire. Each spring he went to Bad Ems. Here he enjoyed tipping his hat to the curtseying ladies as he took his daily stroll through the Kurgarten. From Ems he journeyed first to Coblenz (where Augusta spent a great part of the year), then to the island of Mainau in the Lake of Constance and finally to Gastein where, among the splendid mountain scenery and in that bracing air, he played skittles and attended amateur theatricals. Summers he spent in the somewhat more formal atmosphere of the Babelsberg Palace at Potsdam. In the autumn he attended manoeuvres at Baden-Baden. As he grew older, he had to forgo attending reviews and manoeuvres on horseback and was obliged to sit in his carriage. 'I am ashamed of myself,' he would grumble, 'as I now appear in the eyes of the public as unfit for military service.' Yet it was his presence alone, it was said, that ensured that military reviews and exercises had any 'life' in them.

In late autumn, the Kaiser went to hunt in Silesia. He loved the evenings spent in the smoking-room of his castle after the day's sport. Under the glassy-eyed gaze of stuffed stags' and boars' heads and warmed by the fire roaring in the grate, he and his companions would sit around an old oak table, telling hunting stories, drinking beer out of steins and smoking Turkish tobacco in long clay pipes.

The Empress Augusta's life was very different. She would still rather hold court than relax. Although by now confined to a wheel-chair and with her shaking palsy worse than ever, she remained every bit as sharp and unresigned. A guest described her as 'a thin mummy with her whole breast removed from cancer, yet it was covered with jewels, her head tied on!' Augusta jerked out her orders, she says, like 'an automaton'. Heavy enamelling covered her face, neck and shoulders. It was said that ladies attending the imperial dinner parties were restricted to wearing dresses cut square at the neck, as the Empress, no longer able to present a bare shoulder to the company, was 'enamelled *square*'. Someone attending the Emperor's ninetieth birthday celebrations claimed that Augusta 'quite fresh in mind, but looking like one dug up from the dead, was bent double, painted and covered in precious stones, something of a skeleton and something of a witch. She only lives because she has the will to do so.'

None the less, her interest in affairs, and in politics in particular, was still very much alive. To ensure that she was kept *au fait* with the latest trends in political thinking, Augusta would send for young students and subject them to a somewhat unnerving inquisition. Looking 'more like a waxed figure than a human being', she once questioned the young Prince Blücher, then attending Strasbourg University. 'I am glad to see you, my boy,' she whispered, 'and now will you give me a short résumé (a little *aperçu*) of the political affairs in Alsace?' The poor youngster stammered his way through the audience, managing to work in a few complaints against Bismarck's harsh treatment of Germany's French-speaking subjects. Whether or not this information made any impression he could not tell; the Empress's mask-like face revealed nothing. 'I thank you very much, my child, for what you have told me,' she said, 'it has interested me greatly.' Then, like a corpse, she was wheeled out.

The years had not improved the relationship between the Emperor and Empress. They still bickered as much as before. Once, when the Kaiser was suffering from a slight bilious attack, he refused a slice of cherry cake. 'It is a good thing that you did not take any cherry cake,' commented the Empress. The Emperor, either not having heard or not wanting to hear, said nothing. Augusta repeated her remark. 'What does the Queen say?' asked the Kaiser, for he still insisted on calling her Queen rather than Empress. On being told, he at once beckoned to the footman and helped himself to two large slices of cake.

The Empress, staying at Baden-Baden, once wanted to visit

Geneva incognito. For this she needed her husband's permission. 'May I go to Geneva?' she wired to the Emperor, who was at Ems. 'Go,' he wired back tersely. From Geneva she wanted to go on to Turin. 'May I go on to Turin?' she wired. 'Go,' he answered. From Turin she wanted to go on somewhere else. Again she wired for permission. 'Go, and be hanged!' he replied.

Yet when, in the summer of 1887, she suddenly took ill, the Emperor was desperately worried. 'Wait till you have been married for fifty years and have quarrelled with your wife every day,' explained a member of his suite to a puzzled witness of the Kaiser's misery, 'and then, when you are faced with the alternative of this habit coming to an end, you will be unhappy too.'

Like most old people, the Emperor found himself remembering the distant, more easily than the immediate past. More and more he found his thoughts turning to his boyhood and particularly to his mother, Queen Louise of Prussia, whom he had loved so dearly. Princess Radziwill, attending a dinner at Babelsberg Palace on the anniversary of the battle of Gravelotte in the Franco-Prussian War, was astonished to see tears roll down the old monarch's cheeks as he spoke of the sufferings of Queen Louise at the hands of the Great Napoleon, over three-quarters of a century before. Raising his glass, he thanked his soldiers for avenging, by their victory over the French in 1870, his mother's humiliations. 'His simple words moved his listeners, and gave them an insight into his real character, more than a thousand long speeches would have done,' she said.

And, writing to his aged sister, Princess Alexandrina, he remembered their mother's last birthday, as vividly as though it had been a year or two before instead of almost eighty. 'A long glass had been brought in,' he recalled, 'and I can still see how, when she had finished, she called me and cut a bit off a long white ribbon, which I picked up, also a good many pins which I found and gave to my tutors at their request! I can still see it all! But what I can never forget is that when the polonaises were being danced in the Weisse Saal, and Mamma had danced with the most distinguished Princes, Schilden came and said that Mamma wished to dance a polonaise with me; I was so taken aback that I almost cried with joy and astonishment, for I had never dreamed of such a thing, and afterwards

I kissed her hand with the deepest gratitude! Beside our pretty Mamma I could not have looked very well, small as I was, powdered, and in shoes and stockings, not elegantly dressed as our Princes are now, even at ten years old!'

3

Throughout the winter of 1886–7, Crown Prince Frederick had suffered from a persistent hoarseness. In March 1887 his personal physician, Dr Wegner, unable to alleviate the Prince's sufferings, decided to call in a specialist. He chose Professor Karl Gerhardt. Dr Gerhardt discovered a small growth on the left vocal cord which he tried to remove, first by the use of a wire snare, then with a ring-knife and finally by cauterization. To afford the patient some relief from these painful and still unsuccessful ministrations, Gerhardt decided that he must go to Bad Ems for a few weeks' holiday. At that stage Dr Gerhardt could obviously not have suspected that the growth might be malignant. Although the change of air benefited the Crown Prince, the growth remained. On his return to Berlin in May, he was examined by yet another doctor, Professor Ernst von Bergmann, the eminent surgeon. Between them, Gerhardt and Bergmann came to the conclusion that the growth could be cancerous. They favoured an immediate operation. This would involve the splitting of the larynx. Even if the patient survived the operation, he would, in all probability, be rendered permanently voiceless. It was agreed between the distraught Crown Princess and the doctors that the patient would be told nothing of this until immediately prior to the operation.

Before deciding on so drastic a move, however, the two doctors suggested that a third specialist be consulted. Rejecting, on political grounds, an Austrian and a French doctor, they chose one of Europe's leading authorities on diseases of the throat—an English specialist, Dr Morell Mackenzie. Mackenzie was sent for, and the Crown Princess, relieved at having one of her countrymen called in, backed up the German doctors' summons with a telegram to her mother.

A further examination, conducted before Mackenzie's arrival, resulted in a unanimous diagnosis of cancer by six German doctors. They again recommended a splitting of the larynx. It

151

only remained, therefore, for Dr Mackenzie to give his opinion.

Dr Morell Mackenzie arrived on the afternoon of 20 May 1887. After examining the Crown Prince's throat, he could not agree to the operation until cancer had been confirmed under the microscope. With the consent of Doctors Gerhardt and Bergmann, he removed two fragments of the growth and sent them to Professor Rudolf Virchow, the eminent pathologist, for examination. Professor Virchow's report on these particular fragments was negative. He claimed, however, that they had been too small for him to give a conclusive opinion. Therefore Mackenzie removed yet another fragment. Again Virchow could find no trace of cancer. Mackenzie, backed up by Virchow's analysis, advised against the operation and suggested that the patient come to England for treatment; he should be able to cure Prince Frederick, thought Mackenzie, in a matter of months.

The Crown Princess was immensely relieved. Throughout the various ministrations and examinations she had shown a brave face. She had not wanted to alarm her husband and had all along tried to convince herself that the German doctors' fears had been exaggerated. 'Of course,' she admitted to Queen Victoria, 'the suspense is very trying to me, but I own the hope held out is a very great relief, and as I am sanguine by nature, I easily cling to it. . . .' She simply could not bring herself, she said, to believe the worst. 'I fancy all this will come right somehow and only the remembrance of the scare remain, which was bad enough.'

The German doctors were not nearly as optimistic. They still maintained that the growth was cancerous. This Vicky dismissed as mere professional jealousy on their part; they did not like to admit that Mackenzie had proved them wrong. 'But I am *convinced* of it!' she wrote. 'Fritz *ought* to be under his care and we must see *how* we can carefully effect this.'

That she needed to move carefully there was no question. A great many people at Court, not fully aware of the gravity of the Crown Prince's illness, considered it quite wrong that he should contemplate spending several months in Britain while the health of the ninety-year-old Kaiser was failing so rapidly. However, in that summer of 1887, Queen Victoria celebrated her Golden Jubilee and this gave the Crown Prince and Princess a good excuse to travel to London. They arrived there on 14 June. The Crown Prince took part in the cavalcade preceding the Queen's carriage to Westminster Abbey and, of all the princes, none looked more splendid than the Crown Prince Frederick of Germany. Tall and bearded, in a white uniform, flashing breastplate and towering, eagle-crowned helmet, he looked the very picture of royal dignity and radiant good health. It was difficult to believe that he could not speak above a whisper.

The Jubilee celebrations over, the royal couple went to spend a few weeks at Norris Castle on the Isle of Wight. One catches a glimpse of them during this stay from one of the Crown Princess's nieces: Marie, the sharp-eyed little daughter of her brother, Prince Alfred, who would afterwards become the famous Queen Marie of Rumania. Prince Frederick, looking handsome in his great golden beard, would play with the children on the beach, bombarding them with sand and seaweed. 'He was jolly,' says Marie, 'yet one somehow felt he was condescending, which made us feel shy.'

On the behaviour of her aunt, the Crown Princess, Marie had some telling observations. 'Her eyes were extraordinarily blue, her voice enticing and her smile perfectly delightful. There was great harmony between her smile and her eyes, both of which were astonishingly bright and alive. She was exceedingly sweet to us children and asked us many questions.' Yet to little Princess Marie, the Crown Princess's manner seemed a little too good to be true. She thought her smile forced and mechanical; turned on, she says, 'like electric light'. The smile had 'something of a bite about it'. Nor was the little girl ever convinced that her aunt, on showing amusement, was really amused. Her reaction seemed too stagey, too mannered. What did strike Princess Marie was that the Crown Princess seemed 'ambitious and *tatkräftig*', which she defines as 'forcible, incisive, penetrating'.

All this might have been hindsight. It could be too, that Vicky, sick with worry about her husband's health, had already begun to assume the artificially bright demeanour that was to characterize her in the months ahead.

Crown Prince Frederick spent two months in England under Mackenzie's care but his throat showed almost no improvement. Towards the end of June Mackenzie removed a further particle of the growth and sent it to Virchow for analysis. Again the pathologist could detect no sign of cancer. By the autumn, with Fritz at Balmoral, Mackenzie seems to have convinced both his patient and himself that complete recovery was simply a matter of time and that rest and silence would cure all. 'To think,' wrote the gratified Queen Victoria on hearing Mackenzie's opinion, 'that he should have recovered his dear health so much in England and still more in dear Scotland is an indescribable cause of joy and thankfulness to us.' In a rush of premature relief, Queen Victoria knighted the optimistic doctor.

By now there was considerable agitation in Berlin for the return of the Crown Prince. The Emperor was not expected to last much longer and in certain liberal circles it was feared that Prince Wilhelm was gaining far too much influence. But even at the risk of this, Vicky fought the idea of their return to Berlin 'tooth and nail', as she put it. 'I know the life there,' she said, 'the fatigues, the constant calls upon us and the duties without end!! He would never cure his voice....' The idea that her husband's health might be endangered because the Emperor was suffering 'constant little attacks', seemed to her like sacrificing the future to the present.

Thus, when the couple left Britain in September, it was to Toblach in the Tyrol that they went. When this proved to be too wet for the Crown Prince, they made for Baveno, near Lake Maggiore, by way of Venice. From Venice the Crown Princess reported to Lady Ponsonby that 'the *slightest* thing causes swelling and congestion, pain and hoarseness', and that this made her husband 'much more depressed, impatient and fidgety than he need be'. At Baveno things seemed to be slightly better. The climate was warm, the gardens of their villa were enchanting and Dr Mackenzie expressed himself very satisfied. As long as the Crown Prince neither spoke, nor caught cold, he should be well in three or four months' time. With this reassuring news ringing in his patient's ears, the doctor left for home, leaving his assistant, a Dr Hovell, in charge.

'My English specialist is convinced that he has overcome the real trouble...' wrote the Crown Prince to a friend. 'I am hoping to take up my duties at home at the beginning of the winter.'

German public opinion was not quite so sanguine. It was suspected that the diagnosis of the German doctors had been correct and there were mutterings about the fact that the Crown Prince was in the exclusive care of a British, rather than a German doctor. Such reasoning infuriated Vicky. 'I am

driven quite wild with the newspapers of Berlin . . .' she wrote
to her mother. 'Really it is excessively impertinent of these
people! The Emperor would not have others forced upon him
if he were satisfied; so why should we? It is impossible for Fritz
to be better treated and more carefully than he is! To disturb
the treatment would be to run the risk of spoiling it. Fritz
himself admitted to the Queen that the German doctors had
'nearly killed and totally mismanaged' him, that he would not
allow any of them to come near him and that he was perfectly
satisfied with Sir Morell Mackenzie. To the British Ambassador in Berlin, who had had the temerity to suggest that Dr
Mackenzie share the responsibility for the Crown Prince Frederick's health with some German doctor, Queen Victoria made
clear that it was the German doctors themselves who had asked
the Crown Prince and Princess to consult Sir Morell Mackenzie.

Mackenzie, on hearing of these complaints, published, in the
Munich *Allgemeine Zeitung*, a letter to the effect that he had
'never in any way been opposed to entering into consultation
with any German colleagues'. Should any unfavourable symp-
tom reveal itself, he added, he would be the first to call in a
German doctor.

The letter had hardly been published before more unfavourable symptoms did indeed reveal themselves. The hoarseness increased and the Crown Prince lost his voice entirely.
Imagining that a still warmer climate was needed, Prince
Frederick was moved on from Baveno to San Remo on the
Italian Riviera. Here, at the beginning of November 1887, in a
large villa set in an exotic garden on the shores of the glittering Mediterranean, his sad little Court established itself. They
had not been there twenty-four hours, however, before Dr
Hovell noticed an alarming deterioration in the patient's condition. The Crown Princess immediately telegraphed to Dr
Mackenzie. He came hurrying to San Remo. On examining the
patient's throat, he discovered a new growth. This time he felt
certain that it was malignant. The Crown Prince, begging to
be told the truth, asked the doctor if it was cancer.

'I am sorry to say, Sir,' answered Mackenzie, 'it looks very
much like it, but it is impossible to be certain.'

After a moment or two's silence, Prince Frederick spoke. 'I
have lately been fearing something of this sort,' he said calmly.
'I thank you, Sir Morell, for being so frank with me.'

It was only later, when alone with his wife, that Fritz's remarkable control broke down and his long pent-up anguish burst forth. Sobbing bitterly, he gasped out against the injustice of fate. 'To think that I should have such a horrid, disgusting illness! that I shall be an object of disgust to everyone, and a burden to you all! I had so hoped to be of use to my country. Why is Heaven so cruel to me? What have I done to be thus stricken down and condemned . . . ?'

His long final agony had begun.

CHAPTER SEVEN

SAN REMO

1

Hardly less tragic than the Crown Prince Frederick's martyr-dom was that of the Crown Princess. For there now broke, about her head, a storm of extraordinary violence.

Vicky had always known that she was unpopular but she had never realized the full extent of that unpopularity until now. She did, of course, have friends and admirers in certain liberal and cultural circles, but at Court, in the official world and among the narrow-minded, Junker-dominated society of Ber-lin, she was heartily disliked. 'I am an English woman,' she wrote at this time, 'suspected of liberal, of free-thinking and artistic tendencies; of cosmopolitan and humanitarian senti-ments and the like abominations in the eyes of Bismarck; so I am labelled "suspicious" and "dangerous" by the clique who are all-powerful now.' She was weary, she complained, 'of being constantly blamed and picked to pieces by people who have no right and no business to meddle in our affairs. Whenever any-thing is wrong, it does not matter *what* it be, it is put on *my* back.'

This was never more true than now. The blame for the Crown Prince's condition was laid squarely at her door. She had always been looked upon as headstrong, stubborn, self-satisfied, ambitious and aggressively pro-British; her behaviour throughout her husband's illness was considered to be com-pletely in character. The Crown Prince, always rumoured to be putty in her hands, had never been more dominated by her than during this period. She was so determined, it was said, that her husband should reign and so afraid that he might be passed over in favour of her son that she had persistently mini-mized the seriousness of his illness. She was accused of having distrusted the original diagnosis of Doctors Gerhardt and Bergmann on account of their being German. She had refused to believe that the growth was cancerous and had forbidden her husband to be operated on at a time when such an operation might have saved his life. She had insisted that a British doctor be called in and had herself telegraphed for Dr Mackenzie. She had impressed on Mackenzie ('an unimportant English physician of Radical opinions' as Bismarck subsequently described him) the importance of the growth not being diagnosed as cancerous. She had ignored repeated warnings from Dr Gerhardt and, by whisking her husband away to her beloved England to follow Mackenzie's ineffectual treatment, had kept him from the German doctors who could have helped him. She had buoyed up her husband with false hopes and by her persistent optimism had misled the public about the real seriousness of his illness. That eight precious months had been wasted and that the Crown Prince could no longer be saved was due entirely, it was claimed, to her hatred of Germany, her hatred of her eldest son, her love of power and her notorious wilfulness.

The accusations were nonsense. Of course both she and her husband had lived for the day when his accession to the throne would mean the inauguration of their democratic ideas, and the thought that the splitting of his larynx would make him an Emperor without a voice had horrified her. But, in her devotion to him, Vicky had been ready to agree to anything that would save his life and alleviate his sufferings. This, and not a passion for power, had guided her behaviour throughout his illness. Knowing how much the 'ruling clique' hated their liberalism, she might well, in her highly emotional state, have suspected that they would be only too glad to see Crown Prince Frederick silenced, or even that they would try to force him to renounce his rights to the throne, but she could never have believed that her husband would simply be declared unfit to reign. Bismarck himself claimed that neither the family laws of the House of Hohenzollern nor the German constitution contained any provision for the altering of the succession in the event of physical incapacity. After all, Kaiser Wilhelm I himself had merely acted as Regent for his mentally deranged brother, Frederick Wilhelm IV; not until the mad King died did Wilhelm I succeed to the throne.

In her aversion to the operation which would cost her husband his voice or even his life, the Crown Princess had been backed up by no less a person than Bismarck himself. The operation must not be performed, ordered the Chancellor, without the patient's consent and, speaking to the Crown Princess in what she described as a 'really very nice' manner, Bismarck had told her that his wife had advised her not to allow the operation. 'It is better to fall into the hands of God than into those of man,' the Chancellor had said, by which he meant that they would be better advised to face the dangers of the Crown Prince's illness than to allow him to be operated on. 'I said I had nothing to allow,' Vicky had reported to her mother; 'what the responsible authorities decided on as the best, we should have to submit to.'

In the accusation that the Crown Princess had insisted on the summoning of a British doctor, there is also no truth. It was the German doctors who had been anxious for yet another opinion and it was they who had decided on Dr Morell Mackenzie. That she heartily approved of their choice there is no doubt, but she did not urge it. An announcement, in a German newspaper that November, to the effect that it had been Queen Victoria and the Crown Princess who had summoned Morell Mackenzie, was denied by the British Ambassador. The Ambassador went on to ask Count Herbert Bismarck, the Chancellor's son, publicly to refute the statement. This Count Bismarck, one of the Crown Prince's most dedicated enemies, refused to do. The doctors might contradict his correction, he claimed, and this would simply make matters worse.

The Crown Princess, with her naturally optimistic temperament, had been delighted when Mackenzie expressed his doubts about the cancerous nature of the growth. It is not surprising that she had put her faith in Mackenzie and his cure rather than in the German doctors and their operation. And then, far from insisting that her husband go to England to follow Mackenzie's treatment, she had confessed to her mother that, as some of the German doctors were against it, she dare not suggest it; Dr Gerhardt, however, had been in favour of Mackenzie carrying out the cure himself. 'I now leave it to them to settle their minds amongst themselves and shall not interfere with them,' she had written.

In Berlin, suspicion of Mackenzie was rife. He was accused of being a fraud, anxious for the acclaim which having the Crown Prince under his care in England would bring him. Even members of Prince Frederick's circle described him as 'a shrewd Englishman who desires to advertise himself'. The

Duke of Saxe-Coburg and Gotha claimed that Mackenzie was simply feathering his nest. It was said that, as a liberal, he had agreed to the Crown Princess's scheme of suppressing the true nature of the disease so that her husband would not be prevented from succeeding to the throne. Dr Bergmann claimed that Mackenzie, during his examinations, had harmed the patient's hitherto healthy right vocal cord. Even Sir Rennell Rodd, then a member of the British Ambassador's staff, described Mackenzie as ambitious and aggressive; he was 'a strong and masterful personality, but not a sympathetic one'.

The more Mackenzie was criticized, the more vehemently did the Crown Princess spring to his defence. 'I cannot enough repeat how wise, and kind, how delicate and considerate and judicious Sir M. Mackenzie is—such a real comfort and support—and always calm and collected,' she declared. Queen Victoria, knowing something of her daughter's tendency towards blind partisanship, at one stage tactfully suggested that not only the German doctors, but many in England, did not consider the operation to be so very dangerous and that there were many instances of its success. 'Some people also think that Sir M. Mackenzie's judgement is not quite equal to his great skill in the internal operation,' she added.

But the Crown Princess continued to regard all criticisms of Mackenzie as criticisms of herself. And indeed they were. To the accusation that both she and Mackenzie were too sanguine by half, she replied that it was her duty to remain cheerful. Although it was true that she had allowed herself to be lulled by Mackenzie's bland assurances, she hoped, by a show of optimism, to speed her husband's recovery. 'You know how sensitive and apprehensive, how suspicious and despondent Fritz is by nature,' she wrote to her mother; it was thus up to her to counteract his melancholy by remaining determinedly bright. They were being inundated with letters, telegrams and newspaper articles, each wordier, more pious and more lugubrious than the last. The Jeremiahs were having a field day. Vicky did her best to keep these 'regular funeral operations' from her husband and for this she was accused of falsely building up his hopes and of treating his illness too lightly. But she was convinced that the best thing she could do for her husband was to keep up his spirits; 'we must leave the future in God's hands and not trouble about it', she said, 'but fight this illness as well as we can, by remaining cheerful and hopeful, taking care of

Wilhelm I, the simple, courteous, autocratic King of Prussia, later first German Emperor of the Second Reich.

The liberal, mercurial Queen Augusta of Prussia, who afterwards became the Empress Augusta.

The inauguration of the Second German Reich in the Galerie des Glaces at Versailles. Wilhelm I stands in the centre of the dais with Crown Prince Frederick at his right hand. Bismarck, in white uniform, stands at the foot of the steps.

Otto von Bismarck, the astute and ruthless Iron Chancellor,
who led the Hohenzollern dynasty to greatness.

Kaiser Wilhelm I in old age.

The Empress Augusta in old age.

The liberal, sensitive Crown Prince Frederick of Prussia, afterwards Kaiser Frederick III.

A conference at German Headquarters during the Franco-Prussian War. Wilhelm I is seated left, Bismarck seated right. Crown Prince Frederick is standing left foreground.

The brilliant, emotional Crown Princess Victoria, painted in Venetian costume, at the age of thirty-eight.

The Crown Princess with Prince Wilhelm, aged seventeen, photographed during the less stormy period of their relationship. His crippled left arm is kept hidden from the camera.

The marriage of Victoria (Vicky), the Princess Royal, to Prince Frederick Wilhelm (Fritz) of Prussia, in the Chapel Royal, St. James's Palace.

*The showy, neurotic, vainglorious
Kaiser Wilhelm II.*

Princess Auguste Viktoria (Dona) at the time of her marriage to Prince Wilhelm.

Kaiser Wilhelm II delivering the Speech from the Throne at the opening of the Reichstag, 1888.

The Widowed Empress Frederick.

health, etc.'

She must, at times, have realized that all this was simply whistling in the dark but she was determined that no one else should realize it.

Indeed, if ever a wife acted from the noblest of motives, it was the Crown Princess. Her courage and devotion during this tragic period were of the highest order. In her much criticized trust of Mackenzie, she had simply done what any other woman would have done in the circumstances: both Mackenzie and Virchow were pre-eminent in their fields, so why should she doubt their judgement? She deserved all the sympathy, help and encouragement that she could get. Instead, she was being hounded and insulted by all and sundry. She was even accused, while at San Remo, of having taken her devoted Court Chamberlain, Count Seckendorff, as a lover. At a time when she was tortured by the thought of her husband's fate, when she was forced to put on a smiling front lest he sink into an even deeper depression, when she was both physically and emotionally exhausted, she was being abused, privately and publicly, by her numerous enemies. And by few was she being abused more roundly than by her eldest son, Prince Wilhelm.

2

On 9 November 1887 Prince Wilhelm arrived at San Remo. His appearance in the grief-stricken villa brought the ever-simmering feud between the Crown Princess and himself once more to a head.

He had been sent, announced Wilhelm to his harassed mother in that maddeningly self-important fashion, by the Emperor to find out the truth about the Crown Prince's illness. His arrival had coincided with that of two more doctors, Professor Schrötter and Dr Krause, and he had brought a third, Dr Schmidt, with him. Now that Mackenzie had admitted the possibility of cancer, these three doctors were to examine the Crown Prince and draw up a new report. Speaking to his mother in the presence of several members of the Household, Wilhelm explained that he could not possibly agree to her suggestion of a walk and a private talk as he was going to be much too busy consulting with the doctors. When she answered, with some sharpness, that the doctors would be reporting to her and not to him, he assured her that the 'Emperor's orders' were that he was to insist on things being done correctly, that he was to see that the doctors were not in any way interfered with, and that he was to be responsible for conveying their findings to the Emperor. 'In short,' reported Vicky, 'he was to save his Papa from my mismanagement.'

At the sound of these words, and at the sight of her son, standing with his back half-turned towards her, the Crown Princess lost her control. In her exhausted, anguished and disappointed state, she 'pitched into him', she said, with 'considerable violence'. Considering his behaviour to be 'as rude, as disagreeable and as impertinent' as possible, she lost no time in letting him know it. She assured him that not only would the doctors be reporting to her but that *she* would pass on their report to the Emperor. She would suffer no interference from him whatsoever. Furthermore, she would tell his father of his insolence and see that he was forbidden the house. With this, she swept out of the room.

Realizing that he had gone too far, Prince Wilhelm sent a member of the Household scurrying after her with his apologies. He had not meant to be rude, he said, and begged her not to report the argument to Prince Frederick. The Crown Princess agreed to forgive him; 'but I will not have him dictate to me——' she told her mother, 'the head on my shoulders is every bit as good as his'.

Wilhelm's version of the row was rather different. His mother, he told a friend, had treated him 'like a dog' at San Remo. 'She was doubtless afraid,' he maintained, 'that the house of cards on which she had set her life's hope would now come tumbling down. Standing at the foot of the stairs, I had to allow the flood of her reproaches to pass over me, and to hear her decided refusal to allow me to see my father. . . .' At that moment, claims Wilhelm, he heard a rustling at the top of the stairs and, looking up, saw his father smiling down at him. 'I rushed up the stairs, and with infinite emotion we held each other embraced, while in low whispers he expressed his joy at my visit. During the heavy days that followed we came in spirit very close to one another.'

It makes a touching story but one doubts its accuracy. However, once the row between mother and son had cleared the air, they treated each other more tactfully and there were no more scenes. The Crown Princess could even report that 'all went on quite smoothly and we had many a pleasant little walk and chat together'. The reconciliation, however, could only be in the nature of a truce.

The examination confirmed cancer. When the news was broken to the Crown Prince, he remained quite calm. His wife, terrified lest the truth be told him too brutally, insisted on remaining in the room but, in fact, the doctors were extremely tactful. Prince Frederick was given a choice. Either the larynx must be removed completely (by now the operation would be an extremely dangerous one and the patient would be left, of course, without a voice) or else, as a palliative measure, an incision could be made in his windpipe to avoid possible suffocation. After dismissing the doctors and discussing the matter with Vicky, the Crown Prince decided against the removal of the larynx. If the lesser operation of tracheotomy proved necessary, he would submit to that. A Dr Bramann, assistant to Dr Bergmann, was sent to San Remo to stand by. Prince Wilhelm, satisfied that his duty had been well done, returned to Berlin to report to the Emperor.

By now there could be no doubt that the Crown Prince was a dying man. And with the old Kaiser becoming more feeble by the day, it was a question of which of the two would go first. People began to whisper about a long-forgotten prophecy that the Emperor would live to be ninety-six and be succeeded by a man with one arm. Already the official world was beginning to prepare for the next reign but one; with one sun sinking so fast, it would be as well to turn and face the coming dawn. Lord Salisbury was already asking the British Ambassador in Berlin to do what he could to 'dissipate any prejudices which [Prince Wilhelm] may have contracted against this country'.

By no one, of course, was the future reign being anticipated more eagerly than by Prince Wilhelm himself. He is said to have drawn up an Imperial Edict to be dispatched to the various German princes on the day of his accession. This he sent to Bismarck. The Chancellor, having made a copy of it, wisely advised the Prince to burn it. Both the Kaiser and his Heir Apparent were still alive, explained Bismarck; it really would not do for the public to learn that the Heir Presumptive had already drafted his Imperial Edict.

With the aged Kaiser sometimes proving too befuddled to sign his own name, let alone follow complicated political questions, and with the Crown Prince dangerously ill at San Remo, it was decided to grant Prince Wilhelm the power to sign State papers whenever the Emperor was incapable of doing so. It was a reasonable precaution but the way in which it was inaugurated flung yet another spark into the overcharged atmosphere.

Without even consulting the Crown Prince on the matter, Bismarck sent the Imperial Order to a gratified Prince Wilhelm. Only then did the Chancellor dispatch a notification of what he had done to San Remo. This important information was not even written in Bismarck's own hand, merely signed by him. The Crown Princess, realizing that the news would upset her husband (already he was annoyed by the fact that Dr Bergmann's assistant, and not his English doctor, had been commanded to stand by to perform a possible tracheotomy) decided to keep the dispatch from him. But two days later their second son, the bombastic Prince Henry, arrived from Berlin and handed his father a letter. It was from Prince Wilhelm and it informed the Crown Prince of his appointment as *Stellvertreter des Kaisers*. The Crown Prince was furious. It was not so much that he minded his son being empowered to act for the Emperor, as that he had not been consulted in the matter. He was 'much upset, very angry, and much excited, talked a great deal (which is very bad for him) and said he would go instantly to Berlin . . .' reported the Crown Princess. It took a long time to calm him down.

Prince Wilhelm's appointment encouraged the Crown Princess's suspicion that there was a plot afoot to force her husband to renounce his rights in favour of Prince Wilhelm. In letter after letter to her mother she poured out her fears. The conservatives, she claimed, would go to any lengths to see that their darling, Prince Wilhelm, gained power and continued the Kaiser's and Bismarck's reactionary policies. To this end they were not only spreading alarming reports on the seriousness of the Crown Prince's illness, but were bent on getting his English doctors dismissed so that they could replace them with men of their own choosing. These doctors would then convince their patient of the hopelessness of his case and of the necessity of renouncing his claim to the throne. It was the Junkers who wanted the Crown Prince's larynx removed; it was they who were trying to force an operation which would certainly cost the patient his voice and, in all probability, his life. 'Against this,' declared Vicky, 'it is my duty to fight!'

For this reason, combined with her natural optimism, the

164

Crown Princess would not allow herself to believe that her husband was beyond recovery. She seems even to have convinced herself that he did not really have cancer. In her stubborn belief she was still being backed up by Mackenzie. When, in January 1888, the Crown Prince coughed up a fragment of a new growth in which Professor Virchow could still find no definite trace of cancer, both doctor and wife felt reassured. Although Mackenzie had earlier concurred with the verdict of the other doctors, he now saw fit to assure Queen Victoria that there was nothing malignant in Prince Frederick's throat. Whether or not he really believed this it is impossible to say.

In fact, Dr Mackenzie's incredible changes of mind are one of the most puzzling features of the Crown Prince's illness. This might have been due to the fact that the entire course of the disease was unusual; not really typical of cancer of the throat. Was Mackenzie concealing the true nature of the illness? Did Prince Frederick have syphilis of the larynx? Reports of this certainly appeared in the Paris Press; when they did, the Prince asked Mackenzie to deny them. Dr Schmidt, one of the doctors who examined the patient on 9 November, suggested that he be given large doses of potassium iodide and with this the other doctors present agreed. Potassium iodide was the usual treatment for late syphilis, and Schmidt, after leaving San Remo, announced that the Crown Prince was suffering from a disease of 'contagious origin'. Mackenzie himself is said to have confided to a close friend, Dr Pierce, that the Prince 'had syphilis of the larynx before the cancer appeared'. This opinion has recently been backed up by R. Scott Stevenson in his detailed study of the Crown Prince's illness. Given Fritz's character, it seems unlikely, but there was talk of his association with a Spanish dancer at the opening of the Suez Canal which he had attended some eighteen years before.

Adding weight to the Crown Princess's opinion that her husband did not have cancer was the fact that he still looked so well. His illness seems not to have affected his magnificent appearance in the slightest. Lady Ponsonby, visiting San Remo at this time, reported to her husband that the Crown Prince 'looked beautiful, with a fresh colour and a good appetite, and whom I had the greatest difficulty to prevent talking....' Influenced, no doubt, by the Crown Princess, Lady Ponsonby was able to tell Queen Victoria that the exact nature of the disease remained uncertain and that the latest growth proved nothing one way or the other.

She proved too hopeful by half. Before dawn on 9 February, the Crown Prince staggered to the bedside of his valet gasping, 'Oh God! I can't bear it any longer!' He felt as though he were suffocating. It was decided that the long deferred tracheotomy must be carried out that very day. Dr Bramann performed the operation with great skill and from then on the Crown Prince breathed through a cannula inserted into his throat. The sound of the air through the cannula, reported Vicky to her mother, was 'very horrid'.

During these February days the atmosphere in the villa at San Remo became increasingly tense. Everyone was near breaking-point. The Crown Prince was by turns irritable and depressed; the Crown Princess on the edge of hysteria. Dr Bergmann, who arrived soon after the operation, disagreed with Dr Mackenzie on the choice of cannula for the patient. Mackenzie declared that he disapproved of Bergmann's treatment and that he was staying on only at the insistence of the Crown Princess; Bergmann claimed that he was doing his best 'to keep this abominable colleague within the bounds of medical decency'. The clash ended with Bergmann's temporary withdrawal from the case.

Most members of the Household, agreeing with the German doctors' diagnosis of cancer, found the Crown Princess's blind faith increasingly difficult to countenance; 'Countess Brühl almost cuts me, Fritz's two gentlemen make the longest and stiffest faces', admitted Vicky. To their unspoken disapproval was added the extremely voluble remonstrations of her second son, Prince Henry. Like most people, he not only believed that his father was being killed by his mother and the English doctors, but that the Crown Prince should renounce his rights to the throne in favour of Prince Wilhelm. 'He becomes so rude and impertinent that I really cannot stand it,' wrote the Crown Princess. She dismissed him as 'ignorant, green and misled'. It was hard enough, she complained to her mother, to be torn to pieces by ignorant, excited people, but when one's own children sided with them and refused to believe a word one said, it was almost beyond endurance. 'Henry is quite dreadful in this respect!'

To the air of acrimony within the villa was added the annoying presence of the army of reporters that had taken up residence in the Hôtel de la Méditerranée outside. 'The whole world,' noted one of these journalists, 'had its eyes fixed on this town and on this man. With anxious curiosity everybody was watching the frightful struggle in progress there....' By few was it being watched more eagerly than by the reporters themselves. All day long they prowled around the high walls surrounding the villa or climbed on to the roof of their hotel from which they hoped to catch a glimpse of the dying man on his carefully screened balcony. Cumbersome photographic equipment was for ever being dismantled and moved on to a more promising spot. On the assumption that doors would somehow be opened more readily to them, women reporters were arriving in a steady stream. The presence of this besieging crowd was hardly calculated to improve tempers within the villa.

It was with affairs in this state of tension that Prince Wilhelm turned up once more. This time the Crown Prince took the precaution of scribbling a few lines to his son to tell him that although he was welcome, he was not to interfere in any way. The Prince seems to have taken the warning to heart and behaved with much more circumspection than usual. The Crown Princess, however, still found cause for complaint. 'Not one word of sympathy or affection did he utter,' she said after he had returned to Berlin, 'and I was distressed to see how very haughty he has become, and what tremendous airs he gives himself! It is no doubt the effect of being told so often that he may be Emperor in less than a year.'

It is said that Wilhelm had even gone so far as to claim precedence over his mother as he entered the Lutheran church at San Remo on the grounds that he was there as 'the Emperor's representative'.

Prince Wilhelm had been told by Dr Bergmann that his father had less than six months to live. This information his mother dismissed as nonsense, 'a mere guess and a conjecture'. For, in spite of all evidence to the contrary, the Crown Princess still believed that her husband would recover. The German doctors were simply being obstinate. Although they might convince the Court and the German public, she declared stoutly, they failed to convince *her*. By the end of February she was able to report that the patient had turned the corner and was beginning to mend. A week later she announced that his condition was much improved, that he was eating well and looking better. It needed only six weeks more, she claimed with pathetic insouciance, to set him up. He could then begin his walks and drives once more.

Did she really believe this? Perhaps she simply could not bring herself to admit the truth: that her dying husband might never ascend the throne, that the years of waiting had been in vain, that her long cherished ambitions were about to turn to ashes. Fate could never be so cruel.

But she was fooling no one other than herself.

3

'All our thoughts are at San Remo, where all is going well,' telegraphed old Kaiser Wilhelm to his sister Alexandrina in February 1888. 'If only we could venture to hope!'

By now the Emperor, heartbroken by his son's illness, realized that he himself did not have much longer to live. On 22 March, he would turn ninety-one. He still went driving in his brougham or walking in the Tiergarten and he occasionally attended the Empress Augusta's evening tea parties. Lady Randolph Churchill, visiting Berlin that season, was amazed that he should look so smart and upright. Indeed, it was the Empress in her wheel-chair, with her weak voice and trembling hands and outrageously youthful clothes, who looked the more pathetic figure. But the Emperor was far from well. His hearing was worse, his speech slurred and he felt permanently tired. He often suffered fainting fits. There were times when he simply did not understand what was being said.

On 5 March he caught a chill and was confined to bed. He was still in bed when Prince Wilhelm arrived back from San Remo two days later and by the evening of 8 March it was clear that the Emperor was dying.

He lay in his room in his narrow camp-bed, wearing a white jacket with a red scarf about his neck; his bedside table was a clutter of bottles and glasses. His face, in the light of a single lamp, looked as dignified as ever. The Empress had been wheeled to his bedside and she sat holding his hand. The sick-room was crowded. As the night wore on, so did the Emperor begin to talk and for several hours, with increasing incoherence, he spoke of war. Sometimes it was of the Franco-Prussian War, sometimes of the War of Liberation against the Great Napoleon, sometimes of the possibility of a future war against France. He seemed obsessed by the German alliance with Russia; whatever happened, this must not be allowed to lapse. In the event of another war against France, Germany and Russia must stand together. 'If I should have to go to war,' he muttered, 'I am not afraid of it.'

At four in the morning of 9 March, Bismarck entered the sickroom. Handing his old master the order for the prorogation of the Reichstag for his signature, he indicated that a mere 'W' would suffice. But the Emperor, with his strong sense of duty, insisted that he sign his full name. He could not manage it, 'I've always been pleased with you,' he whispered to Bismarck. 'You've done everything well.'

At daybreak he whispered something to his daughter, the Duchess of Baden. Hurrying into the adjoining room, she returned with the miniature that had stood on his desk for almost seventy years. It was a picture of the love of his youth, Elisa Radziwill. The dying man took it in his trembling fingers.

The Kaiser died at twenty minutes past eight that morning.

Through drifting snow his coffin was carried that night from the unpretentious palace, where he had lived for almost sixty years to the Cathedral opposite the Old Schloss. In the flaring light of the torches and watched by a vast and silent crowd, the procession moved slowly down Unter den Linden. 'A whole period of German history had come to an end,' noted one eyewitness, 'and this crowd that was watching his coffin slowly borne out by soldiers of his First Regiment of Foot Guards, with the snow falling upon it, and the glittering helmets and cuirasses of the escort of the Gardes du Corps riding before and behind it, was vaguely conscious of the solemnity of the moment. Something was gone which could never be replaced....'

With the death of Kaiser Wilhelm I there passed from the German political scene a figure of undoubted significance. It was not that the Emperor, with his many limitations, was a man who had shaped events; it was that—because of these limitations—he had allowed them to be shaped. He had suited Bismarck admirably. His old-fashioned qualities—his conservatism, his despotism, his unquestioning belief in the superiority of the Prussian State—had been exactly what Bismark had needed. Now that he had gone, Bismarck had lost his mainstay. It was no wonder that it was with tears in his eyes that the Chancellor announced the death of his old master to the assembled Reichstag on that morning of 9 March 1888.

Queen Victoria's reaction was less emotional. 'Poor old Emperor,' she noted in her diary that evening, 'he was always very kind to me, but for some years, alas! he was made a tool of for no good!'

PART THREE

KAISER FREDERICK III

CHAPTER EIGHT

THE VOICELESS EMPEROR

1

Crown Prince Frederick was walking in the garden of the villa at San Remo on the morning of 9 March 1888 when he was handed a telegram. It was addressed to 'His Majesty the German Emperor'. From it he learned that his father had died two hours before and that he was now the Emperor Frederick III.

Returning to the house, the new Kaiser entered the drawing-room in which his Household stood assembled. Here, amidst these sad and bourgeois surroundings, he carried out his first imperial duties. A somewhat effusive witness of the scene claimed that 'he had become handsome again, as in the radiant days of his youth. His beard, with a few silver streaks, glowed in the brilliant light cast by the chandelier. Tall and well-built, he dominated the entire company. His blue eyes were slightly misty. His delicate complexion, now heightened with a little colour, seemed to show the real tranquillity which had taken possession of his soul; and his mouth with the red lips had now that fascinating smile which characterized him. . . .'

Seating himself at a small table, the Kaiser wrote out the announcement of his own succession as Frederick III. Then he invested the new Empress with the highest decoration he could bestow—the Order of the Black Eagle. To underline further his appreciation of all she had done, he handed Sir Morell Mackenzie a sheet of paper on which he had written: 'I thank you for having made me live long enough to recompense the valiant courage of my wife.' He let them know that he would be returning to Berlin almost immediately.

His first telegram to Prince Wilhelm was very much to the point. 'I express my confidence, on coming to the throne,' he wired, 'that you will be an example to all of fidelity and obedience.'

Two days later, on the evening of 11 March 1888, the Emperor and Empress arrived in the capital. It was a sombre homecoming. The night was bitterly cold and the streets aswirl with snow. The Emperor, warmly wrapped up, was hurried from the station to the palace of Charlottenburg on the outskirts of the city; he would have more privacy here than in the Kronprinzenpalais on Unter den Linden. To those who caught sight of him at the station, Kaiser Frederick looked surprisingly well; it was the Empress who appeared tired and aged. But no sooner had the Emperor arrived at Charlottenburg than he was obliged to go to bed. The sudden change from the balmy air of San Remo, the fatigues of the journey and the bustle of his arrival had been too much for him. It was hoped that a few days in bed would set him up for the immense task that lay ahead. 'I pray,' the Empress wrote to her mother, 'that he may be spared to be a blessing to his people and to Europe.'

The Kaiser's accession proclamation echoed this thought. 'Not caring for the splendours of great deeds, not striving for glory, I shall be satisfied if it one day be said of my rule that it was beneficial to my people, useful to my country and a blessing to the Empire.'

It was the vainest of vain hopes. However ardently the imperial pair might wish to fulfil the high mission for which they had prepared themselves so earnestly and so long, they were to be given very little opportunity of doing so. The Emperor, according to Dr Bergmann, had about three months to live. It was too late now for any sweeping changes. Realizing this, the Emperor—to the astonishment of a great many people and against his own inclinations—confirmed Bismarck in office. He had no choice. To dismiss Bismarck now, when the Kaiser was incapable of inaugurating a new regime, would be both spiteful and short-sighted: it would lead to political confusion, a weakening of the State and to Bismarck's probable reinstalment as soon as Prince Wilhelm succeeded his father. The Emperor thus wrote his life-long opponent a polite letter setting out the broad lines along which he intended to reign and Bismarck, genuinely touched by the tragedy of the situation, proved himself quite 'civil and nice' to the imperial couple. He had nothing to fear from them now. As the Empress put it, he probably appreciated that they were 'a mere passing shadow soon to be replaced by reality in the shape of William'.

This was certainly the feeling of the majority of Kaiser Frederick's subjects. The Junkers scarcely bothered to hide their gratification. '*L'Empereur est mort; vive l'Empereur mourant,*' quipped the more callous among them. They realized that any changes the Emperor might make would be of little consequence; 'Everyone who is overthrown now will rise again soon,' announced one of the diehards. 'What a terrible misfortune it would have been if we had had a hale and hearty Emperor Frederick!' noted Count von Waldersee in his diary. 'How wonderfully everything has turned out; everywhere people are looking hopefully to the Crown Prince [Wilhelm].' And Count Herbert Bismarck, the Chancellor's son, assured Herr von Bülow that he regarded the Emperor's short expectation of life as a piece of extremely good luck for the Fatherland.

It was the Empress who was being watched more closely. During these months of her husband's reign, the campaign against her reached its peak. 'The Empress now rules the land,' declared Count Waldersee. When Eugene Richther, the liberal politician, tried to refute this allegation in the Prussian parliament, he was simply howled down. Bismarck was quick to compare Frederick's dependence on his Empress with Augusta's influence over the old Kaiser. 'My old master was fully aware of his dependence,' he said. 'He used to say: "Help me; you know very well that I am under petticoat government." But this man is too proud to admit as much. In certain respects, he is as dependent and submissive as a dog; you'd hardly believe to what extent.'

The fact that the Empress had always to be present in order to speak on behalf of her dumb husband seemed to confirm this view. She was very quick, it was noted, to point out to his visitors how well he was looking; she hoped thereby to give the impression that his reign—under her influence—would be a long one. She had refused, they said—while still at San Remo —to allow the tracheotomy to be carried out until the last possible moment; although her husband, whose gasping could be heard six rooms away, had begged for this relief, she had held firm. She was determined that he would retain his voice as long as possible.

She was now accused of forcing him to make public appearances, of plying him with wine and other stimulants to get him through these occasions, of not caring one jot that the effort left him utterly exhausted. Denied the splendours of a coronation, she was said to have insisted on reviving the old Prussian custom of a *Trauercour*—Mourning Court—at which, presiding alone, she could savour the homage of her new subjects. Count von Waldersee, ever malicious, claimed that she was in her element on this occasion. 'Despite the black veil, from my sidelong viewpoint I could get a good look at her face; and reading it, my impression was that she revelled in being the centre of attention.' It was even whispered that she was demanding that the Emperor should appoint her Regent. To this suggestion her two sons, Prince Wilhelm and Prince Henry, lost no time in replying that 'the Hohenzollerns, Prussia and the German Empire would not let a woman rule over them'.

Nor was it only in Berlin that the Empress was suspected of trying to direct affairs. Lord Salisbury, the British Prime Minister, warned his Ambassador in Berlin against giving the impression that the Embassy, together with the Empress, was trying to 'shape Germany to an English pattern'. The Prime Minister had been led to believe that the Empress, in an attempt to make hay while the sun shone, was hoping to utilize the next two or three months to give 'a permanent direction to German policy in an anti-Bismarckian sense'.

Even more upsetting for the Empress than such ill-informed criticism was the antagonism within her own family. The Empress Augusta, assuming that her daughter-in-law would sweep away all traces of Prussianism and anglicize the Court, begged Baron Reischach, who had been appointed First Gentleman-in-waiting to Kaiser Frederick, to 'uphold the old tradition'.

Between the new Empress and her son Wilhelm, relations were as bad as ever. The new Crown Prince made no secret of his impatience to ascend, and his fitness to occupy, the imperial throne. In this he was being backed up to the hilt by his brother Henry and his sister Charlotte. 'I have no words to express my indignation and astonishment about the conduct of your three children,' wrote Queen Victoria to the Empress. 'This must not be allowed.' She advised her daughter to send for them and threaten them with strong measures. Wilhelm and Dona ('his odious ungrateful wife') should be packed off on a journey. They, who had always shown an excessive reverence towards the late Kaiser, must be reminded that their father was now Kaiser.

But it would have needed more than this to bring Prince Wilhelm to heel. Taking advantage of Bismarck's birthday, the Prince made a characteristically thundering speech in which he urged his audience, on account of the new Emperor's incapacity to carry out his duties, to rally round the 'great Chancellor'. That the Prince considered the Emperor to be of little, and Bismarck to be of paramount, importance, there was no doubt. His speech, made at a time when the Emperor was doing his utmost to fulfil his duties, earned him a sharply worded rebuke from his father.

Wilhelm, in his version of affairs at this time, maintained that he was never allowed to see his father alone. Sir Morell Mackenzie, he says, reigned supreme at Charlottenburg. The doctor's rooms were filled with a mob of newspaper reporters who were allowed free and frequent access to the Emperor whereas, whenever he called, he was turned away with the excuse that his father was asleep and his mother out. His every move was spied upon and reported. Finally, with the help of the Emperor's valet, Schultze, Wilhelm was smuggled up a back stairway and into his father's room. The Emperor was delighted. He wanted to know why Wilhelm had not visited him more often. Exactly why he should have been watched and denied access to his father Wilhelm never makes clear.

One of Kaiser Frederick's first tasks was to receive the various dignitaries who had come to attend his father's funeral on 16 March—five days after his own arrival in the capital. A biting wind kept him from meeting them at the station but he was able to greet them at Charlottenburg. 'In full uniform with quick steps, dignified and upright as usual, he went to meet everyone...' claims his wife. All were 'astonished to see him like that after all they had heard'. But the continuing wind kept him from attending the funeral itself. He was forced to stand at his window to see the magnificent cortege, with the resplendently uniformed Prince Wilhelm as chief mourner, pass through the Tiergarten. 'That is where I ought to be now,' he scribbled to Dr Mackenzie as he watched the proudly strutting figure of his son behind the hearse.

This same sense of frustration marked the Kaiser's first ministerial meetings. On being told that the new coins bearing his likeness would take over two months to mint, he could only raise his hands in a gesture of futility.

There was so much that he wanted to do and so little that he could do. Even his most modest attempts at reform were nullified or ignored by Bismarck. He was given no help, no encouragement; no one dared champion his proposals. Even the members of his entourage worked against him by repeating to Bismarck exactly what the Chancellor wanted to hear: that the Emperor was weak, apathetic, little better than a corpse. 'A wall was erected around us so that no independent voices could reach us,' complains the Empress, 'no person came near us who did not belong to the clique....' His plans, whether they concerned an amnesty for political offenders, the improvement of workers' houses, the healing of the breach between the Church and the State, the gradual identification of the throne with liberalism rather than conservatism, all came to nothing. However strongly he might feel, he could insist on nothing for fear of Bismarck handing in his resignation and leaving him with a situation with which he did not have the strength to cope.

Even the few pathetic attempts which he did make to assert his will earned him the condemnation of the conservatives. When he awarded the Black Eagle to Dr Simson, President of the Supreme Court of Justice, and Herr von Friedberg, the Minister of Justice, his critics were quick to point out that not only were both men liberals, but that both were of Jewish descent. 'Fritz considered the anti-Semitic movement ... terrible,' declared the Empress. 'As a modern civilized man, as a Christian and a gentleman, he found it abhorrent.' For this unfashionable attitude, Kaiser Frederick was nicknamed 'Cohen I, King of the Jews' or *Judenkaiser*. To his accession proclamation, carrying the heading 'To my people', vandals had added the word 'Israel'.

Something of the deplorable situation in which the Emperor was placed was described by Colonel Swaine, the British Military Attaché in Berlin. 'We are living in sad times here in Berlin,' he wrote in April 1888. 'Not sad alone because we have an Emperor at death's door, nor sad only because there are family disagreements, but sad, doubly sad, because almost all officials—perhaps with exceptions, but I know them not—are behaving in a way as if the last spark of honour and faithful duty had gone—they are all trimming their sails.

'It seems as if a curse had come over this country, leaving but one bright spot and that is where stands a solitary woman doing her duty faithfully and tenderly by her sick husband against all odds. It is one of the most, if not *the* most, tragic episodes in a country and a life ever recorded in history.'

It was with things in this lamentable state that the German

public was astonished to hear that the Chancellor was about to hand in his resignation.

One of Kaiser Frederick III's first moves on ascending the throne had been to invite Prince Alexander of Battenberg to Berlin. The Emperor, having finally been talked round by the Empress, had decided that the long-delayed marriage between his daughter Moretta and Sandro of Battenberg, so firmly forbidden by the late Kaiser, should now take place. Knowing that Prince Wilhelm was as opposed to the match as his grandfather had been, the Empress was anxious for the matter to be settled while her husband was still alive. After all, with Sandro no longer ruler of Bulgaria, the old Kaiser's reasons for forbidding the match had fallen away. As the Prince now lived in retirement in Darmstadt, there was no possible chance of the marriage causing friction between Russia and Germany. It could have no political consequences whatever.

With this reasoning Bismarck could not, or pretended he could not, agree. In a violently worded protest to the Emperor, he made clear his objections and demanded that the invitation to Prince Alexander to come to Berlin be withdrawn. The whole thing, he maintained, was a British plot, hatched by Queen Victoria to sow discord between Germany and Russia. What he really believed is difficult to say. There was a rumour that his son Herbert had fallen in love with Moretta and that Bismarck was anxious to promote the match. In this he was being backed up by Prince Wilhelm. But it is not impossible that Bismarck imagined that once Prince Alexander arrived in Berlin, the Empress would induce her husband to dismiss him and appoint Sandro Chancellor in his stead. She was known to think very highly of Sandro's abilities and Bismarck was always haunted by the thought of his dismissal.

He therefore played his trump card. He threatened the Emperor with resignation. Unless the invitation to Prince Alexander was immediately withdrawn, he would retire. When it came to dealing with the Empress, the Chancellor behaved more diplomatically. It was not quite so easy to intimidate her. In an adroitly handled interview, he led her to believe that the marriage might be possible at some later date. The result was that the invitation was withdrawn.

Once he had accomplished this, Bismarck strengthened his position by having the Press launch a violent attack on the imperial couple. Although the matter of the marriage had, to all intents and purposes, been settled or at least shelved, Bismarck led the public to believe that he was still on the verge of handing in his resignation. German readers were once more reminded that *die Engländerin* was always ready to sacrifice Germany's great Chancellor to British interests.

However, it was not only at the Emperor and Empress that Bismarck's attacks were aimed: he was hoping to whip up public feeling against Queen Victoria. The Queen, at that time holidaying in Florence, had just announced her intention of visiting Berlin on her way home. Bismarck, convinced that Queen Victoria was coming to force through the Battenberg marriage, was doing everything in his power to stop her. It was given out that the Tsar was violently opposed to the match, that the Chancellor himself was in a towering rage, that the government resented this 'foreign interference' in German affairs, that the Berlin population was likely to be hostile to the Queen. Her arrival in Berlin would be not only undiplomatic but positively dangerous. Heaven only know to what international friction it might lead.

By this artificially created furore the Queen refused to be put off. She referred to Bismarck's conduct as 'disloyal, wicked and really unwise in the extreme!' Russia, she declared firmly, did not care a *straw* about Prince Alexander's marriage; it was simply a nefarious plot on the part of Bismarck, Prince Wilhelm and 'the *cercle vicieux*' surrounding the unfortunate Emperor and Empress. 'How Bismarck, and still more Wilhelm, *can* play such a double game is impossible for us honest, straightforward English to understand,' she fumed. 'Thank God! we *are* English!'

As she seemed to be especially angry with Prince Wilhelm, Lord Salisbury saw fit to warn her, as tactfully as possible, to be circumspect in her dealings with him. With Prince Wilhelm so violently opposed to the match, a meeting between grandmother and grandson might have unfortunate and far-reaching consequences. The Prince's head had been so turned by the prospect of ascending the throne that if he said anything that was likely to draw a reproof from the Queen, he might resent it, 'and a feeling would rankle in his mind which might hinder the good relations between the two nations'. One had to be very careful about how one treated Prince Wilhelm.

But the Queen did not need to be told how she must treat her relations. Indeed, unbeknown to the Empress, the Chancellor or the hot-headed Prince Wilhelm, the Queen herself was no longer in favour of the Battenberg marriage. However much she might disapprove of Wilhelm's impertinence, she realized that a marriage contracted against his wishes would be disastrous for Sandro and Moretta. She had already warned the Empress of this. She knew, moreover, that Sandro himself was not nearly as eager as he had once been. For one thing the match had by now lost its political advantages and, for another, he was pursuing a distinctly less illustrious quarry—an opera singer by the name of Joanna Loisinger. Thus the Queen, far from coming to Berlin to enforce her daughter's wishes, was hoping to pour a little oil on those habitually troubled Hohenzollern waters.

She succeeded admirably. Despite the campaign of vilification in the German Press, she was enthusiastically welcomed when she arrived on 24 April 1888. At the sight of that small, indomitable and undeniably regal figure, all traces of antagonism disappeared and she was met, reported her somewhat astonished Ambassador, by 'dense crowds and hearty cheers'. The Queen herself was impressed by the 'great crowds, who were most enthusiastic, cheering and throwing flowers into the carriage'. She was gratified to hear a continuous shouting of 'Long live the Empress!' whenever she drove out with her daughter.

Victoria's prestige, assurance and sound common sense did much to cheer the unhappy Household at Charlottenburg. She found the Emperor looking deceptively well and was deeply touched by the way he raised both hands at the pleasure of seeing her. When her private secretary, Sir Henry Ponsonby, assured the Empress that her husband was looking better, the Empress's eyes filled with tears. 'No, he is not really better,' she said quietly, 'but it has done him a temporary good to see Mama.' It had done her good as well. The Queen was a great comfort to her daughter. Even Prince Wilhelm listened carefully to his grandmother's advice. He promised to be more considerate towards his mother in future. Victoria visited the widowed Empress Augusta at the Old Schloss and found her 'in deep mourning, with a long veil, seated in a chair, quite crumpled up and deathly pale, really rather a ghastly sight'. Her voice was barely audible, one hand was paralysed and the other shaky. The old Empress was clearly delighted at seeing the Queen again.

The Queen's greatest success, however, was with Bismarck. The momentous interview between them took place on 25 April, the day after Victoria's arrival. At the prospect of coming face to face with the formidable old lady, all Bismarck's self-confidence evaporated. There were no quips now about her arriving with a parson in her travelling bag and a bridegroom in her trunk to ensure that her grand-daughter was well and truly married. He felt sure that he was in for a difficult time. The Queen's aide-de-camp reported him as being 'unmistakably nervous and ill at ease'; he wanted to know where exactly she would be in the Audience Chamber and whether she would be seated or standing. The Empress led him into the room and then left him alone with the Queen.

The meeting passed off admirably. Queen and Chancellor were charmed with each other. The Queen, expecting to meet a brute, was 'agreeably surprised to find him so amiable and gentle'. The Chancellor, expecting her to insist on the Battenberg marriage, was gratified to find that she did not mention the subject. What neither of them knew was that the Empress, believing that Bismarck would sanction a quiet wedding later on, had encouraged her husband to state, in his will, that it was his express wish that Moretta marry Sandro. He imposed, on his successor Wilhelm, the duty of carrying out this wish. The Queen appealed to Bismarck to stand by the poor Empress and, for the sake of 'dear Fritz', not to appoint Wilhelm as Regent. They agreed that Wilhelm was painfully inexperienced, although Bismarck believed that 'should he be thrown into the water, he would be able to swim', as he was certainly clever. Queen and Chancellor parted on cordial terms and Bismarck emerged from the interview mopping his brow and exclaiming, 'That was a woman! One could do business with her!'

The Queen left Berlin the following evening. After an early dinner she went to take leave of the Emperor. It was a poignant parting, for the Queen must have known that she would never again see him alive. For his sake, however, she remained cheerful. Kissing him goodbye, she said that she hoped he would visit her as soon as he was stronger. In return, Fritz handed her a posy of forget-me-nots.

The Empress drove with her mother to the station. She too, was determined to put on a brave front: it would not do for the German Empress to break down in public. She stood there on the beflagged platform—with its guard of honour, its military band and its group of officials—a small, plumpish, straight-backed figure in a black, bustled dress, smiling tremulously as her mother boarded the train and took her place at the window of her saloon. Not until the train started was Vicky suddenly overwhelmed by the utter desolateness of her position. She burst into uncontrollable sobs.

'It was terrible,' wrote the equally heartbroken Queen, 'to see her standing there in tears, while the train moved slowly off, and to think of all she was suffering, and might have to go through. My poor, poor child. . . .'

3

'Sir Morell Mackenzie is particularly satisfied,' wrote Kaiser Frederick III in his diary for 4 April 1888, 'and thinks I have now reached the same state I would have been in directly after the operation and that I will soon be able to speak.'

Sympathy alone must have prompted Mackenzie to give his patient this reassurance for there was by this time no doubt that the Emperor did not have much longer to live. Indeed, a week after Fritz's optimistic diary entry, his condition worsened considerably. On the morning of 12 April the Emperor was seized by a violent coughing fit and Dr Mackenzie decided to replace the existing cannula with one of a slightly different design. To safeguard himself, the doctor summoned his rival, Dr Bergmann, to witness the changeover. Dr Bergmann, with his assistant Dr Bramann, arrived at five that afternoon. According to both the Emperor and the Empress, Bergmann, deciding that he and not Mackenzie must replace the cannula, did so with such clumsiness that a renewed fit of coughing caused a violent haemorrhage. Bramann then took over and effected the insertion with apparent ease. The new cannula afforded the patient some relief but the operation left him utterly exhausted. In his diary the Kaiser mentioned that Bergmann had 'with brutal strength forced in another cannula' and the Empress always claimed that her husband's end had been hastened by Bergmann's clumsy ministerings that day.

The incident led to another flare-up between the doctors. Mackenzie refused to continue in attendance if Bergmann was again allowed to touch the Emperor's throat and the incensed Bergmann once more withdrew from the case. His retirement led to a renewed outburst in the Press against Mackenzie and the Empress. Bergmann's cause was championed by the Emperor's political enemies and even Prince Wilhelm made a point of inviting the doctor to dinner. The Empress, in her overwrought state, claimed that the conservatives saw in Mackenzie an obstacle to their scheme for belittling and intimidating the Emperor. They hated the doctor, she said, for keeping up the patient's strength and spirits. Bergmann's gloomy predictions were much more to their taste.

There can be no doubt that, whatever Mackenzie's shortcomings, his presence was a great comfort to the Emperor and Empress. 'Sir Morell Mackenzie supported me loyally, wisely and with delicacy and feeling,' wrote Vicky after her husband's death. 'He was so devoted to Fritz that he had only one thought, to protect him like a beloved child from every rude contact, physical or moral, and he succeeded.' And as there was by now no doubt that the Kaiser was dying, Mackenzie's bland and reassuring presence was of more value than the realism of the German doctors.

To his friends, the sight of Kaiser Frederick was almost unbearably poignant. 'The Emperor placed his hand on my shoulder and smiled sadly, so that I could hardly restrain my tears,' wrote Prince Hohenlohe. 'He gave me the impression of a martyr; and indeed, no martyrdom in the world is comparable with this slow death. Everyone who comes near him is full of admiration for his courageous and quiet resignation to a fate which is inevitable, and which he fully realizes.'

However, there were still periods when the Emperor felt slightly better. His temperature would subside, his sleep would be undisturbed and he would lose that anxious, hunted look. Then he would sit by the window writing letters or making entries, in pencil, in his diary. On warm days a tent would be erected in the garden and he would lie back in the sunshine, protected from view by a screen of shrubs. The old Empress Augusta would be wheeled to his side and, with nodding head and trembling hand, would sit talking to her son. At night, in order to breathe, he wanted to be fanned continuously. Several times during the night the Empress would get up and stand listening by his door to make sure that all was well. At half-past six each morning she was by his bedside and would sit there, knitting or crocheting, until he woke. On seeing her, he would smile and stretch out his arms. His lips would form the words 'Tell me', and she would be obliged to recount every little detail of her doings; what she had 'done, seen and heard the day before, what I thought, hoped and imagined. . . .' She always made a point of showing him a cheerful and contented face; her one thought was to keep up his courage and his confidence. As late as 31 May, a fortnight before his death, she was assuring Queen Victoria that he was 'continuing to improve' and 'gaining strength'.

To Prince Hohenlohe, who found her 'frank and cheerful manner' astonishing, she said that 'it is perhaps possible that the illness will be of a long duration. The expectation of a speedy end has not yet been confirmed.'

If the imperial couple were distressed by the antagonism of the official world, they were heartened and comforted by the obvious goodwill of a great many of their subjects. The Emperor's rooms were always filled with gifts of flowers from friends or unknown sympathizers. He had often to show himself to the crowds that gathered all day beyond the railings of the palace. At the sight of him, still so tall and handsome, there would be a burst of cheering, a waving of handkerchiefs and a flinging up of hats. Mothers would lift up their children so that they might see his face. Occasionally, if he were feeling particularly strong, he would drive into Berlin. He was immensely touched by the cheering crowds and by the flowers that were tossed into his carriage. But the continual raising of his hand to his cap tired him and a sudden fit of coughing would force them to turn into one of the royal palaces so that the bleeding could be checked and the bandage renewed.

One day during April the Empress drove out alone from Charlottenburg to the Berlin Schloss. She had summoned Bismarck to meet her there on important business. This concerned her future financial position. On arrival she handed the Chancellor an order from the Emperor, signed, countersigned and sealed, to the effect that seventy-five per cent of her portion, together with the dowries of her unmarried daughters and all the daughters' share of the Emperor's property, be paid to her by the Crown Treasury immediately; the rest was to be paid over on the death of Kaiser Frederick, before his successor assumed control of the funds and revenues. The Empress, very wisely, was not going to leave her inheritance to the mercies of her son Wilhelm.

On 24 May her second son, the truculent Prince Henry, married his cousin, Princess Irene of Hesse—daughter of Vicky's late sister, Princess Alice. The ceremony was held at Charlottenburg Palace and, with the Emperor feeling well enough to attend, the Household was afforded one day of celebration. The Court put off mourning for the occasion and with the women in white or grey and the chapel filled with white roses, the atmosphere was almost gay. At the sight of her husband in full uniform, 'so handsome and dignified but so thin and pale', Vicky's heart turned over. 'I kept back my tears with difficulty and felt with bitter sorrow that we should never again see him attending such a festive gathering as Emperor!' Fritz got through the ceremony without coughing but the effort had obviously been too much for him. That night he ran a high temperature and he had to spend the following day in bed.

'I have seen many brave men,' commented Kaiser Frederick's one-time aide, old Field-Marshal von Moltke, 'but none so brave as the Emperor has shown himself today!'

A few days later, on the insistence of Prince Wilhelm, the Emperor sat in an open carriage in the grounds of Charlottenburg Palace to watch a march past of the Second Guards Infantry Brigade, led by the Prince himself. Painfully thin and wrapped in an overcoat, he made a pathetic figure; compared with him, Prince Wilhelm looked the very picture of radiant good health and aggressive soldierliness. The review, boasted the Prince, afforded his father his last great joy on earth; he says that the Kaiser handed him a card on which he had written, 'Have been content and felt great joy.' But the Empress claimed that the occasion had been a terrible trial. 'From that time,' she says, 'he went downhill.'

On 1 June the Court moved, as was customary in the summer, from Berlin to Potsdam. Leaving Charlottenburg, they travelled in the new royal steamer *Alexandria*, to the Neues Palais. All along the river banks cheering crowds collected to see the Emperor pass by and flowers rained down on the slowly steaming vessel. The Kaiser was delighted to be back at the Neues Palais. Having been born there and having spent almost every summer of his married life among its rococo delights, he had always regarded it as home. 'How glad I am to be here at last,' he mounted on his arrival.

He wished the palace to be known, from this time on, as Friedrichskron.

CHAPTER NINE

FRIEDRICHSKRON

1

It was soon after the Court had settled into renamed Friedrichskron that Kaiser Frederick III undertook the only important political act of his short reign. He insisted on the dismissal of the Minister of the Interior, an arch-reactionary by the name of Robert von Puttkamer. Puttkamer had annoyed the Emperor for several reasons. He had been loud in proclaiming that an Emperor who could not speak should not reign; he had been responsible for the official announcement of Kaiser Wilhelm I's death in which no allusion had been made to the new Emperor; and, most serious of all, he had been guilty of unethical behaviour in a recent series of by-elections. Although the Emperor might have been prepared to ignore the first two offences, he was determined not to allow the third to go unpunished. But he had to move carefully; 'there is instantly a ministerial crisis about everything as soon as he remonstrates and one has to be very cautious', said the Empress. However, during the first days of June, he was given the opportunity of getting his way.

At this time Bismarck introduced a bill proposing that the life of the Reichstag be prolonged from three to five years. With the elections of the year before having given the Chancellor a sympathetic majority in the Reichstag, he was determined to hang on to it for as long as possible. The recent by-elections had shown that the voters, no longer influenced by Bismarck's artificially created war scare, were once more swinging left and, with a chance that the future Kaiser Wilhelm II might not prove quite as pliable as his grandfather, Bismarck was anxious to safeguard his position by having an obedient Reichstag at his command. Although he could not prolong the life of the present Reichstag beyond three years, he could ensure that the following—and possibly only slightly less sympathetic—one, would sit for five years.

The bill was therefore introduced, passed and presented to the Emperor for his signature.

Frederick III, who recognized the bill for what it was, decided that he must study it before signing it. The delay infuriated Bismarck. Storming into the Empress's presence, he demanded that the bill be signed immediately. He claimed that the Kaiser had no right to refuse, that he was exceeding his prerogatives, that the Government would resign and the future of the country be jeopardized if the Emperor did not sign. When he had had his say, the Empress assured him that if, in accordance with the constitution, the Kaiser was obliged to give his signature, then give it he would. At this the Chancellor calmed down. When, in a quieter mood, he discussed the matter with the Emperor, Frederick was able to turn the controversy to good account. He made the granting of his signature conditional on the dismissal of the arrogant Puttkamer. The manoeuvre worked and Puttkamer was dismissed on 11 June. The Kaiser had won a round.

Although Puttkamer's dismissal had been a very minor achievement, it fired the Empress's imagination. Once more those irrepressible spirits soared upwards. She described it as 'a great step' and was quite sure that if only Fritz were able to break through the wall of opposition he would be able to carry out all sorts of similar changes. 'If I could think we had a year before us!' she exclaimed. She assured her mother that although she might be sad and depressed, she was not abashed and was determined to 'fight and struggle to the last'.

She allowed herself to be heartened by the fact that her husband, although physically exhausted, was still mentally alert. He signed documents, he wrote letters, he made entries in his diary, he read the newspapers, he issued instructions. His interest in everyday affairs was as lively as ever. Reassured by his wife and his doctor, he could still not accept the seriousness of his illness. 'Do I seem to improve?' he asked the Empress one day. 'When shall I be well again? What do you think? Shall I be ill long? I must get well, I have so much to do.'

There were occasions when he was still capable of making a physical effort. One day, after listening to a deeply moving rendering of 'Salve fac Regem' by a visiting choir in an adjoining salon, he left his chair and walked, upright and unaided, into the room to congratulate them. On 11 June the King of Sweden visited Friedrichskron and the Kaiser insisted on receiving him in proper fashion. Dressed in full uniform and carrying his great helmet under his arm, he led the King to the dais. He spent several minutes listening to his guest's conversation and then smilingly took his leave. But the effort had exhausted him and he had to be put to bed.

It was such instances of the Emperor's devotion to duty that caused his wife to be so infuriated by the slanders of his enemies. They, who knew nothing of his courage, spoke of him as a listless, bemused, half imbecilic creature, propped up and goaded on by his power-hungry wife. There were even wild rumours to the effect that he had already died and that she and her liberal supporters were concealing the fact from the nation.

'The spectacle of a dying hero who remained at his post to the very end, did his duty, thought only of his people, his work, his calling, which at the same time was so moving, affecting, awe-inspiring and heart-rending, did not suggest the sublime to such cynical and mean souls,' declared Vicky. 'The long-drawn-out breath of a noble, courageous man and Emperor was merely a useless waste of time in their eyes!'

On the day after the King of Sweden's visit, Bismarck came again to Friedrichskron. He wished to discuss the matter of Puttkamer's successor with the Kaiser. When the Chancellor was about to take his leave, the Empress entered the room. Taking hold of her hand, the Emperor laid it in Bismarck's. The dumb and dying man then looked from one to the other; both realized that the Kaiser was committing his wife to the Chancellor's care. 'Your Majesty may rest assured,' murmured Bismarck, 'that I shall never forget that Her Majesty is my Queen.'

But Vicky refused to be comforted. She appreciated that Bismarck might harbour a certain feudal loyalty to his master, the Emperor, but she knew that this feeling did not extend to herself any more than it had done to Kaiser Wilhelm I's consort, Augusta. On taking leave of him she fancied she saw, in his bulbous eyes, a 'look of triumph, of relief and joy' at the prospect of the Emperor's obviously imminent death. 'My heart was cold,' she afterwards exclaimed, 'as if death's icy fingers were about it, and the pain was hard and cruel.'

By now even she realized that her husband could not live for many more days. She therefore put into operation a plan which she had been contemplating for some time. Determined that the full story of the campaign against her husband and herself should one day be revealed and that justice should be done to their memory, she had to make sure that their private papers did not fall into Bismarck's—or Wilhelm's—hands. The only way to ensure this was to smuggle the papers out of the country. Already, during their visit to England for the Queen's Jubilee the year before, she had deposited three boxes of papers in a safe at Buckingham Palace. Now, on 14 June, she arranged for yet more personal papers to be secreted to England. A Mr Inman Bernard, special correspondent of the *New York Herald*, was invited to call at Friedrichskron where he was handed a parcel by Sir Morell Mackenzie. This he was asked to deliver to the British Embassy in Berlin with instructions for the Ambassador to send it on to Queen Victoria. Presumably this was done, for on 17 June the Queen noted that the Military Attaché had arrived from Berlin with some of Kaiser Frederick III's papers for her safe-keeping.

That the Empress's somewhat melodramatic precautions had been justified was soon to become startlingly clear.

2

At three o'clock on the morning of 14 June, the Empress was woken by a slight sound in her room. Dr Mackenzie was standing by her bed. 'I wanted to tell you that the pulse has become quicker and weaker and the breathing more rapid in the last half-hour,' he whispered. 'The Emperor seems in no pain or discomfort, the fever is still high. This is a bad sign.' Flinging on a wrap, the Empress hurried to the sickroom. As she did not want to alarm the patient by appearing at such an unusual time, she stood by the door, listening. The Kaiser, who was being fanned all the time, was restless; he coughed incessantly. She could hear the grating sound of the air passing in and out of the cannula.

Towards morning Dr Mackenzie sent a telegram to Queen Victoria. It announced that the Emperor was sinking. Yet during the course of the day there was a slight improvement. As it was the birthday of his third daughter Sophie, the Kaiser was able to hand her a bouquet to mark the occasion. Vicky sat by his bedside for most of the day, soothing him, diverting him, helping him write down his questions. 'What is happening to me?' he wrote at one stage. Telegrams were sent off to Prince Wilhelm, Princess Charlotte and the honeymooning Prince Henry, summoning them to the palace. During the afternoon the British Ambassador, Sir Edward Malet, called. 'The worst is feared within the next twenty-four hours,' he telegraphed to Queen Victoria. 'His Majesty's head is quite clear and he is suffering no pain. The Empress was deeply moved, but collected.'

On receipt of this the Queen sent a telegram to Prince Wilhelm. 'Am in greatest distress at this terrible news, and so troubled about poor, dear Mama. Do all you can, as I asked you, to help her at this terrible time of dreadful trial and grief. God help us!'

That night the Empress slept on a chaise-longue which had been drawn close to the open doorway of the Emperor's room. Again the Emperor lay awake for most of the night, coughing and constantly changing position. During the following morning, 15 June, the sickroom gradually filled up with members of the family, doctors, officials and servants. 'Are the doctors satisfied with my condition?' asked the Kaiser. The Empress assured him that they were. When she asked if he were tired, he nodded, mouthing, 'Very, very!' At a quarter-past eleven that morning he suddenly took three deep breaths, closed his eyes as if in pain and then died.

The Empress crossed to the wall and, taking down the withered laurel wreath which she had given him after the Franco-Prussian War, she laid it on his chest. Then from a corner she fetched his service sword and rested it in his arm. She folded his hands and kissed them. With that, she left the room.

'Oh! my husband, my darling, my Fritz!!' wrote the distracted Vicky to her mother that night. 'So good, so kind, so tender, brave, patient and noble, so cruelly tried, taken from the nation, the wife and daughters that did so need him. His mild just rule was not to be....'

Queen Victoria, in a telegram to the old Empress Augusta, admitted that her daughter's misfortune was far worse than her own had been on the death of Prince Albert. To her grandson, now Kaiser Wilhelm II, the Queen wired, 'I am brokenhearted. Help and do all you can for your poor dear Mother and try to follow in your best, noblest, and kindest of father's footsteps. GRANDMAMA V.R.I.'

The Queen would have been appalled to know what the first acts of the new Kaiser's reign were to be.

3

As soon as it had become apparent that Kaiser Frederick was dying, his son's long-premeditated plan was put into action. Throughout the night of 14 June the grounds and corridors of Friedrichskron were full of stealthy movement and whispered instructions. Everything was being made ready for the moment of the Emperor's death. The minute it arrived, at a quarter past eleven on the morning of 15 June, Major von Natzmer mounted his horse and galloped around the perimeter of the park, shouting his commands. Within seconds a regiment of hussars had surrounded the palace, sealing it off from the outside world. The gates were heavily guarded and soldiers, with rifles at the ready, were stationed within the palace itself. Orders were given that no one, not even members of the imperial family, was allowed to leave Friedrichskron without a signed permit. All outgoing letters and telegrams were to be censored and all parcels examined. Any doctor attempting to leave would be arrested immediately; it was with considerable difficulty that the new Kaiser was dissuaded from arresting Dr Mackenzie there and then.

Once the palace had been successfully cordoned off, it was thoroughly searched. The Kaiser was anxious to lay his hands on his late father's private papers; he probably hoped, imagined the Empress, that he would uncover traces of 'liberal plots'. General von Winterfeld, once considered a devoted friend of Kaiser Frederick, had recently switched his allegiance to the son; he now flung himself on his late master's desk, ripping open anything that might contain incriminating documents. The young Kaiser himself, in his red hussar's uniform, ransacked his mother's room. They found nothing. The late Emperor's personal papers, for what they were worth, were safely stored at Buckingham Palace.

Nor did the Kaiser's callousness end with this particular outrage. In defiance of his late father's instructions and his mother's pleas, he permitted a post-mortem to be conducted on the Emperor's body. Whatever the earlier symptoms, that Fred-

193

erick III had died of cancer of the throat there was no longer any doubt; it was simply to underline the fact—as publicly as possible—that the German doctors had all along been right and the Empress and Mackenzie wrong that the Kaiser allowed the autopsy. The post-mortem was an extremely hurried and haphazard affair, with the verdict being pronounced on evidence of the naked eye only. 'I was mad with sorrow, anger and agitation that they dared to touch his dear, sacred mortal remains...' cried the helpless Vicky.

Then, on opening his father's will, the Kaiser read, addressed to himself, the following words. 'I wish to have it set in evidence as my unbiased personal opinion that I entirely acquiesce in the betrothal of your second sister with Prince Alexander of Battenberg. I charge you as a filial duty with the accomplishment of this my desire....' The Kaiser responded to this injunction by getting a letter off to Prince Alexander, even before Kaiser Frederick was buried, in which he forbade the match, claiming that this was the 'profound conviction previously held by my late deceased grandfather and father'.

Further disregarding the late Emperor's wishes, Kaiser Wilhelm made it clear that he objected to his father's name being perpetuated in the name of his palace; he gave orders that from henceforth the newly named Friedrichskron would again be known as the Neues Palais. Every scrap of writing paper bearing the heading of 'Friedrichskron' had to be handed over and burnt.

And, as a final insult to his father's memory, Kaiser Wilhelm II made a public announcement to the effect that he intended 'to follow the same path by which my deceased grandfather won the confidence of his allies, the love of the German people, and the goodwill of foreign countries'.

Kaiser Frederick III was buried on 18 June 1888. Over his heart his widow laid a medallion containing her picture and a lock of her hair. Then, taking her three youngest daughters, she fled from Friedrichskron to her farm at nearby Bornstedt. The Empress Frederick—as she was henceforth to be known—did not attend the funeral. It was just as well for, according to the new Kaiser's friend, Count Eulenburg, it was a hurried, far from imposing affair. Although 'the troops were dignified, the clergy were laughing and chattering. Field Marshal Blumenthal, with the Standard over his shoulder, reeling about, talking—it was horrible.'

PART FOUR

KAISER WILHELM II

CHAPTER TEN

THE ALL-HIGHEST

1

Kaiser Wilhelm II was twenty-nine when he ascended the imperial German throne. Although he had not yet perfected the theatrically heroic presence—the level stare, the upturned moustaches, the jutting chin, the gorgeous uniform and the aggressive stance—that was to be immortalized in so many hundreds of portraits and photographs, he was none the less an imposing-looking man. Already, in his first public appearances, he revealed signs of the showiness that was to be one of his chief characteristics. He was almost always in uniform, often with his great, gold, eagle-crowned helmet on his head and sometimes with a crimson mantle falling from his shoulders. His speech was emphatic and his manner assertive. His hand-shake was like a grip of iron. His walk was an energetic strut. Only that undersized left arm, which he was always careful to keep bent so as to minimize its shortness, rendered his presentation of himself as a warrior-monarch less than perfect. That, and his tendency to shift his gaze if looked at too hard.

He lost no time in surrounding himself with all the trappings of wealth, position and power. Not for him the austerities of Kaiser Wilhelm I or the aestheticism of Kaiser Frederick III; his court was the most opulent in Europe, almost Byzantine in its splendour. Within a few months of his accession he demanded an increase of six million marks a year. With this he set about renovating, rebuilding and embellishing. In Berlin he took up residence among the rococo splendours of the Old Schloss; at Potsdam he moved into the Neues Palais. 'The new rooms are very gorgeous,' wrote one guest, 'but it is all rather heavy and overloaded and wanting in real refinement.' The sober Court dress of previous days was replaced by something altogether more ornate—three-cornered hats, knee-breeches, silk stockings and buckled shoes. The palace guard was fitted out in the uniform of Frederick the Great's time; the apartments swarmed with costumed pages. A new royal train, painted white and gold, consisted of twelve carriages, with the Kaiser's saloon-carriage decorated in ice-blue silk and hung with dazzling chandeliers. A new royal yacht cost over four and a half million marks.

In these lavish settings, the Kaiser behaved like nothing so much as the leading actor in a never-ending pageant. He loved to display himself. With his gracious, ever-smiling, doll-like Empress by his side, he moved in a whirl of balls, receptions, parades and state visits. One night would find him in the imperial box at the opera; another would see him drinking the health of some royal guest at a banquet. He was never happier than when in some magnificent uniform, astride a great white charger, acknowledging the cheers of an enthusiastic crowd. He craved popularity and feasted on applause.

He had a passion for travel. Because of this, he soon became known as '*der Reise-Kaiser*'. Well over half of each year was spent away from Berlin; a member of the Household doubted if he was home for one hundred days a year. His yacht was for ever cruising the seas; his train was for ever crossing and re-crossing the Empire. His sudden journeys were the despair of his entourage, and his clamorous arrivals the dread of his hosts. 'The Prussians are coming!' would be the cry in the little German courts (as it was in the nurseries of France) when the Kaiser, with a flourish of trumpets and an enormous retinue, came clattering into the courtyard of some provincial Schloss. From then on everything would have to be done at the double; the company would be subjected to a succession of banquets, parlour games, practical jokes and uniform changes. The Kaiser always travelled with dozens of uniforms; his valets were on duty day and night.

His return home would be no less uproarious. Reaching the Neues Palais at midnight, he would make as much noise as if it were noon. His advent would be marked, noted one of Dona's long-suffering ladies, by 'a clatter of wheels and hooves, horses driven at breakneck speed, sentinels shouting and striking their fire-arms on the pavement, seneschal, adjutants, porters, secretaries, footmen and valets standing to attention, or flying hither and thither, and all candles and lamps in the passageways and rooms blazing forth'. Not for nothing did they call the Kaiser *Wilhelm der Plötzliche*—'Wilhelm the Sudden'.

His egotism was notorious. He would always refer to 'my army', 'my navy', 'my fortresses' and 'my ports'; he never missed an opportunity of drawing attention to 'my prowess' or 'my indefatigability'. He was for ever subjecting the older and plumper members of his entourage to rigorous physical exercise so as to point up his own agility. 'You should have seen von Hülsen or von Kessel puff and gasp after our half-hour's fencing,' he would boast, 'while I was as fresh as if I had just stepped from my bath.' Civic visitors' books and regimental bibles throughout Germany carried the Sovereign's vainglorious inscriptions. 'The Will of the King is the supreme law,' read one; and in the bible of the new Berlin garrison church, he wrote—without quotation marks—*Ye shall walk in all the ways which I have commanded you, Wilhelm Imperator Rex.*

That he was exceptionally talented—not only as a ruler and a soldier—he had no doubt. There were few things to which he did not turn his hand. He fancied himself as a poet, a novelist, a painter, a sculptor, an architect, a designer of ships, a sportsman, a strategist and a diplomat. He chose all his wife's hats and put them on display once a year so that all could appreciate the excellence of his taste. He would assure his listeners that, in common with Frederick the Great, he was an inspired composer. Nor, he would add, was this his only resemblance to his famous predecessor. 'Frederick is not dead,' he would declare, with a great thump of his chest, 'he lives here, and his mailed fist will clutch somebody's throat sooner or later.'

With his Empress, the submissive Dona, Wilhelm had very little to do. He paid lavish tribute to her in public (to a regiment in Bonn he once declared that the smile she had bestowed on them that day would henceforth ennoble their lives) but in private he all but ignored her. He seldom took her with him on his journeys and hardly ever wrote to her while he was away. According to one of her ladies, she would usually receive a curt message from an adjutant to say that, 'His Majesty shot so many hares, stuck a prodigious number of pigs, or killed so many deer or buck; weather such and such. ...' Once, when a minister asked her to intervene on some State matter, Dona assured him that the Kaiser would simply say, 'Go away; you don't understand these things.' On another occasion, when she protested at his cancelling of a dinner party, he answered gruffly, 'I decide these things—not you.'

Yet she never complained. Indeed, she would not have had him otherwise. To her adoring eyes his increasing eccentricities were simply manifestations of his genius. She made it her business to see that he was never angered or upset and lived in a constant flutter lest this happen. Apart from this dedication to him, her interests were confined to her large family, her sumptuous clothes and her God. 'Religion,' as one of her more cynical ladies put it, 'makes an excellent cloak for insignificance,' and the insignificant Dona undoubtedly made a great show of her piety. She is said to have been responsible for the building of forty-two new churches during the first ten years of the reign. To her, no less than to her husband, God had a special interest in Germany. 'I am helped,' Kaiser Wilhelm II once said, 'to press forward on the road which heaven has marked out for me by my feeling of responsibility to the Ruler of all and by my firm conviction that God ... who has taken so much trouble over our homeland and our dynasty, will not desert us now.'

Such reasoning made perfect sense to Dona. She was, says Princess Radziwill, 'the perfect German *Hausfrau*, believing firmly that God created supermen when He created Germans, and expecting everybody to believe in this fact as in the Gospels. For her there was only one thing which counted, the prosperity, glory and superiority of Germany over any other nation on earth. She was the living incarnation of *"Deutschland über alles"*....'

Dona hated foreigners. To her all Russians were barbarians, all Frenchmen immoral, all Mediterranean races untrustworthy and all the British 'selfish and unscrupulous hypocrites, for whom she felt even less affection than the rest'.

The Kaiser's closest companion was still the urbane Count Eulenburg. 'I pray from the depths of my soul,' gushed Eulenburg on Wilhelm's accession, 'that Your Majesty will deign to continue the patronage which has become a radiance in my life.' His Majesty was only too happy to oblige and by continuing to favour Eulenburg, was able to benefit from the older man's experience. 'Never forget that H.M. needs praise every now and again,' wrote Eulenburg to an official on one occasion. 'He is one of those people who gets out of sorts if they do not, from time to time, hear words of appreciation from the lips of some important person or other. You will always obtain his consent to your wishes so long as you do not neglect to express appreciation of H.M. whenever he deserves it.'

Prince Bismarck was not altogether happy about Eulenburg's hold over the young Kaiser. Count Eulenburg, grumbled the Chancellor, is 'something of a Prussian Cagliostro ... a mystic, a romantic rhetorician ... particularly dangerous for the dramatic temperament of our Emperor. In that high personage's presence he assumes adoring attitudes which I believe to be perfectly sincere. The Emperor has only to look up, and he is sure to find those eyes fixed worshipfully on him.'

Nor were Eulenburg's the only eyes so fixed. That so ostentatious a personality as Kaiser Wilhelm II should be surrounded by fawners and flatterers was to be expected. He lived in an aura of adulation. His circle was as artificial and theatrical as himself. It was Count Eulenburg's particular qualities—the romanticism, the extravagance, the sentimentality and the effeminacy—which pervaded the entire imperial entourage. Everything was lush, unnatural, larger than life. 'As a personality His Majesty is charming, touching, irresistible, adorable ...' exclaimed a future State Secretary. His officers saw themselves as a band of medieval knights devotedly serving their liege rather than paid servants of the State. Generals bent to kiss the Kaiser's gloved hand, ambassadors overwhelmed him with praise, a Junker once immortalized a royal hunt by having engraved, in gold on a granite block, the inscription: 'At this point His Majesty bagged a white cock pheasant, the fifty-thousandth creature to fall before the All-Highest.'

'Our sublime, mighty, beloved Kaiser, King and Lord for all times, for ever and ever ...' were the opening words of an address to Wilhelm, rendered somewhat less effective by the fact that they had been written by the Kaiser himself and delivered by his brother, Prince Henry.

However, it was not often that Wilhelm left the speech-making to others. He was an enthusiastic orator. In his loud and grating voice, he would harangue his long-suffering audiences for hours on end. To him, the sound of his own voice was only fractionally less pleasurable than the roar of applause that followed its cessation. As what he said was not always tactful ('tactlessness is masculine,' claimed one of his apologists) there were those who came to dread the tireless exercise of what he considered to be his God-given eloquence. 'If Your Majesty would be a little more economical of such a gift,' ventured

Count Eulenburg on one occasion, 'it would be a hundred times more efficacious.'

The Count was right. The Kaiser's first proclamation to the army had sent a shiver of apprehension through Europe's chancelleries. 'We belong to each other—I and the Army——' thundered the Kaiser, 'we were born for each other and will cleave indissolubly to each other, whether it be the Will of God to send us calm or storm. You will soon swear fealty and submission to me, and I promise ever to bear in mind that from the world above the eyes of my forefathers look down upon me, and that I shall have one day to stand accountable to them for the glory and honour of the Army.'

His dead ancestors, presumably, were keeping an eye on his handling of domestic politics as well. In his speeches to civilian audiences, he was no less bombastic. He once assured a group of striking employees at the Krupp Works that if they had anything to do with the Social Democratic Party, he would have them all shot down. For this particular show of statesmanship, the Kaiser was roundly applauded by his sycophantic entourage.

Moving in such a golden glow of approbation, any slight to his dignity cut him to the quick. His sense of inferiority did not lie very far below that assured and brilliant surface. He could never quite shake himself free of the suspicion that some of his relations, and the British royal family in particular, did not take his new status quite seriously enough. Not long after his accession, the Kaiser complained, through official channels, to Queen Victoria, that the Prince of Wales tended to treat him as a nephew rather than as an Emperor. This impertinence earned him one of his grandmother's most withering replies.

'This is really too *vulgar* and too absurd,' wrote the Queen to Lord Salisbury, 'as well as untrue, almost *to be believed*.

'We have always been very intimate with our grandson and nephew, and to pretend that he is to be treated *in private* as well as in public as "his Imperial Majesty" is *perfect madness*! He has been treated just as we should have treated his beloved father and even grandfather, and as the Queen *herself* was always treated by her dear uncle King Leopold. *If* he has *such* notions, he [had] better *never* come *here*.

'The Queen will not swallow this affront.'

This was not the Queen's only complaint against her grandson. She considered the haste with which he embarked on a series of State visits, so soon after his father's death, to be unseemly. Kaiser Frederick III was hardly cold before his son announced his intention of visiting the Courts of St Petersburg, Vienna and Rome. When the Queen advised him, as tactfully as possible, to postpone these tours until some months had passed, he felt it necessary to remind her, rather less tactfully, that, as a fellow sovereign, he had his duties to fulfil. The 'complete stagnation' of his late father's reign had meant that he simply could not afford to wait until the etiquette of Court mourning had been fulfilled. 'I deem it necessary,' he said, 'that monarchs should meet often and confer together to look out for dangers which threaten the monarchical principle from democratic and republican parties in all parts of the world.'

For England's constitutional Queen, this was too much. 'Trust that we shall be *very cool*, though civil, in our communications with my grandson and Prince Bismarck,' she wired to Lord Salisbury, 'who are bent on a return to the oldest times of government.'

As always, Wilhelm's version of the affair was rather different. Queen Victoria had insisted, he writes, that his first State visit be to her. His refusal, delivered with firmness but kindness, had opened her eyes to the fact that her grandson was now the German Emperor. 'From that day onward,' he claims, 'she never treated her grandson except as a sovereign of equal rank with herself.'

Yet, for all his arrogance, Kaiser Wilhelm II did not mean any real harm. His bark was much worse than his bite. He was not nearly as warlike or as reactionary as he liked to appear. He was a sabre-rattler, not a fighter. He preferred military manoeuvres to actual battle; bloodthirsty words to bloodthirsty deeds. He wanted to be a Napoleon, says Winston Churchill, without fighting Napoleon's battles; he wanted victories without wars. He might threaten to shoot down striking workers but he was already beginning to think in terms of legislation for the protection of employees. He wanted, he once announced, to be a *roi des gueux*. If one looked beyond the arrogantly waxed moustache which was soon to become his most prominent characteristic, one noticed a sensitive, almost diffident expression. For all his air of bravado, he was nervous (a loaded revolver lay always beside his bed), given to fits of blind panic and obsessed with his health.

Nor was he quite as foolish as he sometimes sounded. His mind was lively, his memory excellent and his intelligence well above average. He could, on occasion, be utterly charming. If Prince Hohenlohe's early assessment of him as 'a wise, conscientious man', not unlike Prince Albert, was too charitable, there is no doubt that, with his wide-ranging interests and his exceptional energy, Kaiser Wilhelm II was more than just an empty exhibitionist.

In many ways he epitomized the Germany of the Second Reich—militant, thrusting, power-conscious, ostentatious and ultra-sensitive. He was very much the product of his time and his environment. 'In William's soul,' writes Golo Mann, 'influences, traditions and dreams struggled with each other; English and Prussian elements, liberalism and absolutism, pacifism and military pageantry, imperial romanticism and the spirit of modern industrialism.'

Indeed, there were contained in this neurotic young man, almost all the elements which had kept the Hohenzollern dynasty in a state of turmoil for over thirty years. Over half a dozen different threads went to form the knot of his personality. The militarism of Kaiser Wilhelm I, the spiritedness of the Empress Augusta, the impulsiveness of Queen Victoria, the romanticism of Prince Albert, the idealism of the Emperor Frederick, the dogmatism of the Empress Frederick—all these, allied to the authoritarianism instilled into him by Bismarck, warred within the person of Kaiser Wilhelm II. To those who did not know him well, this conflict was not always apparent; his personality seemed merely many-faceted. As a consummate showman he could act out, now one part, now another. But it remained nothing more than a performance. Stripped of his mask, his costume, his props and his setting, he was a confused and unresolved personality.

What better way then, to hide his uncertainties, his sense of inferiority than by making the most of his theatrical trappings; than to stand always in a dazzling spotlight? For his own sake and for that of his regime, the Reich must be kept *en fête* from morning to night. 'William does do the very oddest things,' reported the embittered Empress Frederick to Queen Victoria, 'the element of Show-off—noise and "sensation", dramatic effects, etc—is very preponderant and, in these serious times, seems to me very youthful. *Du sublime au ridicule—il n'y a qu'un pas* is as true now as it ever was! All the clanging bands

... the cannons firing salutes ... crowds hurrah-ing ... William is in his element and his glory.'

'If your father should die before I do,' the Empress Frederick had once written to her son Wilhelm, 'I shall leave at once. I will not stay in a country where I have had nothing but hatred and not a spark of affection.'

Now that she actually faced this situation, the Empress found herself unable to put her robustly expressed resolve into practice. Despite her attempted withdrawal from public affairs, she was too proud—as she put it—to run away and leave the field to her enemies. She knew that nothing would suit Bismarck, or Wilhelm, better than her disappearance; the German Ambassador in Vienna, after an interview with Kaiser Wilhelm II, was able to report that 'the Empress Frederick is a decided embarrassment for the Emperor Wilhelm, for, to his regret, she refuses to live abroad, but is obviously engaged in forming a Court for herself which may well become the centre of oppositional elements. ...'

Although there were no grounds for Wilhelm's fears that his mother might set up some sort of rival court, she none the less decided to stay on. The decision made, the question of her future home caused fresh clashes between herself and her son. She would have liked to remain at Friedrichskron (now the Neues Palais again) or, failing that, the nearby palace of Sans Souci. Neither suggestion found favour. Her request for Sans Souci was 'curtly and rudely refused' and she was told that she could remain at the Neues Palais only until she had found herself another home. She would be allowed to retain her palace in Berlin and could have the use of the castles of Homburg and Wiesbaden.

These unsatisfactory arrangements convinced her that she must have a place of her own and not merely the loan of some State building. About a year after her husband's death she bought herself an estate at Kronberg, near Homburg. Ever *die Engländerin*, she advised her German architect to go to England to study modern British architecture. As a result, there rose, in the chestnut-covered Taunus hills, not a German Schloss, but a vast country house in the mock-Tudor style so dear to English Victorian hearts. She called it Friedrichshof. Above the front porch were inscribed the words, '*Frederici Memoriae*'.

'His spirit shall rule there,' she declared, 'and in that way alone can his poor, forsaken, broken wife have any peace in her loneliness and sorrow.'

But peace eluded her now as surely as it had ever done. For one thing, her passionate nature would simply not allow her to accept the changed circumstances of her life. For years she had been forced to stand waiting in the wings; after a brief, unappreciated appearance, she was back in the wings, without hope of another opportunity. Despite her professed disinterest, she resented the way in which she was being brushed aside as though of no consequence. No one consoled her, no one consulted her, no one deferred to her. Her husband's death was not mourned; her own eclipse not regretted. As soon as she left the Neues Palais it was taken over by the new Court. 'To think of the room our beloved one closed his eyes in now simply used as a passage—strangers going to and fro and laughing, etc. All the rooms we inhabited and where I suffered such untold agonies, after one short year occupied by others, and the home ringing with noise, laughter and merriment before a year is out, pains me so bitterly!' she complained. She considered Wilhelm more insufferable than ever, she found Dona, with her 'grand condescending airs' extremely aggravating, she thought the way in which Bismarck and his clique were trying to wipe out all traces of her husband's reign quite shameful. 'The sooner he is forgotten the better, therefore the sooner his widow disappears, the better also,' she wrote bitterly to her mother.

Queen Victoria, while sympathizing with her bereaved daughter, understood her nature only too well. She thus wrote Kaiser Wilhelm, a few weeks after his father's death, a very sensible letter. 'Let me also ask you to bear with poor Mama if she is sometimes irritated and excited,' she wrote. 'She does not mean it so; think what months of agony and suspense and watching with broken sleepless nights she has gone through, and *don't mind it*. I am so anxious that all should go smoothly, that I write this openly in the interests of you both.'

But she was blowing against a hurricane. The relations between the Kaiser and his mother continued as bad as ever. 'My mother and I,' wrote Wilhelm with some sagacity at this time, 'have the same characters. I have inherited hers. That good stubborn English blood which will not give way is in both our veins. The consequence is that, if we do not happen to agree, the situation becomes difficult.'

Indeed, Queen Victoria was correct in surmising that the fault might not lie entirely with the young Kaiser; there are indications that he did sometimes try to make himself pleasant. Vicky's friend, Lady Ponsonby, tactfully suggested that if the Empress were 'resolutely to abstain from listening to the reports which, perhaps well-meaning, but certainly officious friends hasten to furnish, this would be a great gain.' The Empress's sister, Princess Christian, who was visiting Berlin at this time, decided that the Kaiser's rudeness to his mother was more a matter of thoughtlessness than intention. He meant well; it was simply that his manner was so unfortunate. Nor did the Empress make the slightest effort to meet him halfway. Princess Christian, who came to a quick understanding of the young man's character, advised her sister to flatter him by consulting him about little things; this way she would win his confidence and gain considerable influence over him.

But things had gone too far for such remedies. And they were made worse by the continuing campaign of vilification of the Empress Frederick. It was almost as vicious now as it had been during the late Emperor's lifetime. A few weeks after her husband's death, Vicky heard that a brochure on his illness, written by the German doctors headed by Bergmann, was about to be published. Knowing that it would rake up all the old controversies, she begged her son, verbally, in writing and by telegram, to prevent its publication. He refused. When she threatened that she would get Mackenzie to answer the report, Wilhelm remained unimpressed. 'Let him answer,' he shrugged, 'it's all the same to me.'

The report was published in July 1888 and served as a fresh indictment of the Empress. 'The publication about my darling Fritz's illness, permitted and authorized by William, makes me quite ill!' cried the Empress. 'It is an outrage to all my feelings, I think cruel and disgraceful! He has no heart, he cannot understand how insulting it is to have all the details which concern so harrowing and painful a thing as the illness of one's own dear husband, father of one's children, officially dragged before the public, in order to satisfy the spite and vanity of four people, Bergmann, Gerhardt, Bramann and Landgraf!

They are to be considered first, and I afterwards!'

Sir Morell Mackenzie, smarting under the attack of the German doctors, sought Queen Victoria's permission to defend himself. The Queen, who did not share her daughter's blind faith in Mackenzie, agreed that he should answer the report but warned him that he must confine himself to medical matters. He was not to drag politics, or the Empress, into the controversy. In a letter to Vicky, the Queen explained that Mackenzie was neither popular nor especially highly regarded in British medical circles. But the Empress would not hear a word against him; once she had given her support, nothing would induce her to withdraw it. Thus, when the Kaiser, pursuing his vendetta against his mother and Mackenzie, decorated the German doctors, she was furious. Immediately she dashed a letter off to Queen Victoria, begging her to honour Mackenzie in turn. This the Queen very wisely refused to consider. 'It would not do him any good,' she explained, 'and would do you and me harm. . . .'

She was right. Even without an honour for Mackenzie, the Empress was harmed by his behaviour. When he published his version of the controversy in a book entitled *The Fatal Illness of Frederick the Noble*, it created an uproar. He attacked the German doctors in no uncertain terms, accusing them of incompetence, brutality and even drunkenness. This unethical production earned him, not only the condemnation of the Royal College of Surgeons, but a fresh outburst of vituperation from Germany. Scratching around for what they imagined would be the worst possible insult, his enemies accused him of being a Jew whose real name was Moritz Markovicz. The German translation of his book was confiscated and its sale prohibited. 'They have no right to do so . . .' declared the Empress. 'William and Bismarck have decided that Bergmann's version is alone to be heard and believed.' The ban was simply another example of the police state which now flourished in Germany.

This particular fracas was as nothing, however, compared with the furore over another publication that autumn: this was part of *The War Diary of the Emperor Frederick*.

In late September 1888, the *Deutsche Rundschau* ran a series of extracts said to be taken from a diary kept by the late Kaiser Frederick during the Franco-Prussian War of 1870–1. The extracts revealed to the German public the true story of the negotiations at Versailles which had led to the establishment of the Second Reich. They now learnt, for the first time, that it had been Crown Prince Frederick and not, as they had been led to believe, Wilhelm I and Bismarck, who had been the driving force behind the final realization of this great achievement. It had been he who, in the face of his father's antagonism and the Chancellor's hesitancy, had fought doggedly for the inauguration of the German Empire. The much vaunted proclamation in the Galerie des Glaces at Versailles, for which Bismarck had always taken all the credit, had been the realization of the Crown Prince's, and not of Bismarck's dream.

That the Chancellor was incensed by these revelations can be appreciated. Both he and Kaiser Wilhelm II were said to be in 'a state of fury and excitement' about it. Bismarck lost no time in publishing an official answer to the *Deutsche Rundschau*'s extracts. The diary, he maintained, was a forgery. What he really thought was clear from his frank remark to his confidant, Busch, that 'we must first treat it as a forgery ... then, when it is proved genuine by the production of the original, it can be dealt with further in another way.' In any case, continued Bismarck in his public repudiation of the diary, the Crown Prince Frederick had known nothing of such affairs of State, as he could not be trusted with confidential information: Wilhelm I, asserted the Chancellor, 'feared indiscreet remarks to the English Court which was in sympathy with France'. This, of course, was a thrust at the Empress Frederick whom Bismarck suspected of having given the extracts to the newspaper. To discredit her still further, he let it be known that the person responsible for the publication would be prosecuted for high treason for stealing and revealing State secrets.

The Empress, in fact, had had nothing to do with the matter. 'I was much surprised and also annoyed at the publication which is extremely injudicious and indiscreet!' she wrote to Queen Victoria soon after the appearance of the extracts. 'Of course,' she added, 'it is all true. . . .'

It was indeed, and the person responsible for the publication revealed himself a day or two afterwards. He was Heinrich Geffcken, a Professor of Political Science and one-time adviser to the late Emperor Frederick. It appears that some fifteen years before, the Crown Prince Frederick had had certain extracts from his War Diary copied and circulated among his friends. It was these that Geffcken, on his own initiative, had

had reproduced in the *Deutsche Rundschau*. Bismarck promptly had Geffcken arrested for treason.

The Empress was furious; not only with Bismarck for his brutality but with her family for the way in which they—who knew the truth of the Versailles negotiations and of the circulation of the extracts—supported the Chancellor against her in the controversy. All of them, the Kaiser, Prince Henry, Princess Charlotte, the old Empress Augusta and her daughter and son-in-law, the Duke and Duchess of Baden, kept silent in the face of Bismarck's attacks on the late Kaiser Frederick. Seeing her sons side with her enemies made her realize what Caesar must have felt on being stabbed by Brutus, declared the Empress. Queen Victoria was no less incensed. She felt 'too furious, too, too indignant, too savage, also' to trust herself to speak of Kaiser Wilhelm's behaviour.

Once Geffcken had revealed the source of the extracts, the accusation against him had to be withdrawn. Bismarck kept suspicion against the Empress alive, however, by letting it be known that a list of the late Emperor Frederick's associates had been drawn up by the police and that their houses were likely to be searched. She was even indirectly accused of having stolen the cipher which her husband had used for his secret State correspondence; only by exercising the utmost restraint did the Empress stop herself from suing Bismarck for this particular piece of slander. 'It is obviously to try and exasperate me so that I may leave the country altogether in disgust and return no more,' she told her mother as the innuendoes against her mounted.

It was becoming imperative, however, that she leave the country for a period. To afford her distracted daughter some relief from this persecution, Queen Victoria invited her to spend the winter of 1888–9 with her at Windsor. At this Lord Salisbury, in his anxiety not to upset Anglo-German relations further, took fright. He intimated to the Queen that it might be better, in view of the friction between the Kaiser, his mother and Bismarck, for the Empress Frederick to postpone her visit. The suggestion earned him a sharp rebuke. 'Letter received. Intention doubtless well meant...' wired the Queen. She went on to explain that such timidity would simply 'encourage' the Kaiser and the Bismarcks; 'you all seem frightened of them, which is not the way to make them better', she declared. She wanted no one to mention the matter of postponement again.

Nor did anyone dare to do so. When the Empress Frederick arrived, on 19 November 1888, the Queen saw to it that she was received with all honour due to her. The Prince of Wales was sent across to Flushing in the royal yacht to bring her home; the Queen, accompanied by a galaxy of royal relations and the German Ambassador, went down to Port Victoria to meet her; there were guards of honour, fanfares of trumpets and an abundance of flags. On 21 November, the Empress's forty-eighth birthday, there was a reception at Windsor at which the entire German Embassy and the English Court were presented to her. 'I made darling Vicky go first everywhere,' noted the Queen. That was the way to bring Wilhelm and Bismarck to their senses.

It was while the Empress was in England that she learnt that yet another of her schemes had turned to dust. Prince Alexander of Battenberg announced his marriage to the singer, Joanna Loisinger. In a letter to his brother (the Queen's son-in-law, Prince Henry of Battenberg) Sandro explained that having met with nothing but rebuffs, refusals and insults, he was determined, at least, to have a quiet and happy home life. The Queen, although saddened by the news, was worldly enough to accept the situation. It must be given out, she instructed Lord Salisbury, that the lady bore the highest character, was highly educated and that Prince Alexander 'had never visited her till he had proposed to her'.

The Empress was not so easily resigned. 'I cannot get over it,' she exlaimed with a characteristic blend of loyalty and naivety. 'It wrung one's heart to think of the way he has been persecuted, ill-used, hunted down—and driven to despair!'

Sandro, who had taken the title of Count Hartenau, did not enjoy married life long. In 1893, at the age of thirty-six, he died of peritonitis. He was buried in Sofia, amidst those scenes in which he had experienced such excitements and such heartbreak.

It must have been with almost as much relief as disappointment that Moretta, kept in suspense for a decade, was able to turn her attention elsewhere. The following year she became engaged to Prince Adolf zu Schaumburg-Lippe. 'We were mutually attracted to each other,' she noted in her memoirs, 'and I believe it was a case of love at first sight.'

This was not Moretta's last romance. At the age of sixty-one, some ten years after the death of her husband during the First World War, the Princess married a virile Russian adventurer half her age. His name was Alexander Zubkov. Having squandered her fortune, Zubkov abandoned her and she died two years later, in 1929, homeless, penniless and disowned by her family.

The Empress Frederick returned to Germany at the end of February 1889. There can be no doubt that three months away from the turbulent atmosphere of the German Court, combined with some sound advice from Queen Victoria, had had a calming effect on her. The Kaiser, for his part, seems to have been anxious for an improvement in the relationship between his mother and himself. During her absence he admitted to Count Waldersee that he regretted the differences between them; he hoped that her stay in England would 'put an end to these for ever and make them disappear for good and all'.

Given their characters, this was impossible, but from this point on (if only because the Empress was by now stripped of all influence) their relationship was not so continuously stormy.

3

For the seventy-seven-year-old Empress Augusta, the accession of her grandson, Kaiser Wilhelm II, meant a new lease of life. With her daughter-in-law, the Empress Frederick, being so unpopular at Court and the new Kaiserin, Dona, having so little taste or talent for public life, the Empress Augusta was forced into the limelight once more. This turn of events delighted her. She had always been happiest in the thick of things. The fact that her grandson's despotism was opposed to everything for which she had battled so vehemently in youth and middle-age seems to have bothered her no longer. Her love of pomp, of position and of political involvement had proved stronger than her liberalism. Given the choice of retiring from public life or of associating herself with her grandson's showy regime, she plumped for the more important role. Her liberalism had always been of an emotional rather than a rational variety; she now traded her principles for a taste of power.

The new Kaiser was only too glad of her co-operation. Anxious to identify himself with the glories of his grandfather's reign, Wilhelm II found reassurance in the presence of Wilhelm I's Empress. She lent to his Court a comforting air of continuity. He flattered her, he consulted her, he encouraged her. There was a continuous to-ing and fro-ing between his palace and hers; 'they ask the Empress Augusta about everything', ran one jaundiced report. And she, in turn, deferred to him at all times. She received his protégés, she entertained his friends, she never left Berlin nor even changed her residence without first getting his permission. Unlike his mother, the Empress Augusta always treated the new Kaiser as the Head of the House.

'The Weimar Princess,' wrote Wilhelm II, 'had become to the very core a Prussian Queen and a German Empress. That she was the best of grandmothers to me at the same time, I shall always remember to my dying day.'

Her palace of Babelsberg was almost as busy as it had been in her heyday. There were audiences, dinners and receptions without number. Her spirit remained unconquerable; her vitality unimpaired. Although frail, crippled and aged, she was as tireless as ever. Indeed, Prince Hohenlohe reported her as looking 'better than formerly, her voice clearer and more intelligible'. Her glance was as penetrating, her tongue as sharp and her interest as lively as they had ever been. She looked no less bizarre: 'dressed in pale blue satin, with jewels to her waist, her venerable head crowned with a magnificent tiara, she made a brave, if somewhat pathetic, figure', reported one of her many guests.

She even patched up her life-long feud with Bismarck. Writing from Baden-Baden towards the end of the year 1888, she thanked the Chancellor for having stood loyally by her late husband and for having supported her grandson. 'In hours of bitterness you have shown sympathy to me, therefore I feel myself called upon, before I complete this year, to thank you once again and at the same time to reckon on the continuance of your help in the midst of these painful events of a stirring time....'

And Bismarck, in his turn, was ready to forgive her. He even managed to find something good to say about her. 'She often made things difficult for me,' he mused, 'but she never ceased to be a woman of distinction, animated by a lively sense of duty....'

The embittered Empress Frederick found the Empress Augusta's behaviour inexplicable. On Kaiser Frederick's death, his Empress had sent his mother an anguished telegram: 'For your only son, she, who was proud and happy to be his wife, weeps...! No mother ever had such a son,' ran the heart-broken phrases. Now, a matter of mere months later, the Empress Augusta seemed to have forgotten, not only her son, but everything that he had stood for. 'We wanted nothing else than what she gave herself endless trouble to effect with her own son,' complained Vicky to Queen Victoria. 'She wished him to have less prejudices, *einen freieren, weiteren Blick* [a freer, wider outlook] than the rest of his family and did him an immense service thereby, but she completely turned round of late years....' Backed up by those other erstwhile supporters of the Emperor Frederick—her daughter and son-in-law, the Duke and Duchess of Baden—the Empress Augusta was wasting no time on regretting the past. Although always kind to her son's widow, she made very little effort to sympathize with or comfort her. What a support, declared Vicky, the two of them could have been to each other. Both widowed, enlightened Empresses, they could have tried to keep alive the late Kaiser Frederick's ideals; 'but she has long gone over to the other camp,' sighed the Empress Frederick.

In answer to this complaint, Queen Victoria advised her daughter not to waste 'loving expressions from your warm bleeding heart on one who really is incapable of understanding them or you. Pray don't.'

For all the Empress Augusta's new-found sense of importance, however, she could not last much longer. No amount of rouge could hide the gauntness of her cheek and no wealth of trimming the pathetic frailty of her body. By the end of 1889 she was looking more like a painted corpse than ever. The American Minister, received in audience by her a day or two before the New Year, says that he 'saw at a glance that the task was beyond her strength, and that she assumed it because it was a Sovereign's duty....' He reports her as saying that she had only one wish: 'that is that people will say of me after I am dead, "She was a good woman"'.

Early in 1890 she caught influenza and on 7 January she died. She was seventy-eight years old. 'I suppose that no woman had a sadder youth or middle age than hers,' commented Walburga Paget.

Dead, the Empress Augusta was vouchsafed one last moment of glory: her lying-in-state was magnificent. For a couple of days she not only held the centre of the stage but seemed to have recaptured the youth which she had striven so desperately to maintain. They dressed her in the gown of cloth-of-gold which she had worn for her Golden Wedding. Her false chestnut ringlets were arranged across her forehead, her eyebrows and eyelashes skilfully painted; from the golden myrtle wreath that crowned her head, a gold-spangled tulle veil cascaded over her shoulders, carefully draped to hide the sagging flesh of her chin. At her wrists were her bracelets and on her hand her wedding ring. They laid her in a coffin so surrounded by flowers that it looked more like a bed. The golden train of her dress, lined with ermine, covered her feet and flowed out of the coffin and down the steps of the dais on which she lay. It was almost as though she were about to attend a fête or a soirée.

'She looked wonderfully well and almost like a young person,' reported the Empress Frederick. 'I felt that if she could have seen herself she would have been pleased. She was "the Empress" even in death and surrounded with all the stiff pomp and ceremony she loved so much.'

Judging by the way the Empress Frederick was treated at the funeral, she, too, might just as well have been dead. Standing under the suffocating blaze of lights in the chapel of the Schloss, she was all but ignored. 'I felt so lonely, so helpless among them all . . .' she told her mother. 'No one took me up or down stairs and one feels so set on one side, so forgotten, that to all my pain it gives me a feeling of bitterness difficult to describe.'

The Empress Augusta was buried on 11 January 1890. Of those six characters once caught up in the Hohenzollern maelstrom—the Emperor Wilhelm I and the Empress Augusta, the Emperor and Empress Frederick, the Emperor Wilhelm II, and Prince Bismarck—three now remained. Of these, the Empress Frederick counted for almost nothing. Only the Kaiser and Bismarck still held positions of power.

4

'We Hohenzollerns,' Kaiser Wilhelm II once assured a somewhat startled fellow sovereign, 'are the bailiffs of God.'

That the Kaiser could make this grandiloquent claim was due, not only to his overweening conceit, but to Bismarck's deliberate policy of near-deification of the German Emperor. The Chancellor had organized the state in such a way as to make the Kaiser all-powerful; in theory it was the Emperor who ruled the Reich. Bismarck always claimed that it was the 'Emperor's policy' that he was carrying out. The Kaiser, he once announced to a sceptical Reichstag, was the real Minister–President of the country. The Chancellor was merely the master's mouthpiece.

This exaltation of the Emperor was a major part of the system by which Bismarck had retained control of the destinies of the Second Reich for almost twenty years. Provided the Chancellor was able to manipulate the Emperor, he was able to manipulate the Empire in the Emperor's name. He could be dismissed by no one other than the Emperor. This had always been his strength. Now it was to prove his weakness.

As long as the Chancellor had had to contend with the pliable Kaiser Wilhelm I and the dying Kaiser Frederick III, his position had been secure. His fears that, through the machinations of either the Empress Augusta or the Empress Frederick, he might be dismissed had been groundless; he had always proved indispensable. But now something was beginning to go wrong. In Kaiser Wilhelm II, Bismarck found himself dealing with a much less manageable personality. Despite the fact that he had nurtured him since boyhood, the Chancellor felt that the new Emperor was not showing nearly enough gratitude or respect; indeed, he was revealing an alarmingly independent streak. The Kaiser tended to take what Bismarck had been saying all these years quite seriously: this opinionated young man really seemed to believe that he was all-powerful, that the Chancellor was there to carry out his policy, that he, and not Bismarck, was the 'real Minister–President' of the country. The new Emperor was coming to a realization that he was indeed 'a bailiff of God', answerable to no man, not even Bismarck. More and more, it must have seemed to the apprehensive Chancellor, had his role been that of Frankenstein.

A decade before, Bismarck would probably have known how to handle this uppity young man but by now he was beginning to lose his grip. He was in his seventies already, tired, truculent, set in his ways. He was spending longer and ever longer periods on his estates, away from the worries of the Chancellery in Berlin; for eight of the first eighteen months of the new Kaiser's reign, the Chancellor was away from the capital. 'My father lacks the old hammer stroke,' remarked one of his sons. Faced with the Kaiser's defiance, the Chancellor was quite likely to burst into tears.

In his show of independence, the Kaiser was being backed up to the hilt by his entourage. He would never become a powerful ruler, they whispered to him, while he remained Bismarck's puppet. Frederick the Great, whom the new Kaiser was hoping to emulate, would never have been so splendid a monarch had he allowed himself to be governed by a man like Bismarck. The Chancellor's dismissal would open up a 'mine of popularity' for the Kaiser and serve as proof positive of his greatness. To Wilhelm, who admitted to no doubts about his own capabilities, such innuendoes were melodious indeed. He, who longed, not only to shine but to dazzle, could certainly never do so while he remained in Bismarck's giant shadow.

There were other reasons for the Kaiser's dissatisfaction with Bismarck. They disagreed on so many things. Hitherto, the quarrels which had bedevilled the relationship between the six leading actors in the Hohenzollern drama had never occurred between Wilhelm II and Bismarck. Now they did little else but quarrel. 'In my discussions [with Bismarck],' complained the Kaiser to the British Ambassador, 'he treated me like a schoolboy. When I urged that I believed that the Ministers were really in favour of my views ... he told me that they were all blackguards and cowards. He became so violent on occasions, that I did not know whether he would not throw the inkstand at my head....'

Their main disagreement was over domestic policies. The Kaiser, no less anxious than Bismarck to preserve an authoritarian monarchy, believed that the way to do this was by placating the working classes; some of the causes of their discontent must be removed. Bismarck, now as always, believed in a rigid suppression of this discontent. The Kaiser wanted to be looked upon as undisputed ruler of all the Germans, including the workers; Bismarck continued to consider the largely working-class Social Democratic Party as an enemy of the State. The Kaiser's scheme for doing something to prevent the exploitation of the workers was dismissed by Bismarck as 'humanitarian rubbish'. Indeed, far from conceding any need for reform, the Chancellor was anxious to make the anti-Socialist law—introduced twelve years earlier after Nobiling's attack on old Kaiser Wilhelm I—a permanent one. This the Reichstag refused to do. Their lack of co-operation alarmed and infuriated Bismarck. If the present Reichstag, in which he was usually certain of a majority, defied him, what would happen when he had to deal with a less sympathetic one? If he were to lose the support of both Kaiser and Reichstag, what would happen to him?

He found out soon enough. New elections were held in February 1890. As Bismarck was unable to invent some threat to the Reich and so stampede the electorate into voting for conservative deputies, his supporters suffered a crushing defeat. The *Freisinnige* Party (once known as Crown Prince Frederick's party) and the Social Democrats doubled their votes; together with the other opposition party—the Centre Party— these three now formed a majority against the defeated National Liberals.

Faced with this situation, Bismarck did not know what to do. He began thinking in terms of fresh parliamentary combinations (he tried wooing old arch-enemy, Windthorst of the Centre Party), of changing the constitution, of abolishing universal suffrage, of a brutal campaign against the Social Democrats. There was even a bizarre scheme whereby the various German princes would be asked to dissolve the Reich. He was ready for anything that would keep him in power; anything, that is, short of submitting himself to the new Kaiser's will.

This suited Kaiser Wilhelm perfectly. Assured that Bismarck had lost the support, not only of his colleagues but of the voters, the young Kaiser felt confident to move against him. 'It is now a question of whether the Emperor or the Chancellor has the upper hand,' wrote Wilhelm to his fellow sovereign, the Emperor Franz Joseph of Austria. After one or two further heated arguments on relatively trivial matters, the question was resolved. Bismarck was forced to hand in his resignation on 18 March 1890.

It was scarcely credible. For almost thirty years Bismarck had exercised single-handed control over first Prussian and then German affairs. With unprecedented skill he had played party off against party, parliament off against Kaiser, sovereign off against successor until, in the end, he had been beaten at his own game. He had been so busy outwitting his enemies that he had never had time to make friends.

No one raised a finger to save him. Everyone, from the Emperor to the humblest worker, was glad to see him go. Even the

Junkers had lost faith in him. 'A most repulsive spectacle is offered here by many people who, having until recently kow-towed to Prince Bismarck and to everything connected with his name, now shamelessly dissect his past in order to lay bare insignificant mistakes and minor weaknesses of his,' reported the Austrian Ambassador in Berlin. He, who had always treated his fellow man with scarcely disguised contempt, was now being similarly treated. Of that host of one-time sup-porters, only his son Herbert followed him into retirement.

Kaiser Wilhelm II was now his own master. From out of that welter of political and domestic conflict in which the first thirty years of his life had been spent, he had emerged trium-phant. There was no longer anyone strong enough to check, or even guide him. A mere two years before, he had still had so many restraining influences with which to contend: the rigid-ity of his grandfather, the liberalism of his grandmother and his parents, the might of Bismarck. Now every one of these inhibiting authorities had been swept away. Through Bis-marck's manoeuvrings, the Kaiser had inherited a position of enormous power; too much, in fact, for anyone other than a man of exceptional qualities. Through Bismarck's manoeuvr-ings, too, he had inherited an innocuous parliament and a politically docile people, utterly incapable of curbing, let alone defying him. He could do as he pleased. 'It seems to me,' wrote the Empress Frederick, 'that the German Emperor is to be converted into a sort of Tsar, and Germany to be governed by ukases.'

Before quitting public life for ever, Bismarck carried out a last official duty. He went to take leave of the Empress Fred-erick. There had been a subtle shift in the relationship between these long-standing enemies since Wilhelm's accession to the throne. It may have been that the very length of their enmity had formed a bond between them or that the Empress, having to choose the lesser of two evils—Wilhelm or Bismarck—had chosen Bismarck. Her judgements of his behaviour had cer-tainly come to be less harsh of late; his 'genius and prestige' she now conceded, could still be valuable to Germany, particularly as the new sovereign was so 'inexperienced and imprudent'. And once it had become clear that the new Kaiser was thinking of ditching his Chancellor, the Empress and Bismarck were drawn closer together still. While careful to avoid political topics, Bismarck could pour his complaints about the Kaiser's naivety and ingratitude into the Empress's only too sympathetic ears. The Empress declared Bismarck's attitude towards Wilhelm to be 'prudent and sensible and practical'.

Some time before his dismissal as Chancellor, Bismarck is said to have called on the Empress Frederick and begged her to intercede on his behalf. 'I am sorry,' she had been forced to reply. 'You, yourself, Prince Bismarck, have destroyed all my influence with my son. I can do nothing.'

Thus it was that Bismarck's formal farewell to the Empress Frederick was not without a certain poignancy. Both ambitious for power, the two of them had fought so long and so bitterly for opposing ideals, only to find that, quite suddenly, neither of them counted for anything. The cur had indeed run away with the bone. In their common rejection by one who had come to hold power, the ex-Empress and the ex-Chancellor could take comfort from each other. Appreciating the irony of the situation by which Bismarck, who had consistently championed Wilhelm against her, had in turn been discarded by him, the Empress was careful not to take advantage of it. She did not crow. 'We parted amicably and in peace,' she told Queen Victoria, 'which I was glad of, as I should have been sorry—having suffered so much all these long years under the system—that it should appear as if I had any spirit of revenge, which I really have not.'

She realized, moreover, that although Bismarck had been dismissed, it was he, or rather his system, that had triumphed in the long run. He may have lost this particular battle but he had won the war. 'Bismarck is gone,' she wrote, 'but Wilhelm has learned to play the despot from him.'

nation, Russia asked Germany for a renewal of the treaty between them. The request was turned down. Wilhelm II and Caprivi decided that Germany could no longer be allied to both Russia and Austria. With these two countries always at loggerheads in the Balkans, an alliance with both of them was not really practical politics. Germany must choose between them. Naturally, she chose Austria. The Russian alliance—the somewhat shaky cornerstone of Bismarck's foreign policy—was finished. Russia was henceforth obliged to look elsewhere for friends.

And so was Wilhelm. He began looking, therefore, towards Britain.

The Kaiser's attitude towards his mother's country had always been ambivalent: rather in the nature of a love–hate relationship. He admired England, he envied her, he was attracted to her, he feared her. He criticized her with characteristic vigour yet his criticisms had never quite rung true. They had been shafts aimed at his Anglophile parents rather than at England herself. Now that these parents were safely out of the way, the Kaiser could allow his latent respect for Britain to emerge. Indeed, of all the countries of Europe there was none with which he would rather be associated. Once Bismarck had been dismissed and the Russian alliance broken, the Kaiser began to think in terms of closer friendship with Britain.

The fact that the Queen of England was his grandmother gave him opportunities for friendly overtures denied to other sovereigns. In fact, once he had paid his first State visit to Britain there seemed to be no keeping him away. Every year saw him yachting at Cowes and every visit was followed by a gushing letter of thanks to the Queen in which he would hint at a possible alliance between their two countries. Should 'the Will of Providence lay the heavy burden on us of fighting for our homes and destinies', he wrote on one occasion, 'then may the British fleet be seen forging ahead, side by side with the German, and the "Red Coat" marching to victory with the Pomeranian Grenadier!' Obsessed by uniforms, he was for ever angling for yet another British one. The Queen, who had already made him an Admiral of the Fleet, considered this tireless 'fishing for uniforms' regrettable. When, on giving way to his importunings, she made him an Honorary Colonel of the 1st Royal Dragoons, his delight was almost overwhelming. 'I am moved, deeply moved,' he enthused, 'at the idea that I now too can wear beside the Naval uniform the traditional British "Redcoat".'

Not everyone, however, shared Kaiser Wilhelm II's enthusiasm for closer relations between the two countries. Britain was still determined to remain aloof from any Continental entanglements and a great many Germans, conscious of their country's growing might, saw no reason for allying themselves to anyone. Then, on a more personal level, the Kaiser's English relations were not nearly so enamoured of him as he seemed to be of them. Queen Victoria, finding his ebullience somewhat exhausting, once suggested that the British Ambassador in Berlin drop a hint to the effect that the Kaiser need not come to England *every* year. And there was little love lost between the Kaiser and his Uncle Bertie—Britain's future King. If anything, his nephew's bumptious behaviour made the urbane Prince of Wales more Francophile than ever. There was as yet no suggestion, however, that King Edward VII's England might one day look to France rather than Germany for friendship; during the early 1890s such a possibility seemed remote indeed.

France, none the less, was making a new friend. She and Russia were drawing closer together. It seemed, on the face of it, an unlikely association. Republican France and reactionary Russia would make strange bedfellows. But they had one factor in common and this a very powerful one: a fear of Kaiser Wilhelm II's Germany. In 1891 the French fleet paid a friendly visit to the Russian naval base at Kronstadt and Europe was diverted by the spectacle of Tsar Alexander III, the Autocrat of All the Russias, standing bare-headed while a French naval band blared out the revolutionary strains of the hated *Marseillaise*. Two years later the Russian navy returned the visit by sending a fleet to Toulon and by the end of that year a secret military convention had been agreed upon by the two nations.

Bismarck's great fear had been realized: Germany faced the possibility of war on two fronts.

From this time on, when Wilhelm II should have been making every effort to win Britain's goodwill, he began to lose it. He was too tactless, too boastful and too bellicose to win British confidence. With almost every step he took he seemed to bring the Reich into conflict with British interests. The two countries clashed over colonial policy in Africa and the Far East; German promoting of the Berlin–Baghdad Railway roused British antagonism; the Kaiser's plans to build a powerful navy alarmed and infuriated the Mistress of the Seas. In 1896, when Dr Jameson led his unsuccessful raid into the Transvaal Republic, the Kaiser saw fit to send a telegram to President Kruger, congratulating him on having repelled the band of British invaders. Wilhelm's rashness earned him a stinging rebuke from Queen Victoria (it would have been more stinging still had she known that he had suggested sending German troops to the Transvaal) and raised a storm of indignation throughout England. Although the Kaiser's fears that the incident had put an end to his little visits to Cowes were not justified (he was nothing if not resilient) it did put an end to any hope of an alliance. Some politicians, in Britain and Germany, might still favour co-operation, but from now on public opinion in both countries was against it.

Thus, in the half a dozen years that followed Bismarck's dismissal, the European stage was set for the great drama which was to be played out from 1914 to 1918. Although the Kaiser was to try to win back Russia's friendship and to plan new alliances, and although Britain, isolated during the Boer War, was to think more seriously about an understanding with Germany, the situation would not change. Britain was to be drawn ever closer towards France and Russia, leaving the Reich with only decaying Austria and uncertain Italy as allies. Bismarck's 'nightmare of coalitions' against Germany had come true.

Yet Wilhelm remained sanguine. For one thing Germany was far and away the most powerful nation on the Continent and, for another, he never dreamed that Britain might one day ally herself to France and Russia. Franco-British colonial rivalry was too bitter and Russo-British enmity too long-standing for any chance of an agreement between the three of them. He fondly imagined that he, like Bismarck before him, was the arbiter of Europe; that he needed only to rattle his sabre for lesser nations to tremble.

In his megalomania, Kaiser Wilhelm II had the support of a considerable body of his countrymen. 'We are ready to fall into line when our Kaiser calls...' they cried, 'but in return we demand a prize that makes the sacrifice worthwhile: to belong to a *Herrenvolk* which takes its share of the world and does not seek to depend on the favour and goodwill of another nation. Germany, awake!'

2

If Kaiser Wilhelm II had imagined that by dismissing Prince Bismarck he would have silenced the old man once and for all, he was soon proved wrong. Bismarck's retirement at Friedrichsruh was anything but graceful. At seventy-five the ex-Chancellor was as touchy, as vindictive and as unforgiving as he had ever been. His interest in politics was unflagging. As mercilessly as he had once attacked the Empress Augusta and the Empress Frederick, he now pitched into the Kaiser and his entourage. His still considerable energies were henceforth to be poured into discrediting the man responsible for his eclipse. He published hundreds of articles, he gave dozens of interviews, he made innumerable speeches. In his successor, Caprivi, he had very little faith; Caprivi's relatively liberal policy ran counter to everything Bismarck had stood for. Indeed, Bismarck found himself out of sympathy with almost all the trends of the new regime: the industrialization, the expansionism, the colonialism, the breaking of old alliances. For a man whose talent, once he had established the Reich, had been for subtle manipulation, everything was now too brash by half. That the Fatherland was being led into a 'morass' he had no doubt; it was his duty, he declared, to save it.

Conscious of that bulbous, baleful, all-seeing eye trained on him from Friedrichsruh, the Kaiser took care to isolate his ex-Chancellor as much as possible. The official world was quick to follow the new master's example. Bismarck's mail was intercepted, his pronouncements played down, his visitors discouraged. He, who had always complained of being too busy, now longed for company. One of his rare guests, an American railway magnate not known to the Chancellor, was startled to hear his host enter the room while he was still washing his hands after the journey. 'You are my only visitor this week,' grumbled Bismarck. 'I am boycotted. No one will have anything to do with me. They are all afraid that their names might appear in the papers as guests of mine, and that this would displease our young master on the throne.'

In 1892, when Bismarck travelled to Vienna to attend the wedding of his son Herbert, the Kaiser wrote to the Emperor Franz Joseph, requesting that the Emperor refuse to receive the ex-Chancellor. His 'disobedient subject' was to be ignored, said Wilhelm. Heinrich von Sybel, the historian, was forbidden access to certain documents because of his tendency to glorify Bismarck too much and Wilhelm too little. And it is said that the only occasion on which the ex-Chancellor was able to read the signature of his successor, Caprivi, was when it was penned at the foot of a document demanding a refund of the salary paid to him from 20 March to 31 March 1890; it was claimed that Bismarck, having been dismissed on the 18 March, had already been drawing his pension during that period.

'The Emperor dismissed me like a lackey,' muttered Bismarck on one occasion. 'All my life I have behaved as a nobleman who cannot be insulted without demanding amends. But I cannot demand satisfaction of the Emperor.'

However, there were other things which he could do to avenge himself and, as the months and years went by, so did he have the satisfaction of seeing his tireless speech-making and article-writing begin to take effect. Public opinion began turning in his favour. From being disgraced and ostracized, he gradually found himself enjoying a popularity never accorded him in his days of office. Shorn of power, he seemed less malicious, more detached than he had once been. People began, not only to listen to him, but to applaud him. He developed into a national father-figure, Germany's Grand Old Man—deferred to, respected, even loved. Deputations, ignoring the disapproval of Berlin, paid pilgrimages to Friedrichsruh. while Bismarck, warming to this growing adulation, began to travel about the country, making speeches, inspecting guards of honour, accepting addresses of welcome. 'When my train is approaching a station, has slowed down, and I hear the shouting and the singing of the crowds awaiting me,' he admitted, 'my heart is filled with joy that I am not forgotten in Germany.'

At every opportunity he spoke out against the trends of the new regime. Stumping about the market-place at Jena in the course of a triumphant journey to Vienna, he treated his frenzied audience to no less than nine speeches. 'A man may be a loyal adherent of his dynasty, his King, and his Emperor, without being convinced of the wisdom of all the measures of that King's and Emperor's commissaries,' he thundered. 'I myself am not convinced, nor shall I in future keep my opinions to myself.'

In some cases, these opinions seemed to have undergone a

startling change. So bitter was his animosity towards the Kaiser that he was even willing to advocate a strengthening of the constitution. Owning that he himself might have 'unwittingly' contributed to a lessening of the influence of parliament, he warned against the growing power of the monarch. It seems that the old man, intoxicated by his unwonted popularity among the common people, was almost ready to embrace democracy.

But it was still from the Right that he drew his main support. Among the Junker reactionaries and the new breed of lower middle-class nationalists, there was strong disapproval of Kaiser Wilhelm II's policies: the estrangement with Russia, the new trade agreements, the social reforms. There was a growing awareness of the fact that the Kaiser was not nearly as resolute or as autocratic as he pretended; he was not anything like as unyielding as Bismarck had been. As the ex-Chancellor himself put it, 'the most disastrous element in [the Kaiser's] character is that he cannot be permanently subjected to any influence, while from moment to moment he is accessible to all influences'. The old Chancellor thus became the core of a new opposition—a 'national' opposition as distinct from the opposition of the Left—composed largely of nationalists, anti-Semites and Pan Germans. It was an opposition of which the Kaiser was acutely aware and understandably uneasy. Far from having rid himself of a nuisance, Wilhelm II seemed to have created a positive danger. It was essential that he do something about it.

As the attempted isolation of the ex-Chancellor had failed, Kaiser Wilhelm's only hope was to stage a reconciliation. Unable to beat his opponent, he must join him. Bismarck's illness, in 1893, gave him the opportunity. The Kaiser showered him with attentions and, on his recovery, the ex-Chancellor was obliged to pay his sovereign a somewhat grudging visit of thanks. This led to a series of meetings between them. But the *rapprochement* remained a surface one only: underneath, the mutual antipathy simmered as of old. The Kaiser was effusive but detached while Bismarck scarcely bothered to be polite. The Kaiser's determination to discuss nothing of consequence was always turned to devastating effect by the malicious Bismarck. 'The Emperor was gracious enough to consult Prince Bismarck concerning the important question of lightening the kit of infantry soldiers on active service...' ran one of Bismarck's ironically worded reports to a local newspaper after a visit from the Kaiser. 'With the same intention of making things easier for the men, a change has been made in the collar, which can now be turned down.'

On Bismarck's eightieth birthday, in 1895, the Kaiser arrived in great state to present the old man with a golden sword of honour. The gift was an emblem, declared Wilhelm with a rich mixture of metaphors, 'of that great and mighty constructive period when blood and iron was the cement'. His fulsome speech received no answering one from Bismarck. 'While the Emperor, in his cuirass, reined in his tall horse and addressed me,' said Bismarck of this historic moment, 'I could not take my eyes off a drop of rain which was slowly running down his glittering armour.'

When the Kaiser, obsessed with the idea of building a great German navy, asked the still influential Bismarck to give the project his sanction, the old man assured the Kaiser's messenger that he was no tom cat, ready to send out sparks when stroked. 'Tell the Emperor,' he growled, 'I want nothing but to be left alone, and die in peace.'

They met for the last time, these two rivals, a few months before Bismarck's death in 1898. Wilhelm II, surrounded by his galaxy of flamboyantly uniformed, sycophantic officers, descended on Friedrichsruh and spent the entire time in noisy and inconsequential chatter. Whenever the old Chancellor tried to introduce politics into the conversation, the Kaiser would ignore him by making yet another quip or asking yet another conundrum. Finally Bismarck, exasperated beyond endurance, sounded a warning. 'Your Majesty,' he said with deceptive nonchalance, 'so long as you have these officers around you, there is no doubt that you may do exactly as you please. But if ever that should not be so, it will be quite another matter.'

As though he had not heard this exhortation, the Kaiser prattled loudly on.

'I will not do him the pleasure of dying,' Bismarck had once said apropos of the Kaiser but, for all the vehemence of his hatred, he could not expect to go on living much longer. He finally died, aged eighty-three, in July 1898. Wilhelm II, relieved to be rid at last of that critical and overpowering presence, came to Friedrichsruh to pay his final respects. He would have been distinctly less relieved had he known that Bismarck's most deadly thrust was yet to be delivered. The old Chancellor had left instructions for his memoirs to be published as soon after his death as possible. In this skilfully written, three-volume work, Bismarck had made a biting attack on Kaiser Wilhelm II. Indeed, so embittered was this one-time royalist that he could find very little to say in praise of the House of Hohenzollern to which he had devoted so much of his life.

But the Kaiser was spared this indictment. Bismarck's heirs considered the chapter on Wilhelm II to be too inflammatory and they withheld the third volume from publication.

As far as the unsuspecting Kaiser was concerned, however, the published volumes of Bismarck's *Reflections and Recollections* were bad enough. The Chancellor's detached, statesmanlike and Olympian attitude and his lavish praise of Kaiser Wilhelm I seemed to underline the present Kaiser's inadequacies. Wilhelm II was quick to take offence. When someone sympathized with him at this treatment at the hands of Bismarck, Wilhelm's defence was richly typical. 'I perfectly understood the terrible task which Heaven had shaped for me: the task of rescuing the Crown from the overwhelming shadow of its minister...' he declared. 'When the strife waxed hot and Bismarck began his most daring tricks against me, not recoiling before even High Treason, I sent a message to him saying: it seemed to me as if he was riding into the lists against the House of Hohenzollern for his own family; if it were so I warned him, that this was useless as in that case he must be the loser. The reply was what I had expected, and I felled him, stretching him in the sand, for the sake of my Crown and our House.... Where is he now? The storm has calmed, the standard waves high in the breeze, comforting every anxious look cast upwards; the Crown sends its rays "by the Grace of God" into Palace and hut, and—pardon me if I say so—Europe and the world listen to hear "what does the German Emperor say or think", and not what is the will of his Chancellor....'

3

'I am completely cast off from the official world,' complained the widowed Empress Frederick to Queen Victoria; 'not a single official person ever comes near me and what used to be *mein tägliches Brot* [my daily bread] has quite ceased. How I used to work for Fritz and how he used to tell me everything! Now I might be buried alive.... Influence on the course of events I have not the smallest, or faintest.... Now that my experience is perhaps worth something there is a dead silence and one's existence is forgotten.'

But not quite. The Kaiser, conscious of the ever-increasing isolation of Germany, was casting about for some way in which to improve relations with her most bitter enemy, France. A royal visit was the customary palliative in such cases but not even Wilhelm was quite so conceited as to imagine that he would be welcome in Paris. He therefore decided to send his mother. She had paid several private visits to France during the past few years and had always been well received. She would now pay an official visit to Paris. As patron of a forth-coming art exhibition in Berlin, she would be going to thank those French artists who had agreed to show their pictures. It seemed a harmless enough mission.

The visit was a disaster. The German Press, hinting that it was the first step towards a *rapprochement* between the two countries, whipped the chauvinistic French into a fury. Every move of the Empress was criticized in the French papers. They claimed that by calling on certain artists, she had neglected others. Her trips to Saint-Cloud and Versailles (both closely associated with the Franco-Prussian War) were considered to be tactless and insulting. But it was her visit to the Ministry of Fine Arts that brought things to a climax. When it was learnt that a laurel wreath, placed at the foot of a monument to a painter killed in the war, had been removed just before her arrival lest the sight of it offend her, public passions soared to such a pitch that the Empress was obliged to leave Paris in a hurry. The French artists refused to exhibit in Berlin and the German Press retaliated by heaping abuse on the French nation.

Even now, despite the fact that she had been a blameless victim of circumstances, the Empress received no sympathy from the official world in Berlin. On the contrary, she was roundly attacked for the failure of her mission. She was accused of being undiplomatic, miserly and of having associated with Jews. In what she called her 'tormented' state, she began to wonder whether the Kaiser had sent her to Paris purposely to discredit her. When a friend hotly denied such a possibility, the Empress shook her head. 'Ah! You don't know him!' she answered.

This disastrous mission was the Empress Frederick's last excursion into politics. Her interest in world affairs remained as active as ever and she never ceased to be alarmed at the truculence of her son's behaviour but henceforth she withdrew from public life almost entirely. She devoted herself, more and more, to Friedrichshof, her new home in the Taunus hills. Into this steep-roofed, many-windowed, multiple-chimneyed mansion, she poured all her energies. Here were collected her paintings, her furniture, her *objets d'art*, her well-thumbed books, even the little scraps of paper on which her voiceless husband had scribbled his last pathetic messages. The lavishly decorated rooms were always filled with flowers, gathered by the Empress herself from her magnificent garden. To the people of Kronberg she was a kindly châtelaine and to the cultural world an informed and intelligent hostess.

When she was not in residence at Friedrichshof, she would be travelling. For so active a personality, movement was essential. The winter season she was obliged to spend in Berlin but each year she managed to get away from Germany for a few months. She loved visiting England. London's shops and museums were a source of endless delight; in the rooms at Windsor, Osborne and Balmoral, with their brightly blazing fires and their bowls of freshly picked flowers, she felt eminently at home. She remained devoted to Italy. Each summer found her scrambling about its ruins, wandering through its palazzi, studying its sculpture or sitting in its hot, white sunlight, painting in the bright colours she loved so well. When her third daughter Sophie married the Crown Prince of Greece, she began visiting Athens. 'In sheer beauty *nothing* comes up to the Greek landscape for colour, purity of outline, transparent atmosphere, and everywhere the lovely sea ...' she wrote to Sophie after one of her visits. 'Wedell says Italy is dethroned in my admiration and my heart since I have become so fond of Greece, and it is quite true!'

She seldom saw her eldest son. His occasional visits to Friedrichshof, always marked by much state and bustle, caused people to talk of a reconciliation between them but their relationship remained uneasy. If, in his presence, she held her tongue, in private she aired her views on his increasing megalomania with all her old spirit. She was still capable of flinging a newspaper to the floor and of stamping about in exasperation. His provocative statements, his sudden whims, his appalling lack of finesse, distressed her considerably. If only, she declared, he would make no more of those terrible speeches and would not write those braggartly messages in books and on photographs of himself. It was enough to 'make one's hair stand on end'.

Despite the outward decorum of their relationship, it needed very little to spark off a row. Try as she might, there were times when she simply could not live, as she put it, 'with a padlock on my mouth'. The Greco-Turkish War of 1897, in which Wilhelm favoured Turkey and she Greece, was one cause of friction between them; it led to innumerable scenes. The situation was aggravated by the fact that the Kaiser had fallen out with his sister Sophie, Crown Princess of Greece. Sophie's announcement, after the birth of her first child, that she intended being received into the Greek Orthodox Church, infuriated her brother. It annoyed Dona, his Empress, even more. Sending for Sophie, Dona (about to give birth to a sixth strapping son) primly announced that Wilhelm would never stand for the change of religion. If Sophie persisted in this headstrong course, she would end up in Hell. Sophie, very much her mother's daughter, flared up and told Dona to mind her own business. At this the pregnant Dona became so excited that the doctors were sent for and her baby was born three weeks prematurely. 'If my poor Baby dies it is solely Sophy's fault and she has murdered it,' wrote the agitated Kaiser to Queen Victoria. But the baby flourished and Sophie, ignoring her brother's disapproval, entered the Orthodox Church. At this Wilhelm, suddenly alive to his sacred duties as Head of the Church, threatened to expel her from both Germany and the Hohenzollern family.

The threat caused a violent scene between mother and son. 'William is convinced that I had tried to persuade you to become Greek,' reported the Empress Frederick to Sophie. Having berated her son for his intolerance, she fled to Kiel to escape his anger. Her outburst had no effect, and the Kaiser banned Sophie from Germany. When Sophie protested, Wilhelm held firm. On hearing this, Sophie sent her mother a telegram—through the public post offices at Athens and Homburg —to say, 'Received answer. Keeps to what he said in Berlin. Fixes it to three years. Mad. Never mind. Sophie.'

'That such heartlessness and *Rücksichtslosigkeit* [lack of consideration] have left a deep impression on me you cannot wonder,' wrote the Empress to her mother, 'and it has again revealed to me the spirit in which I have been treated. . . .'

Had Wilhelm's blusterings been confined to such relatively minor matters, the Empress might not have been quite so perturbed; but she saw, only too clearly, into what dangers he was leading the country. 'One is inclined to smile,' she noted after one of the Kaiser's particularly autocratic speeches, 'if it were not so serious and so dangerous.' What Wilhelm should be doing, she wrote perceptively, 'is building up a strong, firm and sound edifice on a broad foundation, if Germany is not to slip down the steep path which leads to a Republic or even a Socialist state. The latter would never last, there would be chaos, then reaction, dictatorship and God knows what further damage. . . .'

She found his handling of Germany's foreign relations equally inept. His blundering behaviour towards England caused her particular anxiety. The Empress, as always, longed for an alliance between the two countries. This was to have been the cornerstone of the Emperor Frederick's foreign policy; the Prince Consort's dearest wish. She watched the growing friendship between France and Russia with mounting alarm. When the French fleet, having just paid its friendly visit to Russia, was invited to Portsmouth and its officers presented to Queen Victoria, the Empress immediately grasped the significance of the occasion. The fact that the Queen had had to stand up while the 'horrid *Marseillaise*' had been played, appalled her; not, one suspects, because of its violently revolutionary sentiments, but because of the fact that the incident had pointed to the coming *entente* between the two nations.

'Oh, if Fritz had only been spared, all this would never have happened!' she once cried out.

In the year 1898, forsaking for once her negative role, she made one more effort to bring about the cherished alliance. In secret she approached both the Kaiser and the British Ambassador, claiming that she had information to the effect that the time for a formal alliance was never more opportune than at present.

In this, as far as Britain was concerned, she was correct. Certain British statesmen were indeed ready for an approach to Germany but by now Germany had lost interest. The Reich was becoming more self-sufficient by the day and its politicians resented what they considered to be Britain's patronizing attitude. When the Empress Frederick spoke to the new Secretary of State. Bernhard von Bülow, of her fears that the building of a great German navy would put paid to all hopes of an *entente*, he simply treated the warning as another instance of her Anglomania. 'She believed...' he wrote in his memoirs, 'the best Germany could do was to make herself useful to England and England's high aims and at the same time ennoble herself by keeping in the course of English policy, like a tiny boat in the wake of a great frigate....'

By the summer of 1899 the Empress had to admit to the final fading of her dream. The gulf between the two nations was widening too fast. 'Such a thing as an alliance is too good to be true,' she sighed. The Prince Consort's plans, mulled over at such length and with such optimism half a century before, had come to nothing. Indeed, every one of those schemes with which, as a young, idealistic bride she had arrived in Berlin, had turned to ashes. There must have been times when she was overwhelmed with a sense, not only of frustration, but of utter failure.

'It is not my fault,' she once told her daughter Sophie, 'but the fault of circumstances, which I had against me ever since I set foot there in 1858, as a young girl only anxious to please, and be pleased with everybody. It was my *misfortune*. Had dear Papa been spared to reign for ten or twenty years, things would have changed very much in that respect, and I would have had the *possibility* of rendering many a service which has been denied me, the means and the opportunity not having come to me.'

Again and again her thoughts would turn to her husband's tragic death. She once wrote to Sophie to tell her of a certain Count S. who had recently been operated on for cancer of the throat by the same Dr Bergmann who had wished to operate on the Emperor Frederick. The Count died soon after. 'I always feel so thankful we listened to the excellent Sir Morell,' she claimed, 'and that dear Papa was not murdered in this fashion, though there were some who for their own political reasons and selfish ambitious plans, would have preferred it to be so, and that dear Papa should never have reigned at all. I need not tell you who these people were, as you know them. They tell me that poor Count S.'s state *after* the operation, with half his throat gone, was so dreadful that to die was a mercy and a relief. It is horrible even to think of. If he had been left alone he might have lived for months, and perhaps a couple of years. . . .'

The anniversary of her husband's accession always brought a pang. 'Ah! that day at San Remo,' she once exclaimed; 'shall I ever forget it!'

In the autumn of 1898, at the age of fifty-seven, the Empress was thrown by her horse and was obliged to spend a few days in bed. It appears that the doctor who was called in to examine her after the accident discovered that she had cancer. Whether or not he advised an operation is not certain; a specialist, examining her some six months later, claimed that an operation at the time of the discovery might have been successful. But she would do nothing about it. It is not unlikely that the Empress derived a certain perverse satisfaction from the thought that she would die of the same disease as her beloved husband. She imagined, however, that her body was strong enough to withstand the ravages of the disease for as much as ten years (her grandmother, the Duchess of Kent, had fought against cancer for eight years) by which time she would have lived her allotted span. She therefore swore the doctor to secrecy and gave out that she was suffering from lumbago.

'I should *not* like the people in Berlin to know that I am ill . . .' she wrote. '[They] would be only too pleased to get rid of me! That was shown, written and said too plainly in 1888 for me to forget and misunderstand it.'

Not until the following year did the Empress tell the Kaiser, the Marshal of her Household and one or two close friends. Queen Victoria was never informed.

But the Empress Frederick's estimate of ten more years of life had been too optimistic. The disease spread rapidly and by the end of the year 1900 she was in almost continuous pain. One of the last glimpses one gets of her before she was completely bedridden is from Princess Catherine Radziwill. The two women met in a hotel room at Bordighera, in Italy, where the Empress was spending the winter of 1899. 'Mentally she was as alert as ever, and as interested in what was going on in the world,' says Princess Radziwill. 'Her beautiful eyes retained their expression of kindliness, intelligence and comprehension of all the problems of life. As ever, she used the most fitting words to say what she thought, and was all sympathy, and made one feel that she was always ready to pick up those whom existence had wounded, with the same ease that she would lift from the ground a fallen child. We talked of many things for a long time, which, however, appeared to me much too short, and then it was that she uttered these remarkable words, when the name of a person whom had done her a great deal of harm happened to crop up; "Let us forget the past," she said, and one could see she meant it absolutely. . . .

'She got up and kissed me as she dismissed me, and I shall never forget her as I saw her then, for what proved to be the last time, standing in that hotel room at Bordighera, a solitary figure in deep mourning, with fragrant flowers all around her, and that far-away look upon her face which only appears when one stands at that turning in the road of life which leads to the end.'

Within a few months of this meeting she was indeed nearing the end of her road. 'The terrible nights of agony are worse than ever, no rest, no peace,' she confided to her daughter Sophie. 'The tears rush down my cheeks when I am not shouting with pain. The injections of morphia dull the pains a little for about quarter of an hour, sometimes not at all, then they rage again with renewed intensity, and make me wish I was safe in my grave, where these sufferings are not. So my nights are spent.' It was clear that she could not hope to live for many more months.

By now her mother, Queen Victoria, was also sinking fast. It was wondered which of the two would go first. As they had done for the past half-century almost, the two women still exchanged letters, although both were now obliged to dictate them. The Queen still believed that it was lumbago which prevented her daughter from writing herself. 'Darling Vicky's sixtieth birthday,' ran the entry in the Queen's Journal for 21 November 1900. 'To think of her, who was so wonderfully active and strong, now so ill and suffering, is heartbreaking. . . . We pray daily that she may suffer less.'

Queen Victoria died on 22 January 1901. Supporting her pillow to the very end was her eldest grandson, Kaiser Wilhelm II. He was henceforth to claim that the Queen had died 'in his arms'.

The Empress Frederick lived on, in frightful pain, for another six months. At the end of February 1901 her brother, now King Edward VII, visited her at Friedrichshof and the Empress, possibly remembering how the Kaiser had ransacked the rooms after the death of the Emperor Frederick, asked the King's private secretary, Sir Frederick Ponsonby, to take some of her letters back with him to England. These were bound copies of her correspondence to her mother which the Empress had once borrowed, possibly with a view to publishing them. As they formed such an indictment of the Kaiser and such a vindication of her own behaviour, she probably suspected that her son would never allow them to see the light of day. They were her one means of clearing her name.

Ponsonby, who claims that considerable ingenuity was necessary to get the boxes of letters out of her castle, took upon himself the task of publishing them. He did not do so, however, until ten years after the flight of the Kaiser from Germany in 1918. The *Letters of the Empress Frederick* remain the most vivid testimony to the sufferings of that much-maligned, misunderstood and unhappy woman—surely one of the most tragic figures in the history of the nineteenth century.

The Empress Frederick died, at the age of sixty, on 5 August 1901. It was a day of brilliant sunshine and as, surrounded by members of her family, she lay dying, a butterfly flew in by the open window and fluttered about her head. As it returned to the window and floated out into the sunlit garden, the Empress died.

By dying in the year 1901, the Empress Frederick was at least spared what would probably have been the crowning agony of her life: the terrible war between her husband's country and her own.

Calumnies pursued her beyond her death. Despite the fact that her orders for a simple funeral were faithfully carried out (she was buried beside Kaiser Frederick III at Potsdam) the most scurrilous stories about her dying wishes circulated in Berlin. She had insisted, they whispered, that she be buried, not as a German sovereign, but as an English princess. An Anglican bishop was to conduct the funeral service according to the rights of the Anglican Church. She was to be laid naked, wrapped in a Union Jack, in a coffin specially brought over from England and the body then sent back to England for burial at Windsor. Only an admirable firmness on the part of the beloved Kaiser had prevented such scandalous proceedings. One could imagine, clucked one of her enemies, how hurt the people of Berlin had been by the behaviour of this Princess 'who in dying showed her contempt for everything that was German'.

She was *die Engländerin*, they nodded vigorously, to the very end.

4

The deaths of Bismarck and the Empress Frederick coincided with the end of an era in Germany. Not only did their passing ring down the final curtain on the Hohenzollern family drama, but it happened to come at a turning-point in the history of the Reich. While Bismarck and the Empress had been alive, a little of the atmosphere of the early days of the Second Reich had lingered on. There had still been something left of that loose federation of princes reigning over pastoral, provincial states and headed by a courtly old gentleman who had preferred being called King of Prussia to German Emperor. Now, with the turn of the century, everything changed. The 'new course' of the 1890s was forgotten and Germany launched on its resolve to become a world power. The divisions between the various German states became increasingly blurred; even Prussia lost its identity—if not its influence; and the Kaiser was regarded, not simply as the leading German sovereign, but as the sole ruler of a Greater Germany. It was no longer enough for the Reich to be the first nation on the Continent; she must be a great power. The end of the nineteenth century marked the beginning of the policy of *Weltpolitik*.

This, of course, was in harmony with the spirit of the times. This was the great age of world powers, of the spread of European civilization, of high-flown theories of racial superiority, of land-hungry visionaries, of aggressive nationalism. The great nations were expanding, trading, colonizing, establishing spheres of influence and founding empires. It was the high noon of imperialism.

No movement could have suited Kaiser Wilhelm II better. He fancied himself as a World Emperor *par excellence*. It gave him endless opportunity for those *grands gestes*, half-romantic, half-militant, that he adored. With the beginnings of *Weltpolitik*, he came finally into his own. 'Bülow, be my Bismarck,' he said to his latest Chancellor, and Bernhard von Bülow, who was certainly no Bismarck, set about trying to emulate his predecessor's iron policies. Once more Germany had a mission: she must equal, or even outstrip, those other great world powers—Russia, France, the United States and particularly Great Britain.

'The German Reich has become a *Weltreich*,' thundered the Kaiser. 'Thousands of our countrymen live in far-flung corners of the earth. German goods, German knowledge, German industriousness, cross the sea. German ships carry goods worth thousands of millions. You, gentlemen, have the important duty of helping me to link this greater German Reich firmly to ours at home.'

He did not have to ask twice. The majority of his subjects were quite ready for this new imperial venture; indeed, social and economic pressures within the industrially burgeoning Reich made it imperative. But that these ideas should flourish so well was largely due to the climate created by the newly-formed Pan German League. This league was made up of a hotch-potch of idealists, nationalists, racialists, imperialists and militarists, dedicated to the idea of a Greater Germany. They dreamed, not only of a vast new German state embracing Holland, Belgium, Luxembourg, Switzerland and Austria, but of a great Empire beyond the seas. For them, even the most expansive of the Kaiser's gestures was never quite expansive enough.

The first decade of the twentieth century saw the theories of *Weltpolitik* put into practice. Germany expanded in Africa, China and the Pacific. She moved into the Middle East and embarked on that most exotic project—the building of the Berlin to Baghdad railway, thereby linking the icy waves of the North Sea with the balmy waters of the Persian Gulf. The Kaiser, sporting an assortment of the most spectacular uniforms, toured the decaying Ottoman Empire. From Damascus he blandly assured 300 million Mohammedans (a great many of whom owed allegiance to Britain and Russia) that he was their real friend. When the Boxer Rebellion broke out in the Far East he organized a military expedition, made up of European powers and commanded by General Waldersee, to put it down. For years he had been ranting against the 'Yellow Peril'; now, in one of his most unfortunate speeches, he urged his soldiers to make the name 'German' as feared in China as the name 'Hun' had once been in Europe. He even designed a vast allegorical painting in which an angel, with gleaming armour and flaming sword, urged several buxom, helmeted and fiery-eyed matrons, each representing a European nation, to protect their 'most sacred possessions' against the Asiatic hordes.

But it was in regard to building a German navy that the Kaiser's emotions were most deeply involved. Jealous of British sea power, he was determined that Germany should have as magnificent a fleet. His motives were not necessarily belligerent; a powerful navy would deter any would-be aggressor and would establish the Reich as a great maritime power. It would be a symbol of national greatness. In an atmosphere of almost hysterical chauvinism, two vast navy bills were passed in the Reichstag and the Kaiser's great shipbuilding programme put in hand. It was this building of a big battle fleet, more than anything, that aroused British fears and suspicions; from the turn of the century on, the frantic naval race between the two nations simply deepened the mutual distrust.

Prince Bismarck, being taken on a tour of the gigantic shipyards at Hamburg shortly before his death, was appalled by what he saw. In this noisy manifestation of German might he sensed the ruin of his own, delicately balanced system. With frightened eyes, the old man turned away. 'Another world, a new world...' he muttered.

It was indeed. And the fact that Bismarck had helped lay its foundations did not make it any easier for him to accept.

Chancellor von Bülow was not far wrong, however, when he claimed that the Kaiser's motives were not really belligerent. 'What Wilhelm II most desired...' said Bülow, 'was to see himself, at the head of a glorious German fleet, starting out on a peaceful visit to England. The English sovereign, with his fleet, would meet the German Kaiser in Portsmouth. The two fleets would file past each other, the two monarchs each wearing the naval uniform of the other's country ... would then stand on the bridge of their flagships. Then, after they had embraced in the prescribed manner, a gala dinner with lovely speeches would be held in Cowes.'

But even the vainglorious Wilhelm wanted something slightly more tangible than this from his navy. What he was hoping for was that Britain, impressed by German naval might, would be compelled to join the Triple Alliance of Germany, Austria and Italy, as a full member, thus converting it into a Quadruple Alliance. This Britain refused to do. She was certainly anxious for a limited alliance with Germany, and three times between the years 1898 and 1902 she approached her with this in view. Each time she was rebuffed. Germany, assuming that Britain needed her more than she needed Britain, would accept her as a full additional member of the Triple Alliance or not at all. She accepted her therefore, not at all. The end of the nineteenth century thus coincided with another turning-point in the history of the Reich—the loss of all chance of an alliance between these two great Teutonic nations. The twentieth century, announced Bülow on finally rebuffing the British overtures, would decide whether Germany or Britain was to be 'the hammer or the anvil'.

From this time on, Britain drew ever closer to France and, through France, to Russia. King Edward VII—'the Peacemaker' in the eyes of his own countrymen and 'a Satan', bent on isolating Germany, in the fevered imagination of the Kaiser —lent his full support to the *Entente Cordiale* which was signed between Britain and France in 1904. Wilhelm's belated efforts to revive his country's alliance with Russia (an effort confined very largely to the writing of page after page of ill-considered advice to 'Nicky'—the young Tsar Nicholas II) was unsuccessful. Russia remained firmly allied to France. What Wilhelm was to call 'the encirclement' of the Reich had begun.

Yet this, in itself, need not have led to war. One of the main reasons for the great conflict of 1914–18 was that Europe had developed into a series of rival power-blocs, all competing with each other, all striving to be larger, stronger, more magnificent than each other. Each wanted a bigger navy, a stronger army, a greater empire than the other; each was anxious to score diplomatic victories over its neighbours. It had become a vicious circle. Germany was probably no worse than the rest of them. It was simply that her diplomats had isolated her in a hostile world and that, like her Kaiser, she had become too self-confident, too boastful and too militant. Sooner or later she would have to prove herself. 'The only nations which have progressed and become great have been warring nations,' thundered the Kaiser on one occasion. 'Those who have not been ambitious and gone to war have been nothing.' This was hardly the sort of talk to still the apprehensions of Germany's neighbours.

Of the many flamboyant titles by which it pleased Kaiser Wilhelm II to be known—'the All-Highest', 'Admiral of the Atlantic', 'Instrument of the Almighty'—that of 'Supreme War Lord' was undoubtedly his favourite. It was not going to be easy to retain it without actually going to war.

It was inevitable, perhaps, that the Second Reich, born in war and nurtured with militarism, should go down in war. The last great European struggle had seen its beginnings; the first great world struggle was to see its end. In the same Galerie des Glaces at Versailles in which the Empire had been so triumphantly proclaimed in 1871, a defeated Germany would be obliged to accept the humiliating peace terms of the victorious Allies. The Kaisers, whom Frederick III had seen as heirs to the Holy Roman Empire—the successors of Charlemagne—reigned for a relatively brief period of Germany's history. The First Reich had lasted for over a thousand years. The second was to last for less than fifty.

EPILOGUE

DOORN 1918–1941

1

Bismarck, a year or two before his death in 1898, predicted that 'the crash will come twenty years after my departure'. His prediction was correct—to the month almost. In November 1918 the Second Reich collapsed and Kaiser Wilhelm II fled to Holland. On the very day that the Kaiser arrived at Amerongen, his temporary place of exile, the armistice was signed. The 'Kaiser's War' was over.

In point of fact, Kaiser Wilhelm II had had very little to do with the waging of it. He was not even directly responsible for its declaration. On the contrary, its outbreak, which was the almost inevitable result of the positions into which the various countries of Europe had manoeuvred themselves, completely unnerved him. He had never looked more haggard nor sounded more pessimistic than during the first few days of the fighting. 'Here is a man whose world had collapsed and who had some premonition of impending disaster,' wrote a friend at the time.

As usual, Wilhelm blamed everyone but himself for the outbreak of hostilities. And it was Britain that he blamed most of all. Ever wont to overestimate the powers of reigning sovereigns, he accused King George V of conspiring with Tsar Nicholas II to complete the nefarious policy of encirclement begun by the late King Edward VII. 'To think that George and Nicky should have played me false!' he exclaimed. 'If my grandmother had been alive, she would never have allowed it.'

Once his first fears had been stilled, his volatile nature reasserted itself and he threw himself into the role of generalissimo with customary gusto. As the Supreme Commander, he considered it essential that he identify himself with the army as much as possible. He lost almost all contact with the government of the country; 'idiotic civilians', he announced firmly, were to keep their mouths shut. He lived, for most of the time, at headquarters, either in some comfortable mansion or in his luxurious white and gold train. At long last, in fact as well as in fancy, he had become the Supreme War Lord.

The pose did not last long. The first reverses—in East Prussia—plunged him back into deepest gloom. By then, moreover, the military authorities were beginning to get his measure. It had taken the war to reveal the Kaiser for what he was: a panicky, despairing, vacillating neurotic, incapable of sustained effort or even coherent thought. Indeed, the chief Staff doctor was preparing himself for a complete mental breakdown of 'this highly nervous man of whom before the war we all entertained such an entirely false impression'. Within weeks he was being allowed almost no say in the conduct of the campaign and before many months had passed he was scarcely more than a puppet in the hands of the High Command. Control of the destinies of the Reich passed to that much more resolute pair—Field Marshal von Hindenburg and General Ludendorff.

Kaiser Wilhelm spent the four years of the war travelling, with a vast retinue, to and fro across the Reich, almost completely divorced from the military, political and civilian life of the country. He, who should have been a rallying-point for the nation, proved to be nothing more than an encumbrance. Of this, he was acutely aware. 'If people in Germany think I am the Supreme Commander, they are grossly mistaken,' he once sighed. 'The General Staff tells me nothing and never asks my advice. I drink tea, go for walks and saw wood. . . .'

The autumn of 1918 found him at Grand Headquarters, at Spa in Belgium, and it was here that his last scene as German Emperor was played out. His troops were falling back on all fronts, his cities seething with discontent. It was essential that Germany ask for an armistice. But President Wilson had made it clear that he was not prepared to negotiate with 'military leaders and monarchical authority'; the Kaiser, in other words, would have to go and a peace be negotiated with the government. By the second week in November, with revolutionary clamour spreading through the Reich and the soldiers refusing to continue the fight, even the High Command came to the conclusion that Wilhelm must abdicate.

At first he refused to hear of it. He countered the suggestion with several wild schemes of his own. He would lead his troops against the revolutionaries; he would renounce his imperial title and become simply King of Prussia; he would form an alliance with Britain and Japan to fling the Americans out of Europe. But the High Command persisted and after still more anguished argument, the Kaiser agreed to take their advice. He appealed to Queen Wilhelmina of Holland for asylum and on 10 November he crossed the frontier. He was offered temporary accommodation at Amerongen, the home of Count Godard Bentinck. By that time Germany had already been declared a republic.

Thus it was that the man who had kept the world on tenterhooks for years, who was known as 'the bane of Europe', who was regarded—in England particularly—as a bloodthirsty, bloodstained monster, took his leave of the struggle in which thirteen million men had lost their lives.

'Now,' said the Kaiser briskly to his host as they drove up to his place of exile, 'for a cup of really good English tea!'

2

Kaiser Wilhelm II's reign had lasted for thirty years; his exile was to last for twenty-two. He was to die, at the age of eighty-two, in 1941.

Once his initial anger at what he considered to be his unfair treatment by his subjects had worn off, his exile became as notable for its dignity as his reign had been for its turbulence. Relieved of the pressures of his position, his personality mellowed. He became, if no wiser, certainly more relaxed, more friendly and more benign. He had once claimed that he had always wanted to be an English country gentleman; he was as close to being one now as he would ever be. With his white beard, his tweed suits and his passion for dogs, gardening and chopping wood, he made the perfect country squire. To his Dutch hosts, he was always 'a great gentleman'.

Ten days after his flight from Germany Dona joined him at Amerongen, and in the spring of 1920 they bought the country house at Doorn, some five miles away. The war years had improved the relationship between husband and wife and exile was to bring them closer together still. But by now Dona was a broken, embittered woman, desolate at the overthrow of the Reich, violent in her hatred of Britain, and suffering from a weak heart. She died, in her early sixties, on 11 April 1921, two months after their fortieth wedding anniversary. Ever devoted to her husband, she left instructions that he was to marry again as soon as possible.

He did not wait long. During the course of the following year Wilhelm received a letter of admiration from a little boy. Touched by the letter, he invited the youngster and his widowed mother to visit him at Doorn. The mother was the thirty-five-year-old Princess Hermine of Schönaich-Carolath, and six months after her visit she and the Kaiser were married. Lively, ambitious and argumentative, Princess Hermine was quite different from the passive Dona, but there is no doubt that the marriage was a happy one and that Hermine's presence at Doorn was a great comfort to the ageing Kaiser. 'I have found peace and happiness again after such terrible years of loss and trials through the affection of this winning lady who has consented to be my wife and to bring sunshine into this house of darkness, sorrow and mourning,' wrote Wilhelm to a friend.

In common with all royal exiles, Kaiser Wilhelm II was soon immersed in a process of self-justification. There was, of course, a great deal to be explained away, particularly with regard to the responsibility for the outbreak of the war. For this Wilhelm persisted in laying the blame on everyone else. Chief among that host of villains—his advisers, his generals, rival diplomats, foreign rulers—was his uncle, the late King Edward VII—'the encircler'. The 'peace of Europe,' argued Wilhelm, 'was never in such danger as when the King of England concerned himself with its maintenance'.

But it was to the great Hohenzollern vendetta of his youth that the Kaiser seemed to be drawn back most frequently and compulsively. Indeed, it was almost as though that bitter ideological struggle was being waged all over again. The first salvo was fired by the dead Bismarck. As soon as the Reich collapsed, Bismarck's publishers released the controversial third volume of the great man's memoirs. It was every bit as damning as had been expected. The Chancellor attacked the Kaiser for his duplicity, his vanity, his shallowness, his instability and his lack of experience. 'With the transition from the Hohenzollern spirit to the Coburg-English conception,' argued Bismarck, 'an imponderable factor was lost which will be difficult to restore....' To be described as Coburg-English, rather than Hohenzollern, was indeed an insult to Wilhelm.

The Kaiser replied to Bismarck in his *Memoirs,* published in 1922. From them the Chancellor emerges as a stubborn, dictatorial and old-fashioned despot, intent on establishing his mastery over the idealistic and enlightened young Emperor. In *My Early Life,* published soon after, Wilhelm gave a somewhat rose-coloured version of his role during those tempestuous years. He is revealed as the adoring grandson of an exceptional grandfather, the respectful pupil of an admired Chancellor and the dutiful son of a devoted father and an emotional and politically misguided mother.

'My father's goodness of heart amounted to tenderness, and even to softness,' he wrote. 'He had the most genuine sympathy with any and every form of suffering....' Wilhelm's portrait of his mother was both restrained and shrewd. 'Assuredly my mother was a woman of great gifts, full of ideas and initiative. If, however, she was never quite as appreciated as she deserved, the fault was not wholly that of others. I am convinced that history will give her the full recognition that, like so much else, was denied her in her lifetime. The tragedy of my father's life was hers: perhaps hers in even greater measure.'

It was with extreme reluctance, claimed Wilhelm, that he could bring himself to write about his father's short reign. 'It was so full of pain and suffering, so full of cabals and intrigues against myself, that even today the memory of it oppresses me like a nightmare.'

Others did not show the same reluctance. Embroidering on Wilhelm's version of this period, several German writers depicted Kaiser Frederick III as nothing more than a milksop, entirely at the mercy of his hard-hearted wife. Emil Ludwig's portrait of her, in his widely read life of Kaiser Wilhelm II, was particularly damning.

This impression was corrected, in no uncertain fashion, by the publication of the *Letters of the Empress Frederick,* which had remained, for all these years, in the hands of Sir Frederick Ponsonby. For the first time the world was able to learn something of the sufferings of this impetuous but high-minded woman at the hands of Bismarck and her eldest son. The Kaiser did his utmost to prevent publication of the letters but, being unsuccessful, insisted on writing a preface to the German edition of the book. His mother, he wrote, had always had a quick temper and had suffered severely from her nerves after her husband's tragic death. 'Everywhere,' he maintained, 'she saw enemies harbouring aversion for her, hate even. She was sensitive. Anything hurt her. She was used to quick words and wrote them down. . . .'

Wilhelm's last, full-length book to touch on the subject was entitled *My Ancestors* and the final in this series of short character sketches deals with his father, the Emperor Frederick II. 'Politically his clever, highly intellectual mother had brought him up to hold liberal views: and liberalism was the basis of his opinions,' wrote Wilhelm. 'It was strengthened more than ever when he married my mother, the daughter of the great Queen Victoria of England and the highly talented, noble-minded Prince Consort, for she had grown up in the midst of British Parliamentary Constitutionalism and introduced its ideas effectively into her husband's world of thought. In time this gave rise to friction. . . .'

As the years of exile went by, so did the Kaiser's attitude towards his mother's country soften. Britain, unlike Germany and despite all his and Bismarck's predictions, was still a monarchy, and for this reason alone the Kaiser was kindly disposed towards it. Compared with Germany during the 1920s and 1930s, it seemed like a haven of stability. The British, in their turn, had come to view the ageing Kaiser more sympathetically. He was clearly not the bloodstained tyrant which they had once assumed him to be; when set against Germany's new master, Adolf Hitler, he seemed mild indeed.

Hitler's rise to power had thrown the Kaiser into a quandary. Favouring a strong national movement and imagining that it would lead to a restoration of the Hohenzollerns (in this his new wife was even more optimistic than he) Wilhelm at first approved of the Nazi upsurge. Only after the regime was firmly established and Hitler had made it clear that he had no need of the Hohenzollerns did Wilhelm change his ideas. In 1938, after Neville Chamberlain's journey to Munich, the Kaiser wrote an impassioned letter to the widowed Queen Mary; his first to any member of his mother's family since the war.

'May I with a grateful heart relieved from a sickening anxiety by the intercession of Heaven unite my warmest, sincerest thanks to the Lord with yours and those of the German and British people that He saved us from a most fearful catastrophe by helping the responsible statesmen to preserve peace!' ran the feverish phrases. 'I have not the slightest doubt that Mr N. Chamberlain was inspired by Heaven and guided by God who took pity on his children on Earth by crowning his mission with such relieving success. God bless him. I kiss your hand in respectful devotion as ever.'

A link had once more been forged between the two families and four months later, on the Kaiser's eightieth birthday, he received several congratulatory telegrams from the British royal family. In 1940, at Winston Churchill's instigation, King George VI offered the Kaiser refuge in England from Hitler's invading army. For a moment Wilhelm thought of accepting but, on reflection, he decided to stay where he was. It would not do for even a rejected Hohenzollern to crave protection from his country's enemies. Despite Hitler's orders that there was to be no fraternization between the German army and its former Supreme War Lord, the Kaiser received several officers and would often stroll down to the gatehouse at Doorn to talk to the guards stationed there. When Paris fell to the victorious *Wehrmacht*, the Kaiser sent Hitler a telegram of congratulation. How *he* would once have adored to have ridden his horse at the head of a triumphal march down the Champs Elysées.

Kaiser Wilhelm II died in June 1941 and was buried at Doorn. His death passed almost unnoticed. The world was too caught up in the holocaust which had originated, in no small measure, in the Hohenzollern vortex of over half a century before.

3

The conflict of the three Kaisers, dramatic in itself, was symptomatic of a still greater struggle: it was a microcosm of the ideological battle which was being waged throughout Germany during the nineteenth century. It was a clash between liberalism and conservatism, between democracy and authoritarianism, between parliamentary rule and military dictatorship, between the spread of enlightened ideas and the exaltation of force, between the Coburg theory of constitutional monarchy and the Hohenzollern belief in the Divine Right of Kings, between opposing concepts of patriotism and national greatness. 'Why were we, so to speak, in opposition?' explained the Empress Frederick after the death of her husband. 'Because our patriotism wanted to see the greatness of our fatherland connected with the noble sense for right, morality, for freedom and culture, for individual independence, for the improvement of the single person as man and as German, as European and as cosmopolitan. Improvement, progress, ennoblement—that was our motto. Peace, tolerance, charity—these most precious possessions of mankind, we had to see them trampled upon, laughed at.... *Blood and iron* alone made Germany great and unified—all national vices were called patriotism!'

It is tempting to speculate on what might have happened if these passionately expressed ideals had been put into practice; if the Crown Prince Frederick had come earlier to the throne. In the Hohenzollern drama, his is the most important yet, at the same time, the most negative figure. His accession could have made the world of difference to the history of Germany and Europe whereas, when it finally took place, it was valueless.

But what would have happened if King Wilhelm I had carried out his threat to abdicate in 1862, before Bismarck was summoned to take charge of affairs in Prussia? Would Frederick have come to terms with the refractory parliament and set Prussia along a different course? Would Bismarck have played any significant role in German affairs? Would Germany have been unified quite so speedily and would it have been achieved in accordance with Frederick's progressive ideas? If Kaiser Wilhelm I had lived a natural lifespan, or even if he had died at the hands of Nobiling in 1878, at the age of eighty-one, would Frederick have been able to handle Bismarck? By then the Chancellor was thoroughly entrenched. He not only controlled the Press and the State officials but had reduced parliament to a state of complete docility. The Reichstag had no real sense of responsibility; unaccustomed to asserting themselves, its members simply came to arrangements with the Chancellor. He had blunted almost all sense of individual freedom and independence of mind in Germany. The middle classes, having achieved what they wanted socially and economically, were content to leave political power in the hands of the ruling caste. They could not but help admire the way in which the forces of conservatism had unified Germany; they could not shake off their fear of the proletariat. Their sense of values had become distorted. For the majority of Germans, force had become the most important thing.

Were these institutions too strong and these attitudes too ingrained for Frederick to alter? And was he a strong enough man to effect the necessary changes? Could he have defied the reactionary Junker elite and the powerful military caste; could he have awakened the conscience and the political potential of the German people? On the other hand, was he somewhat less committed to liberalism than a great many people supposed? Was he not too conscious of the power and dignity of the Hohenzollerns to relinquish some of the rights of the crown? His son Wilhelm certainly thought so. 'Whether he would have developed these [liberal] ideas in action if his reign had been longer I cannot say. I do not believe it,' wrote Wilhelm of his father in *My Early Life*. Kaiser Frederick III, he claimed, 'was an authoritarian in his bones, and not too tolerant of opposition'.

With this, Fritz's friend, Gustav Freytag, was inclined to agree. 'Had destiny allowed him a real reign,' he wrote in his study of Frederick III's character, 'this [Hohenzollern pride] would probably have shown itself at times in a manner unpleasantly surprising to his contemporaries.'

In spite of all these reservations, there can be no doubt that there would have been some attempt at a change of course in Germany during the 1880s if Frederick had come earlier to the throne. Somewhere between 1871 and 1890 the Reich would have taken a different road. Supported by his wife, his mother and the considerable body of liberal opinion in the country, Frederick III might well have used the power granted the monarchy by Bismarck to undermine the Chancellor's position or to dismiss him altogether. Of this, Bismarck had lived in constant fear. Frederick would probably have appointed what the Chancellor always called a 'Gladstone Ministry'. He would have encouraged the bourgeoisie to play a greater part in the affairs of the State. He would almost certainly have worked towards an alliance with Great Britain and so kept her out of the arms of France and Russia. Had he lived as long as his father, or even his eldest son, or even his allotted span, Frederick III would have reigned into the twentieth century and the subsequent history of Europe might have been very different. An older Wilhelm II, inheriting a much less powerful constitutional position, an effective parliament and a country allied to Great Britain, might have vouchsafed Germany, Europe and the world a very different sort of future.

It is one of Germany's tragedies that Kaiser Wilhelm I—a man of the eighteenth century—lived too long and that by the accession, three months after his death, of a man of the twentieth century, his grandson Kaiser Wilhelm II, a generation was missed out. The State passed from the blood and iron autocracy of Wilhelm I's Bismarck to the militarily dominated autocracy of Wilhelm II. It was denied the services of Frederick III—the monarch who, for all his shortcomings, personified the liberalism of the nineteenth century.

BIBLIOGRAPHY

BIBLIOGRAPHY

Albert, Harold A.: *Queen Victoria's Sister*. Robert Hale, London, 1967.

Alice, Grand Duchess of Hesse: *Letters to Her Majesty The Queen*. John Murray, London, 1885.

Anon: *The Empress Frederick: A Memoir*. James Nisbet, London, 1913.

Balfour, Michael: *The Kaiser and His Times*. Cresset Press, London, 1964: Houghton Mifflin, Boston, 1964.

Barkeley, Richard: *The Empress Frederick*. Macmillan, London, 1956: St Martin's Press, New York, 1956.

Benson, E. F.: *The Kaiser and English Relations*. Longmans, Green, London, 1936: New York, 1936.

Bernstorff, Count Johann: *Memoirs* (translated by Eric Sutton). Heinemann, London, 1926.

Beust, Count von: *Memoirs*. Remington, London, 1887.

Bismarck, Prince Otto von, *Reflections and Reminiscences* (2 vols). Smith, Elder, London, 1898.

—— *New Chapters of Bismarck's Autobiography* (translated by Bernard Miall). Hodder & Stoughton, London, 1930.

Blowitz, Henri Stephan de: *My Memoirs*. Edward Arnold, London, 1903.

Blücher, Prince: *Memoirs*. John Murray, London, 1932.

Bonnin, Georges (ed.): *Bismarck and the Hohenzollern Candidature for the Spanish Throne*. Chatto & Windus, London, 1957.

Bülow, Prince Bernhard von: *Imperial Germany* (translated by Marie A. Lewenz). Casell, London, 1914: New York, 1914.

—— *Memoirs* (4 vols). Putnam, London, 1931: New York, 1931.

—— *Letters of Prince von Bülow* (translated by Frederic Whyte). Hutchinson, London, n.d.

Bunsen, Marie de: *In Three Legations*. T. Fisher Unwin, London, 1909: C. Scribner's Sons, New York, 1909.

Burghclere, Lady (ed.): *A Great Lady's Friendships*. Macmillan, London, 1933.

Busoh, Dr Moritz: *Bismarck: Some Secret Pages of His History* (3 vols). Macmillan, London, 1898: New York, 1898.

—— *Our Chancellor*. Macmillan, London, 1884.

Carr, William: *A History of Germany 1815–1945*. Edward Arnold, London, 1969.

Chamberlain, Sir Austen: *Down the Years*. Cassell, London, 1935.

Churchill, Winston: *Great Contemporaries*. Macmillan, London, 1937: G. P. Putnam's Sons, New York, 1937.

Cohen, Lucy: *Lady de Rothschild and Her Daughters*. John Murray, London, 1935.

Cook, Sir Edward: *Delane of The Times*. Constable, London, 1916.

Corti, Egon, Count: *The English Empress*. Cassell, London, 1957.

—— *Alexander von Battenburg*. Cassell, London, 1954.

Cowles, Virginia: *The Kaiser*. Collins, London, 1963: Harper & Row, New York, 1963.

Dawson, William H.: *Germany and the Germans*. Chapman & Hall, London, 1894.

Dino, Duchess de: *Memoirs*. Heinemann, London, 1910.

Disraeli, Benjamin: *Letters of Disraeli to Lady Bradford and Lady Chesterfield*. Ernest Benn, London, 1929: D. Appleton & Co., New York, 1929.

—— *Letters from Benjamin Disraeli to Frances Anne, Marchioness of Londonderry*. Macmillan, London, 1938.

Dugdale, E. T. S.: *German Diplomatic Documents 1871–1914*. Methuen, London, 1928.

Eckardstein, Baron von: *Ten Years at the Court of St. James 1895–1905* (translated by Prof. G. Young). Thornton Butterworth, London, 1921.

Eich, Hermann: *The Unloved Germans* (translated by Michael Glenny). Macdonald, London, 1965: Stein & Day, New York, 1965.

Elkind, Louis: *The German Emperor's Speeches*. Longmans, London, 1904.

Ernest II, Duke of Saxe-Coburg-Gotha: *Memoirs*. Remington, London, 1888.

Esher, Reginald Viscount: *Journals and Letters*. Ivor Nicholson & Watson, London, 1934.

Eyck, Erich: *Bismarck and the German Empire*. Allen & Unwin, London, 1950.

Fischer, Henry W.: *The Private Lives of William II and His Consort*. Heinemann, London, 1905: W. C. Adams & Co., New York, 1909.

Forbes, Archibald: *William of Germany*. Cassell, London, 1888: New York, 1888.

Frederick III, Emperor of Germany: *Diaries of the Emperor Frederick* (translated by Frances A. Welby). Chapman & Hall, London, 1902.

—— *War Diaries of the Emperor Frederick* (translated by A. R. Allison). Stanley Paul, London, 1927.

Freytag, Gustav: *The Crown Prince and the German Imperial Crown*. George Bell & Sons, London, 1890.

Grant, N. F. (ed.): *The Kaiser's Letter to the Tsar*. Hodder & Stoughton, London, 1920.

Greville, Charles: *The Greville Diary*. Heinemann, London, 1927: Doubleday, Page & Co., Garden City, New York, 1927.

Hamilton, Lord Frederic: *The Vanished World of Yesterday*. Hodder & Stoughton, London, 1950.

Harden, Maximilian: *Word Portraits* (translated by Julius Gabe). Blackwood, London, 1912.

Hardman, Sir William: *A Mid-Victorian Pepys*. Cecil Palmer, London, 1923.

Headlam, James W.: *Bismarck and the Foundation of the German Empire*. Putnam, London, 1911: G. P. Putnam's Sons, New York, 1899.

Hoche, Jules: *Bismarck at Home*. John McQueen, London, 1899.

Hohenlohe, Prince Chlodwig: *Memoirs* (2 vols, translated by George W. Chrystal). Heinemann, London, 1906.

Holstein, Friedrich von: *The Holstein Papers* (4 vols, edited by N. Rich & M. Fisher). Cambridge University Press, 1958.

Howard, Michael: *The Franco-Prussian War*. Hart-Davis, London, 1961: Macmillan, New York, 1961.

Kennedy, A. L. (ed.): *My Dear Duchess*. John Murray, London, 1956.

Kürenberg, Joachim von: *The Kaiser* (translated by H. Russell & H. Hagen). Cassell, London, 1954: Simon & Schuster, New York, 1955.

Kurtz, Harold: *The Second Reich*. Macdonald, London, 1970.

Lee, Sir Sidney: *King Edward VII* (2 vols). Macmillan, London, 1925: New York, 1925.

Legge, Edward: *The Public and Private Life of Kaiser Wilhelm II*. Eveleigh Nash, London, 1915.

Longford, Elizabeth: *Victoria R.I.* Weidenfeld & Nicolson, London, 1964.

Louise, Princess of Schleswig-Holstein: *Behind the Scenes at the Prussian Court*. John Murray, London, 1939.

Lowe, Charles: Bismarck's Table Talk. H. Grevel, London, 1895.

—— *Prince Bismarck* (2 vols). Cassell, London, 1885: New York, 1886: Roberts Brothers, Boston, 1895.

—— *The German Emperor William II*. Bliss, Sands & Foshe, London, n.d.

Ludendorff, Erich: *Ludendorff's Own Story, August 1914–November 1918* (2 vols). Harper, New York, 1920.

Ludwig, Emil: *Kaiser Wilhelm II* (translated by E. C. Mayne). Putnam, London, 1926.

—— *Bismarck* (translated by Eden and Cedar Paul). Allen & Unwin, London, 1926.

—— *The Germans* (translated by Heinz and Ruth Norden). Hamish Hamilton, London, 1942.

Lynx, J. J.: *The Great Hohenzollern Scandal*. Oldbourne, London, 1965.

McClintock, Mary Howard: *The Queen Thanks Sir Howard*. John Murray, London, 1945.

Mackenzie, Sir Morell: *The Fatal Illness of Frederick the Noble*. Sampson, Low & Marston, London, 1888.

Magnus, Philip: *King Edward the Seventh*. John Murray, London, 1964: Dutton, New York, 1964.

Malet, Sir Edward: *Shifting Scenes*. John Murray, London, 1964.

Mann, Golo: *The History of Germany Since 1789* (translated by M. Jackson). Chatto & Windus, 1968: F. A. Praeger, New York, 1968.

Marie, Queen of Roumania: *The Story of My Life*. Cassell, London, 1934.

Martin, Theodore: *Life of His Royal Highness the Prince Consort* (5 vols). Smith, Elder, London, 1877–80.

Moltke, Count Helmuth von: *Essays, Speeches, and Memoirs*

(2 vols). James R. Osgood, London, 1893: Harper & Brothers, New York, 1893.

Morier, Sir Robert: *Memoirs and Letters* (2 vols). Edward Arnold, London, 1911.

Müller, Admiral Genge von: *The Kaiser and His Court* (translated and edited by Walter Görlitz). Macdonald, London, 1961.

Nelson, Walter Henry: *The Soldier Kings: The House of Hohenzollern.* G. P. Putnam's Sons, New York, 1970.

Paget, Lady Walburga: *The Linings of Life.* Hurst & Blackett, London, 1928.

—— *Embassies of Other Days* (2 vols). Hutchinson, London, 1923.

Pless, Daisy, Princess of: *Diaries.* John Murray, London, 1928: E. P. Dutton Co., Inc., New York, 1929.

—— *From My Private Diaries.* John Murray, London, 1931.

—— *What I Left Unsaid.* Cassell, London, 1936: E. P. Dutton Co., Inc., New York, 1936.

Ponsonby, Arthur: *Henry Ponsonby.* Macmillan, London, 1943: New York, 1943.

Ponsonby, Sir Frederick: *Recollections of Three Reigns.* Eyre & Spottiswoode, London, 1951.

Ponsonby, Mary: *A Memoir, Some Letters and a Journal.* John Murray, London, 1927.

Pope-Hennessy, James: *Queen Mary.* Allen & Unwin, London, 1959.

Poschinger, Margaretta von: *Life of the Emperor Frederick.* Harper & Brothers, London, 1901: New York, 1901.

Radziwill, Princess Catherine: *My Recollections.* Isbister, London, 1904: J. Pott & Co., New York, 1904.

—— *Germany under Three Emperors.* Cassell, London, 1917: Funk & Wagnalls Co., New York, 1917.

—— *The Empress Frederick.* Cassell, London, 1934.

—— [pseud. Count Paul Vassili]: *Berlin Society.* Sampson, Low & Marston, London, 1885.

Ramm, Agatha: *Germany 1789–1919.* Methuen, London, 1967: Barnes & Noble, New York, 1967.

Redesdale, Lord: *Memories.* Hutchinson, London, 1915.

Reischach, Baron Hugo von: *Under Three Emperors* (translated by Prince Blücher). Constable, London, 1927.

Roberts, Brian: *Cecil Rhodes and the Princess.* Hamish Hamilton, London, 1969.

Rodd, Sir James Rennell: *Social and Diplomatic Memories* (3 vols). Edward Arnold, London, 1922–5.

—— *Frederick, Crown Prince and Emperor*. David Scott, London, 1888: Macmillan & Co., New York, 1888.

Schwering, Count Axel von: *The Berlin Court under William II*. Cassell, London, 1915: New York, 1915.

Simon, Edouard: *The Emperor William and his Reign* (2 vols). Remington, London, 1888.

Somerset, Duke of: *Letters and Memoirs*. Richard Bentley, London, 1893.

Stevenson, R. Scott: *Famous Illnesses in History*. Eyre & Spottiswoode, London, 1962.

Strauss, G. L. M.: *Men Who Have Made the New German Empire* (2 vols). Tinsley Bros., London, 1875.

Sudley, Lord (ed.): *The Lieven–Palmerston Correspondence 1828–1856*. John Murray, London, 1943.

Taffs, Winifred: *Ambassador to Bismarck: Lord Odo Russell*. Frederick Muller, London, 1938.

Taylor, A. J. P.: *The Course of German History*. Hamish Hamilton, London, 1945: Coward-McCann, Inc., New York, 1946.

—— *Bismark*. Hamish Hamilton, London, 1955.

Taylor, Lucy: *"Fritz" of Prussia*. Nelson, London, 1891.

Treitschke, Heinrich von: *History of Germany in the Nineteenth Century* (7 vols). Jarrolds, London, 1915: McBride, Nast Co., New York, 1915–19.

Varé, Daniele: *Twilight of the Kings*. John Murray, London, 1948.

Vassili, Count Paul: See under Radziwill, Princess Catherine.

Victoria, Empress of Germany: *Letters of the Empress Frederick* (edited by Sir Frederick Ponsonby). Macmillan, London, 1928.

—— *The Empress Frederick Writes to Sophie* (edited by A. Gould-Lee). Faber & Faber, London, 1955.

Victoria, Queen of Great Britain: *Letters of Queen Victoria* (9 vols). John Murray, London, 1907–32: Longmans, Green & Co., 1907.

—— *Leaves from the Journal of Our Life in the Highlands*. Smith, Elder, London, 1869: Harper & Bros, New York, 1868: S. C. Griggs & Co., Chicago, 1868.

—— *Dearest Child: Letters between Queen Victoria and the Princess Royal* (edited by Roger Fulford). Evans Bros.

London, 1964: Holt, Rinehart, Winston, New York, 1965.

—— *Dearest Mamma: Letters between Queen Victoria and the Crown Princess of Prussia* (edited by Roger Fulford). Evans Bros., London, 1968.

Victoria, Princess of Prussia: *My Memoirs*. Eveleigh Nash, London, 1929.

Vizetelly, Henry: *Berlin under the New Empire*. Tinsley Bros., London, 1879.

Waldersee, Count von: *A Field Marshal's Memoirs* (translated by Frederic Whyte). Hutchinson, London, 1924.

Ward, Mrs Humphry: *A Writer's Recollections*. Collins, London, 1918: Harper & Bros., New York, 1918.

West, Mrs George Cornwallis: *The Reminiscences of Lady Randolph Churchill*. Edward Arnold, London, 1908: The Century Co., New York, 1908.

Whitman, Sidney: *Imperial Germany*. Trubner, London, 1889: Flood & Vincent, New York, 1897.

—— *Personal Reminiscences of Prince Bismarck*. John Murray, London, 1902; D. Appleton Co., New York, 1903.

Whitton, Lt-Col. F. E.: *Moltke*. Constable, London, 1921.

Wiegler, Paul: *William the First* (translated by Constance Vesey). Allen & Unwin, London, 1929

Wilhelm I, Emperor of Germany: *Correspondence of William I and Bismarck*. Heinemann, London, 1903: F. A. Stokes Co., New York, 1903.

—— *Briefe Kaiser Wilhelmsdes Ersten*. Insel Verlag, Leipzig, 1911.

Wilhelm II, Emperor of Germany: *My Memoirs 1878–1918*. Cassell, London, 1922: New York, 1922.

—— *My Early Life*. Methuen, London, 1926: George H. Doran Co., New York, 1926.

—— *My Ancestors* (translated by W. W. Zambra). Heinemann, London, 1929.

Zedlitz-Trutzschler, Count Robert: *Twelve Years at the Imperial German Court*, Nisbet, London, 1924.

INDEX

Adolf, Prince zu Schaumburg-Lippe, 211

Albert, Prince Consort, 27, 39–45, 47–8, 50–1, 61–2, 65, 67, 72, 86, 109, 117, 133, 139, 192, 204, 234, 250

Alexander II, Tsar of Russia, 87, 112, 127–8, 142

Alexander III, Tsar of Russia, 130–2, 136–8, 180, 223

Alexander (Sandro), Prince of Battenberg, 126–34, 136, 143, 179–83, 194, 211

Alexander, Prince of Hesse, 126

Alexandra, Queen, as Princess of Wales, 68, 72, 108

Alexandria, S.S., 186

Alexandrina, Grand Duchess of Mecklenberg-Schwerin, 35, 150, 168

Alfonso XII, King of Spain, 143

Alfred, Prince, Duke of Edinburgh, 153

Alice, Princess, Grand Duchess of Hesse, 113, 121, 126, 127, 186

Allgemeine Zeitung, 155

Amerongen, 245, 247

Argyll, Duke of, 72

Armida, 126

Arnim, Count von, 106

Augusta, German Empress, 19, 25, 29–37, 39–41, 42, 46, 56, 60, 64, 71, 81, 84, 90, 97–108, 112, 114, 118, 123, 125, 128, 129, 130, 148–50, 168, 175–6, 182, 184, 190, 192–3, 204, 210, 212–16, 225; character and girlhood, 31–6; marriage, 33;

Catholicism, 35, 105–6; coronation, 53; feud with Bismarck, 59, 105–7, 213; golden wedding, 123; death, 214

Auguste Viktoria (Dona), German Empress, 125–7, 130, 138, 198, 206, 212, 232, 247; character, 125, 138, 199–200; death, 248

Babelsberg Palace, 33, 148, 150, 213

Baden, Grand Duke of (*see* Frederick, Grand Duke of Baden)

Baden, Grand Duchess of (*see* Louise, Grand Duchess of Baden)

Balmoral Castle, 40, 45, 127, 153, 231

Balzac, Honoré de, 33

Bamberger, Ludwig, 145

Battenberg, House of (*see also* Alexander, Louis, etc), 126, 129

Bavaria, King of (*see* Ludwig II)

Beatrice, Princess, 130

Bentinck, Count Godard, 247

Bergmann, Professor Ernst von, 151, 157, 160, 163–4, 166–7, 174, 183, 184, 207, 234

Bernard, Inman, 191

Bernhard, Prince of Saxe-Meiningen, 121, 143

Beust, Count, 65–6

Bismarck, Count Herbert von, 132, 159, 175, 179, 219, 225

Bismarck, Prince Otto von, 16–17, 30, 44, 55–9, 60, 66, 83–4, 89–90, 95–6, 100–1, 105–7, 113, 115–21, 123–5, 127–8, 131–2, 134–7, 141–7, 149, 157–9, 163–4, 169, 174–5, 176–82,

A SELECTION OF FINE READING AVAILABLE IN CORGI BOOKS

Novels

- [ ] 552 08651 7   THE HAND REARED BOY   *Brian W Aldiss* 35p
- [ ] 552 09018 2   A SOLDIER ERECT   *Brian W. Aldiss* 35p
- [ ] 552 09274 6   A KIND OF LOVING   *Stan Barstow* 40p
- [ ] 552 09156 1   THE EXORCIST   *William Peter Blatty* 40p
- [ ] 552 09376 9   TREAD SOFTLY IN THIS PLACE   *Brian Cleeve* 40p
- [ ] 552 09217 7   THE DWELLING PLACE   *Catherine Cookson* 45p
- [ ] 552 09381 1   FEATHERS IN THE FIRE   *Catherine Cookson* 35p
- [ ] 552 09380 7   THE ORDEAL OF RUNNING STANDING   *Thomas Fall* 40p
- [ ] 552 09174 X   A CHEMICAL ROMANCE   *Jenny Fabian* 35p
- [ ] 552 09303 3   BLACKSTONE   *Richard Falkirk* 35p
- [ ] 552 09121 9   THE DAY OF THE JACKAL   *Frederick Forsyth* 50p
- [ ] 552 09158 8   THE GOD BENEATH THE SEA   *L. Garfield & E. Blishen* 30p
- [ ] 552 09125 6   CATCH 22   *Joseph Heller* 40p
- [ ] 552 09279 7   STEAMBOAT GOTHIC   *Frances Parkinson Keyes* 50p
- [ ] 552 09379 3   LARRY VINCENT   *Frances Parkinson Keyes* 40p
- [ ] 552 09302 5   SITKA   *Louis L'Amour* 40p
- [ ] 552 09304 1   ESTHER   *Norah Lofts* 30p
- [ ] 552 09364 5   DRUMS ALONG THE KHYBER   *Duncan MacNeil* 35p
- [ ] 552 09394 7   JEREMY   *John Minahan* 30p
- [ ] 552 09256 8   THE LOTUS AND THE WIND   *John Masters* 40p
- [ ] 552 09240 1   THE DRIFTERS   *James A. Michener* 75p
- [ ] 552 09378 5   THE HARVEST BURNS   *Helga Moray* 35p
- [ ] 552 09358 0   LOLITA   *Vladimir Nabokov* 40p
- [ ] 552 09306 8   THE HIGH ROOF   *Joy Packer* 40p
- [ ] 552 09140 5   SARAH WHITMAN   *Diane Pearson* 35p
- [ ] 552 09377 7   GENTLE GREAVES   *Ernest Raymond* 75p
- [ ] 552 08930 3   STORY OF O   *Pauline Reage* 50p
- [ ] 552 08597 9   PORTNOY'S COMPLAINT   *Philip Roth* 40p
- [ ] 552 08372 0   LAST EXIT TO BROOKLYN   *Hubert Selby Jr.* 50p
- [ ] 552 07807 7   VALLEY OF THE DOLLS   *Jacqueline Susann* 40p
- [ ] 552 08523 5   THE LOVE MACHINE   *Jacqueline Susann* 40p
- [ ] 552 08384 4   EXODUS   *Leon Uris* 50p
- [ ] 552 08481 6   FOREVER AMBER Vol. 1   *Kathleen Winsor* 40p
- [ ] 552 08482 4   FOREVER AMBER Vol. 2   *Kathleen Winsor* 40p

War

- [ ] 552 09369 6   THE BRAVE WHITE FLAG   *James Allen Ford* 35p
- [ ] 552 09383 1   DANGEROUS TRADE   *Gilbert Hackforth-Jones* 30p
- [ ] 552 08874 9   SS GENERAL   *Sven Hassel* 35p
- [ ] 552 09178 2   REIGN OF HELL   *Sven Hassel* 35p
- [ ] 552 09368 8   THREE CAME HOME   *Agnes Keith* 35p
- [ ] 552 09324 6   FIGHTER EXPLOITS (illustrated)   *Edward H. Sims* 40p
- [ ] 552 08986 9   DUEL OF THE EAGLES (illustrated)   *Peter Townsend* 50p
- [ ] 552 09367 X   SLAVES OF THE SON OF HEAVEN   *R. H. Whitecross* 35p
- [ ] 552 09382 3   FLAME THROWER   *Andrew Wilson* 35p

Romance

- [ ] 552 09208 8   BRIDAL ARRAY   *Elizabeth Cadell* 30p
- [ ] 552 09329 7   CONSIDER THE LILIES   *Elizabeth Cadell* 30p
- [ ] 552 09417 X   THE NIGHT PEOPLE   *Kate Norway* 30p
- [ ] 552 09312 2   NO SINGLE STAR   *Alex Stuart* 30p
- [ ] 552 09389 0   LIFE IS THE DESTINY   *Alex Stuart* 30p

Science Fiction

- [ ] 552 09237 1   FANTASTIC VOYAGE   *Isaac Asimov* 35p
- [ ] 552 09289 4   STAR TREK 8   *James Blish* 30p
- [ ] 552 09333 5   THE GOLDEN APPLES OF THE SUN   *Ray Bradbury* 35p
- [ ] 552 09313 0   NEW WRITINGS IN S.F. 21   *ed. John Carnell* 35p
- [ ] 552 09334 5   THE MENACE FROM EARTH   *Robert A. Heinlein* 53p

General

☐	552 09332 7	GO ASK ALICE	*Anonymous* 30p
☐	552 09292 4	LOVE, LIFE AND SEX	*Barbara Cartland* 35p
☐	552 09185 5	THE FUNDAMENTALS OF SEX (illustrated)	
			Dr. Philip Cauthery & Dr. Martin Cole 50p
☐	552 09392 0	THE MYSTERIOUS UNKNOWN (illustrated)	
			Robert Charroux 50p
☐	552 09151 0	THE DRAGON AND THE PHOENIX	*Eric Chou* 50p
☐	552 08800 5	CHARIOTS OF THE GODS? (illustrated)	*Erich von Daniken* 35p
☐	552 09073 2	RETURN TO THE STARS (illustrated)	*Erich von Daniken* 40p
☐	552 09331 9	OPERATION RHINO (illustrated)	*John Gordon Davis* 40p
☐	552 07400 4	MY LIFE AND LOVES	*Frank Harris* 65p
☐	552 98748 4	MAKING LOVE (Photographs)	*Walter Hartford* 85p
☐	552 09062 X	THE SENSUOUS MAN	*'M'* 35p
☐	552 09293 2	GOLF'S WINNING STROKE: PUTTING (illustrated)	
			Tom Michael 50p
☐	552 09290 8	INTIMATE BEHAVIOUR	*Desmond Morris* 40p
☐	552 08010 1	THE NAKED APE	*Desmond Morris* 30p
☐	552 09232 0	SECRET OF THE ANDES	*Brother Philip* 30p
☐	552 09390 4	CANDLELIGHT	*T. Lobsang Rampa* 35p
☐	552 09266 5	ANY WOMAN CAN	*David R. Reuben M.D.* 50p
☐	552 09044 1	SEX ENERGY	*Robert S. de Ropp* 35p
☐	552 09250 9	THE MANIPULATED MAN	*Esther Vilar* 35p
☐	552 09145 6	THE NYMPHO AND OTHER MANIACS	*Irvine Wallace* 40p
☐	552 09391 2	OMNIVORE	*Dr. Lyall Watson* 30p

Western

☐	552 09095 6	APACHE	*Will Levington Comfort* 30p
☐	552 09227 4	YOU'RE IN COMMAND NOW, MR. FOG No. 71	
			J. T. Edson 30p
☐	552 09298 3	THE BIG GUN No. 72	*J. T. Edson* 30p
☐	552 09327 0	SET TEXAS BACK ON HER FEET No. 73	*J. T. Edson* 30p
☐	552 09191 X	TREASURE MOUNTAIN	*Louis L'Amour* 30p
☐	552 09264 9	THE FERGUSON RIFLE	*Louis L'Amour* 30p
☐	552 09387 4	THE MAN FROM SKIBBEREEN	*Louis L'Amour* 30p
☐	552 09287 8	KILLING FOR THE LAW No. 21	*Louis Masterson* 25p
☐	552 09328 9	THE BUTCHER FROM GUERRERO No. 22	
			Louis Masterson 25p
☐	552 08810 2	SUDDEN—OUTLAWED	*Oliver Strange* 25p
☐	552 09388 2	HIGH PLAINS DRIFTER	*Ernest Tidyman* 30p

Crime

☐	552 09384 X	DEATH IN HIGH PLACES	*John Creasey* 30p
☐	552 09385 8	DEATH IN FLAMES	*John Creasey* 30p
☐	552 09386 6	THE BARON COMES BACK	*John Creasey* 30p
☐	552 09310 6	CAGE UNTIL TAME	*Laurence Henderson* 35p
☐	552 09262 3	THE EXECUTIONER: CHICAGO WIPEOUT	
			Don Pendleton 30p
☐	552 09325 4	THE EXECUTIONER: VEGAS VENDETTA	*Don Pendleton* 30p
☐	552 09326 2	THE EXECUTIONER: CARIBBEAN KILL	*Don Pendleton* 30p
☐	552 09111 1	THE ERECTION SET	*Mickey Spillane* 40p
☐	552 09273 8	SHAFT HAS A BALL	*Ernest Tidyman* 30p
☐	552 09309 2	SHAFT AMONG THE JEWS	*Ernest Tidyman* 35p

All these books are available at your bookshop or newsagent: or can be ordered direct from the publisher. Just tick the titles you want and fill in the form below.

CORGI BOOKS, Cash Sales Department, P.O. Box 11, Falmouth, Cornwall.
Please send cheque or postal order, no currency, and allow 7p per book to cover the cost of postage and packing in the U.K. (5p if more than one copy) 7p per book overseas.

NAME ....

ADDRESS ....

(NOV. 73) ....